The End of Illusions

ROWMAN & LITTLEFIELD PUBLISHERS, INC.

Published in the United States of America
by Rowman & Littlefield Publishers, Inc.
A wholly owned subsidiary of The Rowman & Littlefield Publishing Group, Inc.
4501 Forbes Boulevard, Suite 200, Lanham, Maryland 20706
www.rowmanlittlefield.com

PO Box 317
Oxford
OX2 9RU, UK

British Library Cataloguing in Publication Information Available

Library of Congress Cataloging-in-Publication Data

The end of illusions : religious leaders confront Hitler's gathering storm
 / edited by Joseph Loconte.
  p. cm.
Includes bibliographical references and index.
ISBN 0-7425-3498-7 (cloth : alk. paper) — ISBN 0-7425-3499-5
(pbk. : alk. paper)
  1. Europe—Church history—20th century. 2. Church and state—Europe
History—20th century. 3. Hitler, Adolf, 1889–1945. I. Loconte, Joe, 1961–

BR735.E53 2004
270.8'23—dc22

                                                          2004010168

Printed in the United States of America

∞™ The paper used in this publication meets the minimum requirements of
American National Standard for Information Sciences—Permanence of Paper
for Printed Library Materials, ANSI/NISO Z39.48-1992.

For Mom and Dad,
whose love gives me courage

Contents

Acknowledgments

The idea for this book emerged after I discovered an essay by theologian Reinhold Niebuhr, where he broke ranks with his pacifist and socialist colleagues to argue that Nazism must be confronted militarily. His critique of the moral and spiritual weaknesses of pacifism in the 1930s seemed eerily relevant to the contemporary debate over the war on terrorism. I initially envisioned a collection confined to the writings of the "hawks" of the era. But a dinner conversation with John Wilson, editor of *Books and Culture*, opened my mind to broadening the book's scope. John gave me a terrific concept, and his excitement about the project propelled me forward.

There are others to thank. My dear brother, Mike, and sister, Suzanne, offered many timely words of support. Friends Os Guinness and Jeane Bethke Elshtain interrupted busy schedules to provide invaluable guidance about framing the contents of the book. Laura Roberts Gottlieb at Rowman & Littlefield also made very important suggestions. Literary agent Rebecca Kurson and husband Ken Kurson gave me great encouragement at just the right moments. Research assistant Claire Burgess brought boundless enthusiasm and intellectual curiosity for every task. She also found the most gripping of photographs to serve as the book's cover. Mac Brodt brought Jewish thinker Stephen Wise to my attention, and Charissa Kersten and Tim Holbert cheerfully researched hard-to-find articles at the Library of Congress.

I am deeply grateful to the Heritage Foundation for giving me the freedom to pursue the project. I also want to give a special word of thanks to William E. Simon Sr. and his family, whose generous endowment continues to support my writing and research.

"Do not suppose this is the end. This is only the beginning of the reckoning. This is only the first sip, the first foretaste of a bitter cup which will be proffered to us year by year unless by a supreme recovery of moral health and martial vigour, we arise again and take our stand for freedom as in the olden time."

—Winston Churchill, before the House of Commons, after the
sell-out of Czechoslovakia to Germany, October 5, 1938

"We have learned that God-fearing democracies of the world which observe the sanctity of treaties and good faith in their dealings with other nations cannot safely be indifferent to international lawlessness anywhere."

—Franklin Roosevelt, address to Congress
and the nation, January 1939

"For it is one thing to see the Land of Peace from a wooded ridge. . .and another to tread the road that leads to it."

—St. Augustine

Introduction

The Politics of Appeasement and the War on Terrorism

B y the fall of 1940 in America, the landscape across the Atlantic must have looked surreal. The German military machine, devastated and humiliated barely twenty years before, was on the move. *Wehrmacht* tanks occupied major European capitals. France, arguably the lead power in the region, had collapsed almost overnight. Thousands of British troops barely escaped with their lives at Dunkirk. German bombers were terrorizing London. At one point President Franklin Roosevelt asked Winston Churchill what the conflict should be called. The British prime minister replied at once: the unnecessary war. "There never was a war more easy to stop than that which has just wrecked what was left of the world from the previous struggle," he wrote much later. "Virtuous motives, trammeled by inertia and timidity, are no match for armed and resolute wickedness."[1]

Of all the lessons to be drawn from World War II, perhaps none is more appropriate for our own time: the failure to face international aggression realistically only invites dangers on our own shores.

True, the al Qaeda terrorist attacks against the United States on September 11, 2001, introduced the nation to a new kind of enemy. Here were men linked to a global network of killers who quietly infiltrated American society and readied themselves to die in suicide attacks—fully persuaded their mission was a divine calling. They did not represent any sovereign state or make political demands of any kind. Their weapons were box cutters, and they used them to turn commercial airplanes into missiles of doom. The reality is now frighteningly plain: The United States and the West face a religious-political movement desperate to acquire the world's most destructive weapons to inflict the greatest possible harm on civilian populations.

1

Yet at another level, this new danger is not so new after all. The more that's learned about Islamic radicalism, the more it appears to be drawing inspiration from another ideology—European fascism. Islamic scholar Bernard Lewis has noted how German fascism influenced the founders of the Ba'ath Party in Syria and Iraq (a pro-Nazi group, for example, seized control of Iraq in April of 1941).[2] Cultural critic Paul Berman sees a strong philosophical link between Nazism and the tenets of Islamic radicals in Iraq and Iran. "At a deep level, totalitarianism and terrorism are one and the same," he writes. "The Ba'ath Party and the Islamists were two branches of a single impulse, which was Muslim totalitarianism—the Muslim variation on the European idea."[3] *Washington Post* columnist Charles Krauthammer also discerns fascist fingerprints at the crime scene of September 11. "In its nihilism, its will to power, its celebration of blood and death, its craving for the cleansing purity that comes only from eradicating life and culture, radical Islam is heir, above all, to Nazism."[4]

The similarities are not only philosophical. Judged by their militarism, their ruthless ambitions, and their global reach, the Islamists threaten the international order in a way that rivals their fascist heroes.

This, at least, is the conviction of the Bush administration, which was quick to connect radical Islam to the fanatical doctrines of the 1930s. Addressing the nation during a joint session of Congress barely a week after the September 11 attacks, President George W. Bush called the perpetrators "the heirs of all the murderous ideologies" of the twentieth century. "By sacrificing human life to serve their radical visions—by abandoning every value except the will to power—they follow in the path of fascism, and Nazism, and totalitarianism." Bush picked up the theme again in an address to the United Nations General Assembly, just a few weeks later. "In a second world war, we learned there is no isolation from evil," he said. "And we resolved that the aggressions and ambitions of the wicked must be opposed early, decisively, and collectively, before they threaten us all. That evil has returned, and that cause is renewed."

Whatever one thinks of this argument, the killing of nearly three thousand innocents on U.S. soil has transformed America's approach to national security more profoundly than the end of the Cold War. The Bush doctrine is as brazen as it is controversial. America will forcibly confront what amounts to "an axis of evil"—that is, terrorist networks and the nations that give them weapons and sanctuary. The new doctrine was invoked to justify the U.S.-led wars in Afghanistan and Iraq. "Nowhere, after all, could have been more distant than Afghanistan, yet that remote and desperate place was where the attacks of September 11 were prepared," writes Michael Ignatieff of Harvard's Kennedy School of Government. "Terror has collapsed distance, and with this collapse has come a sharpened American focus on the necessity of bringing order to the frontier zones."⁵ Similarly, the decision to forcibly disarm Saddam Hussein, writes Bill Keller of the *New York Times Magazine*, was "the most audacious attempt to change the rules of arms control in half a century."⁶

The administration's approach has set off an intense debate about U.S. foreign policy, one in which religious voices have been especially engaged. In the fall of 2001, a coalition of intellectuals and religious leaders drafted a document justifying aggressive military action to combat terrorism. In "What We're Fighting For," sixty public leaders agreed that radical Islam represents an "unmitigated global evil" that can be stopped only by military action. "Organized killers with global reach now threaten us all," they declared. "In the name of universal human morality . . . we support our government's, and our society's, decision to use force of arms against them."⁷ Though some conservatives remain fiercely opposed to the administration's approach, most of the critics are found on the Left: academics, politicians, journalists—and ministers. Indeed, no segment has found the Bush doctrine as morally offensive as the liberal wing of Christianity. Church leaders have called the war on terrorism an excuse for "imperialism." They chastise U.S. officials for ignoring the "root causes" of Muslim rage, which they argue are political and economic. They reject the president's description of the terrorist threat as arrogant and simplistic. The National Council of Churches, for example, warned that "demon-izing adversaries or enemies denies their basic humanity." Liberal clerics opposed the U.S.-led wars in Afghanistan and Iraq, demanding that the Bush administration "lay down the muscle of weapons" and employ the "muscle of the heart."

Any serious student of the 1930s is struck by the familiarity of this debate. When Germany began to reassert itself after World War I, the mood in America was isolationist. Gallup polls in 1938 showed that about 95 percent of the population opposed participation in another war.⁸ Religion was a major part of the reason: churches were the driving force behind the peace movements that punctuated the interwar period. At the beginning of the 1930s, there were perhaps two hundred peace societies. Though many of these groups were ostensibly secular, religious influences were usually close at hand. As one historian observes, the leadership of the peace movement was "deeply religious." Church members made up the majority of the peace workers, and Protestant denominations became "the most effective agencies through which the peace advocates reached public opinion."⁹ Prominent ministers strongly supported the League of Nations and virtually every diplomatic scheme to preserve world order. Then came the lightening bolt, Hitler's march on Europe. For many on the Left, it intensified their activities. Others were shocked into abandoning their pacifism.

As the essays in this volume suggest, what followed was a debate marked by passion as well as serious moral reflection. The doves fiercely resisted American military support for the European democracies. Instead, they opposed the "rush toward intervention." They warned churches against becoming "an adjunct to a war department." They denounced the "devil nation" rhetoric aimed at Germany. They viewed the European conflict as an "unhappy game of power politics." It was not a war for democracy, they said, but a "a clash of imperialisms." America must address the "real" causes of Nazi aggression in order to "dissipate the fears which incubate warlike moods."[10] The hawks, meanwhile, insisted that America end its policy of neutrality and support the Allied cause. They rejected peace proposals as "a euphemism for surrender." They derided the "utopian illusions" of the diplomats who thought Nazism could be appeased. As one of their leading lights put it: "We are not permitted the delightful dream-worlds, the irresponsible fancies, the recourse to resolutions and conferences which are the stock-in-trade of the pulpit." They accused the isolationists of holding a "preference for tyranny" over democratic freedom. And they ultimately urged U.S. military action against "a virtual AntiChrist" whose doctrines threatened the foundations of civilization. Both sides invoked the teachings of Jesus and the moral principles of Christianity. Both accused the other of betraying those principles and leading their flocks astray.

Some will ask: why bother about the views of ministers and theologians, since religion, particularly Christianity, has often served as a handmaiden to state-sponsored aggression? It can't be denied that leaders in the Christian Church have been among the most zealous for war. Constantine's vision of a fiery cross in the skies over Rome in 312 AD, which he took as God's vindication of his defeat over Maxentius, aided in his conversion. It also smoothed the way for an alliance of church and state that caused the partial militarization of Christianity.

The eighth century, for example, witnessed Charlemagne's savage assault and conversion of the Saxons (not to mention butchery: he once ordered 4,500 prisoners executed in a single day). Nevertheless, he received Pope Leo's blessing as emperor of the Holy Roman Empire. By 1095 Pope Urban II helped inaugurate the church's first holy war. "How glorious are the victors who return from battle!" exclaimed St. Bernard. "How blessed are the martyrs who die in battle!" Of course, more than martyrs perished in those battles: there were Muslims, Jews, and plenty of local heretics. Faith-based aggression would start up again in the religious wars that followed the Reformation. Passions were so intense, for example, that after the massacre of French Protestants by Catholic mobs in 1572, Pope Gregory XIII issued a medal honoring those involved in the violence. Europe's wars of religion nearly submerged the continent in blood, and the memory of that era still makes Western leaders (especially Europeans) deeply suspicious of a religious rationale in foreign policy. As R. Scott Appleby writes in *The Ambivalence of the Sacred:* "The core values of secularized Western societies, including freedom of speech and freedom of religion, were elaborated in outraged response to inquisitions, crusades, pogroms, and wars conducted in the name of God."[11]

If Christianity seems to have given its blessing to war, however, it has done so with an uneasy conscience. The church always has produced a nonviolent, dissenting tradition. Anabaptists, Brethren, Mennonites, Moravians, Quakers—all have endured the scorn of fellow believers to speak out against war. Augustine formulated a "just war" theory, which set limits on when and how states might engage militarily, as early as the fourth century AD. A thousand years later Protestant reformer Martin Luther invoked this same theory to denounce the crusading impulse. The Christian just war concept remains the most important moral contribution to the practice of modern warfare. As scholar James Turner Johnson argues, the impulse to holy war has all but vanished in the Christian West. Religion has certainly played a role in fueling political and ethnic strife, he writes, but for quite a long time now, not the central role. "The last time wars were fought for religion in the West was during the century after the Protestant Reformation."[12]

All of this suggests that Christianity's posture toward armed conflict is much more complex than many critics contend. Church historian Roland Bainton has observed that the three basic attitudes to war and peace sustained by the Christian church—pacifism, the just war, and the crusade—often have competed for dominance.[13] Few periods in American history illustrate this complexity more vividly than the 1930s. The religious thinkers included in this volume knew well the history of church-sanctioned aggression. Some had ministered in World War I. Others witnessed firsthand the effects of the carnage on European cities. Nearly all had been deeply affected by it. Together they made the dispute over American participation in war as morally charged as any issue in the nation's history. Writes historian Donald Meyer: "The political debate over American foreign policy broke out of the bonds of mere political pragmatics and into ethics, philosophy, and theology."[14]

AN ERA OF SHOCK AND AWE

It's not surprising that the debate steered itself in this direction. The period between the two world wars was a season of economic, political, and spiritual upheaval. There was, first and foremost, the psychological trauma of the devastation of The Great War. "For those who witnessed the slaughter first hand, as well as for those who stayed home to brood on the collapse of Wilsonian idealism . . . the years between 1917 and 1920 were profoundly disillusioning," writes cultural historian Richard Pells.[15] How could they be otherwise? Over 8.5 million men and women were cut down in their prime; at least 21 million were wounded. Nations were starved into submission, civilians were bombed and brutalized. "It is difficult to grasp the public innocence of that earlier generation," writes historian William Manchester, "and how it recoiled when confronted at last by the monstrous crimes which had been committed in the name of patriotism. As time passed, the yeast of bitterness worked in the public mind and its emotions."[16] Though Manchester spoke mainly of Europeans, he fairly described the American temperament as well. Only the most naive could go on believing blithely in the upward march of human progress.

Many could no longer believe at all. Nietzsche had declared in 1886 that "belief in the Christian God is no longer tenable." By the 1920s, his wish was becoming reality. America was still a religious nation, but traditional Christian doctrines were being marginalized from the centers of intellectual life. Reviewing the decade that followed the war, theologian Walter M. Horton observed "a wave of spiritual depression and religious skepticism, widespread and devastating."[17] Radical thinkers such as Sigmund Freud, who viewed the religions of the world as a "mass delusion," got a warm reception in academic circles. Harry Elmer Barnes, the celebrated revisionist historian, published *The Twilight of Christianity*, which praised the liberalizing social gospel movement while attacking biblical concepts of sin, salvation, and the supernatural. Writing in *The Atlantic Monthly* in 1925, Justin Wroe Nixon complained that liberal Protestants were fending off attacks from the fundamentalists, but surrendering too much ground to humanistic philosophy.[18] In 1929 journalist Walter Lippmann created a stir with his work, *A Preface to Morals*, in which he lamented the loss of traditional faith and its influence in shoring up national morality. Though a skeptic, Lippmann lauded "the gifts of a vital religion" that allow individuals to live coherently in the real world of their everyday experiences. "Our forefathers had such a religion," he wrote. "It is plain we have succeeded only in substituting trivial illusions for majestic faiths."[19]

Several distinct philosophical moods coalesced from this ferment. The emotion shared most widely was a deep revulsion for war. Opinion polls in the 1930s showed that a large majority of Americans considered U.S. participation in World War I a tragic mistake. Franklin Roosevelt spoke for most Americans when he said in a 1936 speech in Chautauqua: "We shun political commitments which might entangle us in foreign wars; we avoid connection with the political activities of the League of Nations. . . . We are not isolationists except in so far as we seek to isolate ourselves completely from war."[20]

The feeling was acute among the nation's ministers, and for good reason: Thousands had given World War I their eager blessing; many turned it into a holy crusade. The story of their naïveté was baldly exposed in the 1930s bestseller *Preachers Present Arms*. Author Ray Abrams, a University of Pennsylvania sociologist, chided the clergy for their uncritical, even hysterical embrace of the conflict. "The members of the cloth and their followers were susceptible to war psychology and crowd-thinking in the same manner as were the other citizens," he wrote. "They possessed no prophylactic against the mob mind."[21] Many ministers had painfully confessed to this sin by the time peace negotiations were concluded. By the early 1920s, churches had passed hundreds of resolutions renouncing war. All the major denominations got into the act. In 1924, the Chicago Federation of Churches, representing fifteen denominations, went on record: "In humble penitence for past mistakes and sincere repentance . . . we declare ourselves as unalterably opposed to war."[22] Peace societies cropped up all over the country, advancing absolute pacifism as their new standard. Thus, a 1931 survey of nearly 20,000 clergymen found that 54 percent would not sanction "any future war or participate as an armed combatant." Nearly half refused to serve as military chaplains in wartime.[23]

If the preacher as pacifist had finally come into his own, he had soul mates: the "outraged utopian" would become another vital force of the prewar period. Such was philosopher Lewis Mumford's phrase for a generation that entered the 1920s as hopeful internationalists, only to be embittered by the failure of Woodrow Wilson's League of Nations to keep the peace. Writing in March of 1941—when much of Europe already was in Nazi hands—Mumford observed that sunny, humanistic views of man and society had collided headlong with political realities. Many religious believers were among the casualties: virtually every major denomination had endorsed the League; over 14,000 clergy signed a petition calling for its ratification by the U.S. Senate.[24] Writes Dana Robert of Boston University's School of Theology: "The vision of one world, united by peace . . . was essentially a product of the 'civilizing' aspect of Protestant missions."[25] Likewise, leading clergy lobbied hard for America to endorse the 1928 Pact of Paris, in which signatories from fifty-nine nations agreed to abandon war as a tool of national policy. The Methodist Peace Commission, for example, circulated a petition with 90,000 signatures demanding ratification. When the Senate approved the treaty the following year, church leaders lavished it with heavenly praise. Opined editors at *The Christian Century*: "Today international war was banished from civilization."[26]

Not quite banished. Within a decade most of the nations that had signed the pact were mobilizing for war. By the mid-1930s, a series of political crises had rendered the agreement moot: Italy's Mussolini captured Ethiopia; Hitler occupied the Rhineland; Germany, Italy, and the Soviet Union were intervening in the Spanish Civil War; and the Japanese invaded China. With each event the resentments of the utopians multiplied and deepened. Nevertheless, they continued to place their trust in international agreements. "Having waged a war to make the world safe for democracy," write historians William Langer and S. Everett Gleason, "the country watched with bitter disillusionment the rise of dictatorships and . . . aggression and conflict."[27] As Hitler began his rampage through Europe, the idealists directed their wrath not at the fecklessness of the League of Nations, or the false security of the Pact of Paris, or the dictator in Berlin. The object of their loathing: the punitive treaty that followed World War I. The reality of German aggression contradicted their most sacred beliefs and hopes. But, as one contemporary observer put it, "instead of understanding themselves better, they made the war bear the burden of their frustrated idealism."[28]

A third intellectual trend tugged in the opposite direction: cynicism about democratic values and institutions. Reflecting on the decade before the threshold crisis of 1938, Protestant thinker Lynn Harold Hough observed that millions of young men were "engrossed by their own psychopathic glooms." They came to deny America's accomplishments and despise its virtues. The new breed of social critic, Hough wrote, is "so color blind that he cannot see the good which exists because of his preoccupation with the evils which betray that good." No wonder: universities were teaching him to regard democratic institutions as havens of economic injustice and Hobbesian politics. Far from being a model of liberal, enlightened government, America seemed a cauldron of moral contradictions. Religious liberals, whose politics already inclined them toward the Socialist Party, were especially prone to this temperament. A poll taken by *World Tomorrow* in 1934 found that 28 percent of the nation's clergymen preferred socialism to capitalism. The editors concluded: "Among all the trades, occupations, and professions in the country, few can produce as high a percentage of Socialists as can the ministry."[29]

The Great Depression, which threw roughly half the population into poverty, provided all the evidence they needed. As one historian summarizes it, the Depression represented for social gospel advocates "a massive challenge to the integrity and moral rationale of American society."[30] To many it was overwhelming. In its more extreme forms, the new agnosticism displayed what Hough called a "cynical delight in the failure of democracy." That perhaps explains why many leaders had trouble recognizing the threats to democratic ideals rising in Moscow, Rome, and Berlin. Writing in 1933 in the *New York Times*, Samuel McCrea Cavert, general secretary of the Federal Council of Churches, pleaded for "a less superficial appraisal" of Hitler's National Socialist Party.[31] That was the year Hitler became chancellor, burned down the Reichstag, declared a one-party state, and imposed laws excluding Jews from government and public life. The cynics excused all of it by invoking the indignities Germany suffered at the hands of the capitalist democracies after World War I. Even as Hitler launched his blitzkrieg across Europe, editors at *The Christian Century* held out hope that he might "give the rest of the world a system of interrelationships better than the trade-strangling and man-exploiting system of empire capitalism."[32]

A final defining mood of the period was its "pitiless perfectionism." Theologian Reinhold Niebuhr applied the term to those who would hijack Jesus and his "gospel of love" to construct ideal political and economic systems. Domestically, it produced moralists obsessed with America's shortcomings. Internationally, it made treaties and peace conferences the highest good: war involved too many ethical ambiguities to be a just alternative. In *Jesus or Christianity* (1929), peace activist Kirby Page dismissed 1,600 years of Christianity as a corruption of the teachings of Jesus. A new politics, based on an ethic of love, was needed. For Page and for the thousands of ministers who absorbed his work, that meant socialism at home and pacifism abroad. "If the Sermon on the Mount is not meant to be followed here and now it is of little value to mankind," wrote Page. "Religion can never be effective in international relations until its advocates . . . devote themselves to the task of replacing international suspicion, fear and enmity with sympathy, confidence, and friendliness."[33] The United States couldn't be trusted to execute an aggressive foreign policy; the regime behaved as any other imperialistic power. After all, the nation that was failing to live out its calling as a "city on a hill" had no business instructing others. Besides, they argued, there were problems at home demanding attention. "We are not the moral censors of the world," opined Francis Talbot in *America*, the nation's leading Catholic weekly. "Our business is to take care of our domestic affairs." And that meant keeping America out of the dirty affairs going on in Europe. "They were implementing the ideal of entire sanctification," writes Donald Meyer, "of complete personal union with Jesus Christ, of—in a word—perfectionism."[34]

THE PEACEMAKERS

The essays in this volume bear the marks of these philosophical moods. The hawks savaged these notions; the doves seemed guided and energized by them. Indeed, one of the remarkable aspects of the noninterventionists was their resoluteness in the face of political reality. In this sense, they thought like many Americans at the time. They remained deeply ambivalent about the nation's international obligations, even as the threat of fascism became more ominous. Indeed, American public opinion steadfastly, and almost universally, opposed involvement in another war.[35] The religious Left, however, clung to peace proposals long after all rational hope of negotiations had collapsed. Many pressed on even as Hitler's armies threatened to swallow the whole of Europe.

Consider some of the major events from early 1938, when Hitler took over the German Army and became total dictator, to December 7, 1941, when Japan's attack on Pearl Harbor forced American entry into the war. In March of 1938, Hitler directly violated the Treaty of Versailles by annexing Austria. In September he forced the allies at Munich to redraw the borders of Czechoslovakia, absorbing 800,000 Czechs and forty of the best-equipped divisions in Europe. Political and religious leaders hailed the Munich Pact as a masterpiece of statecraft that averted all-out war. As Catholic thinker John LaFarge wrote in *America*: "The peace of Munich was possible because of the habits and methods of peacemaking learned through two decades of international intercourse in the halls of the League of Nations."[36] For hawks such as Winston Churchill, such "methods of peacemaking" were precisely the problem. Churchill, who had been observing the fearful rise of Nazism for over a decade, called the agreement a "total and unmitigated defeat" for the cause of peace. Hitler would not stop with the Czechs, he warned, and Britain must prepare for war. "You have to consider the character of the Nazi movement and the rule which it implies," Churchill told the House of Commons in October. "There can never be friendship between the British democracy and the Nazi power, that power which spurns Christian ethics, which cheers its onward course by a barbarous paganism, which vaunts the spirit of aggression and conquest, which derives strength and perverted pleasure from persecution, and uses, as we have seen, with pitiless brutality the threat of murderous force."

It would not be long before Churchill was tragically vindicated. The year 1938, in fact, marked a political and spiritual turning point—the year in which Hitler's "final solution" for European Jews was launched in earnest. On November 9–13, Hitler staged *Kristallnacht*, the Night of Broken Glass, a national campaign of violent anti-Semitism. Shops were looted, synagogues were burned, Jews were beaten by mobs and arrested by the thousands. By December, German Jews were banned from public schools, stripped of their property rights and subject to curfews and arbitrary imprisonment. The camps at Dachau, Sachsenhausen, Buchenwald, and Mauthausen filled up with the newly arrested. The pattern would be repeated in every state that fell under the shadow of the Third Reich. And they fell with frightening speed.

In March of 1939, Hitler invaded and occupied what was left of Czechoslovakia. In May he formed a military alliance with Italian Fascist Benito Mussolini. By September he pushed into Poland. Britain and France declared war, but help was too little and too late. Nearly sixty German divisions had sliced their way into the heart of the country, reaching the outer edges of Warsaw after only eight days of advancing. The government went into exile as the Germans shut down schools and churches and deported thousands. Within weeks the ghettoization and resettlement of Polish Jews had begun. In April of 1940, German tanks invaded Denmark and Norway. In May they swept into Belgium and Holland, and in June rumbled into France. Within ten days France was defeated and forced to submit to a Nazi-installed regime in Paris. That same month Hitler launched the Battle of Britain, and in September began the massive bombing of London. What followed were nearly seventy-six nights of consecutive raids against the city. "They were nights of fire and ruin," writes historian John Lukacs. "The people became accustomed to the new landscape of jagged blackness, to the awful smell of pulverized brick, to the swift onrush of death."[37]

Hitler's appetite for war and death was insatiable. In April of 1941, he attacked Yugoslavia and Greece. In June he set his sights on the Soviet Union, sending three-fourths of his military juggernaut into its wilderness. In a matter of days, half of the Soviet Air Force was destroyed. Hitler's *Wehrmacht* seized more ground in a week than the Imperial German Army had managed in three years during World War I. By August they reached the outskirts of Leningrad. Hitler issued an unprecedented "Commissar Order," instructing that captured political officers of the Red Army be shot immediately. Trained death squads (*Einsatzgruppen*) joined the campaign, with specific orders to kill the "Jew-Bolsheviks." Indeed, wherever Hitler went his hatred of Jews went with him—from one end of the European continent to the other. "Each in its turn became victim, not only of German and Nazi occupation, but of the . . . persecution, transportation and extermination of Jews from these countries," writes historian Robert Ross. "No conquered nation escaped."[38]

Yet even as Hitler's panzer divisions laid waste to much of the continent, religious leaders were blaming the outbreak of hostilities on America or the Allied nations. "If evil is today rampant, this has a cause," explained the Federal Council of Churches. "Through our action or non-action we exerted a profound influence on the course of world events. That course has generated widespread unrest, great violence and immense disaster." Christian fundamentalists also raged against America—not for its foreign policy, but its lack of piety. Rampant immorality and skepticism, they said, were inviting the judgment of God through war. "God pity America!" said Will Houghton, president of Moody Bible Institute. "It looks as if we are about to reap in tragedy for our sowing of unbelief." Most clergymen, however, faulted American and European foreign policy in the interwar period. Baptist luminary Harry Emerson Fosdick claimed almost unanimous support for the view that "we, the democracies, are just as responsible for the rise of the dictators as the dictatorships themselves, and perhaps more so." Reverend John Haynes Holmes, a Unitarian minister in New York, spoke for many when he called Hitler "the veritable incarnation of our nationalistic, capitalistic and militaristic era." A German victory, he intoned, should be viewed as "the punishment for our transgressions."

The transgressions most had in mind centered on that "wicked treaty." By the early 1930s, the Treaty of Versailles had become an object of almost universal scorn. It stood near the heart of the political and economic factors endlessly cited to explain German aggression. There's little dispute that the accord helped cripple the Weimar economy: the effort to force Germany to balance everyone else's books virtually destroyed her currency.[39] Many clerics, however, had surprisingly little trouble jumping from an imperfect treaty to a mass murderer with global territorial ambitions. Reverend Ernest Fremont Tittle, leader of the peace movement in the Methodist Church, joined many who speculated that Nazi aggression had its genesis at Versailles. Germany, he wrote, "may be provoked by bitter belief . . . that there is now no peaceful way of solving a desperate economic problem." Most clergymen, in fact, had come to believe that the punitive measures of Versailles had made the emergence Hitler almost inevitable.[40]

Like the majority of the nation's political leaders, antiwar ministers assumed the European conflict was merely a repeat of World War I. And that war, they agreed, was nothing more than a clash of selfish national interests. The National Council of Churches expressed the typical view: "The war arose chiefly as the result of deep-rooted economic competition to control the raw materials and markets of the world."[41] They wanted no part of a bloody sequel to this horror show; they'd seen the previews.

This attitude helped spawn the U.S. Neutrality Acts, passed from 1935–1939, which sought to cut off American aid and trade to either side in a European or Asian war. For the first time in U.S. foreign policy, all sides in a conflict were treated as "belligerents." Historian Paul Johnson calls the Neutrality Acts "a complete departure from previous American policy, which had always permitted the U.S. government to make moral distinctions between participants in foreign wars."[42] Nevertheless, isolationist clergy sounded alarms whenever they imagined the acts were being violated. Hence the General Conference of the Methodist Church, in a statement urging U.S. neutrality, assumed craven motives among all concerned: "The mood of either victor or vanquished in war cannot aid peace. Only those who have escaped the blood lust of actual fighting can see a world situation steadily and see it whole." Similarly, ministers such as John Haynes Holmes decried the "fundamentally immoral clash of imperialisms" at work again in Europe. "If America goes into the war," he wrote, "it will not be for idealistic reasons but to serve her own imperialistic interests."

The leading mainline Protestant journal, *The Christian Century*, advanced this theme with missionary zeal. Beginning in the mid-1930s, its editorial page issued strident warnings against American entanglement in "the old rivalries and hatreds of Europe." As late as November 26, 1941—with most of Europe effectively under Nazi rule—the magazine denounced Franklin Roosevelt's efforts to assist Churchill through the Atlantic Charter. In an editorial titled, "A War for Imperialism," Charles Clayton Morrison apparently feared a successful Anglo-American alliance more than an Axis victory; it would simply replace one tyranny with another. "The American citizen, with his boundless belief in his own capacities, is asked to prepare to fight a war so that he and his kind can take over the control of the world. The world is in a mess; now let the omnicompetent Anglo-Saxon step in to straighten it out!" Morrison wrote. "But how many Americans stop to realize that behind this simple picture there awaits the prospect of the most ambitious imperialism ever projected, an imperialism which will gradually but inevitably bring to focus against itself the jealousies and hatreds of all the other nations and races on Earth?"

The claim that greedy capitalist states were the greatest obstacle to peace rested on a grotesque assumption: that the differences between the German Reich and Anglo-American democracy didn't really amount to much. This perhaps explains why the isolationists assumed that mobilizing for a fight in Europe meant the end of democratic freedoms on the home front. "Our participation in war would not establish 'democracies' abroad," wrote Francis Talbot for *America*. "But it would certainly destroy what we have left of democracy at home."[43] Harold Fey, executive secretary of the Fellowship of Reconciliation, denounced militarization plans as a ruse to turn America into a dictatorship no different from those in Germany or the Soviet Union. "The men behind this plan are now working night and day pouring out unprecedented public funds for the realization of this totalitarian military system."[44] President Roosevelt was even vilified in the religious press as "the Fuhrer of this inchoate fascism."[45]

Strangely, these critics rarely became as exorcised over the actions of the actual führer in Germany. Albert Palmer, president of Chicago Theological Seminary, rejected denunciations of Hitler as the "short-circuited, adolescent hatred of individual leaders." Yes, he admitted, the war in France had been terrible. But, he reasoned—even as German storm troopers were executing French nationals—"would not the Allies have done much the same thing in Germany if they had got there first?" A. J. Muste, a minister-turned-peace activist, likewise saw no important distinctions between the warring factions. He even compared the Allies to "the men who tortured and killed the victims of the Inquisition," mistakenly believing they were advancing the cause of God.[46] "There are no victors and vanquished in any important sense in modern war," he claimed. "It makes no difference, therefore, which side 'wins.'"[47] It was the same at *The Christian Century*. "It is not a war to preserve civilization!" its editors exclaimed. "It is the war itself that is destroying civilization—destroying it increasingly with each day that the war lasts, and destroying it definitively if it lasts to the point of victory, *no matter which side wins*" (emphasis added). From 1938 to 1941, Protestant groups issued no less than fifty statements about how to achieve a just and durable peace. Yet barely a handful argued that the defeat of Nazism was essential to international justice.

This approach meant painting a softer portrait of life under Nazi rule than the known facts demanded. Antiwar statements simply avoided unpleasant topics: the complete militarization of German society, Hitler's broken promises about his territorial ambitions, the subjugation of entire populations, the anti-Semitic campaigns in Germany, and the deportation and ghettoization of Jews across Europe. There was, indeed, little mention of this feature of Nazism amid the rhetoric of American neutrality, despite widespread press coverage.

Following *Kristallnacht* in November 1938, for example, various political and religious leaders met to denounce the brutalities. Yet Catholic figures such as Paul Blakely quickly complained that these noisy domestic protests resembled "a fit of national hysteria."[48] A few months later, on January 30, 1939, Hitler delivered an ominous Reichstag address, in which he warned of "the destruction of the Jewish race in Europe." The Protestant press ignored it.[49] Even after undeniable reports of mass executions in Poland, liberal apologists dismissed charges that Jews were being killed and processed into soap as "one of the propaganda triumphs of the First World War." They knew better. Hitler had made clear his intentions toward the Jews since *Mein Kampf*, and spent more than a decade whipping up anti-Semitic ugliness. In *So It Was True: The American Protestant Press and the Nazi Persecution of the Jews*, Robert Ross details the "reluctant witness" of church leaders to the mass murder of Jews in Germany and elsewhere in Europe. "The churches in the United States were thought not to know much about such things prior to the discovery of the death camps at the end of World War II," Ross concludes. "Such was not the case."[50]

Most religious organizations and intellectuals that opposed American intervention did not consider themselves isolationists: they were internationalists with a Christian conscience. Their platform included foreign aid, international trade, and commitment to the League of Nations and the World Court.

Yet when it came to dealing with threats to international security, the practical policy was pacifism. America might offer material aid, they said, but let England and France fight Hitler. Even if Nazism prevailed, the Western Hemisphere was safe from military attack. "I am not an isolationist," insisted Georgia Harkness, a Methodist theologian and ecumenical leader. "But . . . America's supreme duty is to remain out of war."[51] Ministers helped form the America First Committee, which soon became a leading noninterventionist group in the United States. The organization even opposed assistance to Britain and France because it "weakens national defense at home and threatens to involve America in war abroad."[52] Harry Emerson Fosdick, chairman of the Emergency Peace Campaign, could foresee no circumstances justifying U.S. engagement. "We see clearly that a war for democracy is a contradiction in terms, that war itself is democracy's chief enemy," Fosdick said. "For the United States to become a belligerent in this conflict would be a colossal and futile disaster."

The major church denominations took a similar view. The General Conference of the reorganized United Methodist Church, representing about 8 million members, declared that America could provide relief for war-stricken populations, but must "remain in a position to preserve democracy within its own borders"—that is, stay out of the European imbroglio.[53] The editorial voice at *America*, which represented mainstream Catholicism, claimed to be "keenly interested" in promoting world peace, but judged U.S. rearmament as a certain path toward war. "When the Government bends itself to its proper work, which is to promote the welfare of the American people, it will have no time to worry about the entanglements of other nations," the editors wrote. "If that policy means 'isolation,' then let us be happy in our isolation, far from Europe, a scene of unending war."[54] Throughout the decade, Christian groups passed hundreds of antiwar resolutions, sponsored international conferences, and organized numerous peace organizations.

None of it, however, could prevent the appearance of Mussolini, Stalin, Franco, and Hitler. It is almost impossible to overstate the problem that totalitarianism created for the churches.[55] American Christians had forged their pacifism in an era of peace and prosperity. That era was over, and they were now living in a nation that, even in the mid-1930s, invested next to nothing in military defense. "At each step in the disintegration of the European order," writes historian Donald Meyer, "the need for rationalization grew more agonizing."[56] And more desperate. The German *Wehrmacht* smashed the European states like rag dolls, making the prospect of a secure and isolated democracy in North America look absurd. Nothing would prevent the Axis states from either strangling America economically or threatening her militarily. Nevertheless, the liberal response was always the same: convene a peace conference. Numerous organizations offered peace proposals and resolutions to establish a "political and economic framework in which the tensions over these pre-war issues would disappear." Groups such as the Fellowship for a Christian Social Order, the Fellowship of Reconciliation, the National Council for Prevention of War, the National Peace Conference, and the Ministers No War Committee led the charge.

Clerics kept up their appeals for talks until the moment America entered the war. "Non-violent victory over the enemies of peace and freedom demands a skill and a heroism quite as great as those ever displayed on the battlefield," argued Albert Day, vice president of the National Council of Churches. "I am convinced that a nation which would employ this strategy would lead the world out of this maddening circle of war breeding war which threatens to destroy civilization."[57] Methodist leader Ernest Tittle was equally unyielding. As late as February 1941, after Hitler had conquered most of Europe and imperiled Great Britain, Tittle held on to hope. "It would not, in my judgment, be an act of insanity to seek an official statement of peace aims" from Germany, he wrote, but rather "an act of high statesmanship." Pacifism as a national strategy, he added, "would pursue a policy not of appeasement but of reconciliation." Editors at *The Christian Century* even suggested that massive peace movements outside Germany would soften the Third Reich. "The internal effects upon the populations of even dictator countries would surely weaken their military morale as they contemplated a prospective world order in which the real causes of the war . . . would at least be on the way to being removed."

The doves rooted their position in a theological claim—that the ethics of Jesus flatly contradicted a resort to war to solve international crises. The primary obligation of the Christian, they argued, was to rid himself of any desire for revenge and to adopt a posture of love and forgiveness. "Let us pray not for security, or for national victory," implored Georgia Harkness, a professor at Garrett Biblical Institute in Evanston, Illinois. "Let us pray for the purging of our impulses to hate, to retaliate, to think evil of others, to have recourse to military might in those areas where only the curative processes of world cooperation and brotherhood can prevail."

The teachings of Jesus not only opposed war, these leaders claimed, but pointed the way toward its resolution. Love—Christian love—could topple tyrants. "The Son of God . . . resists evil but never with its own weapons," wrote Reverend Tittle. "He resists it with truth and love even unto death." Reverend Fosdick, of New York City's Park Avenue Baptist Church, deeply regretted his earlier support of war. "The whole business of war," he said, "the causes that produce it, the processes that characterize it, the moral consequences that accompany it, are too obviously the denial of everything that Jesus taught." Albert Palmer, a leader in the Congregational Christian Church, admitted that world domination by the Nazis would likely follow an invasion of Britain—yet remained untroubled by the prospect. "Can military force do much against soul force which folds its arms and bides its day?" he asked. "Without military opposition the Hitlers wither away." Christian forgiveness, they insisted, would provide the solvent. "Forgiveness heals wounds and prevents new ones from being made," wrote Palmer, who liked to quote from the Sermon on the Mount. "If your enemy hunger, feed him—and understand him. Love your enemies and do them good." Or as John Haynes Holmes asked rhetorically: "Can anyone read Jesus' gospel, and study his life in fulfillment of that gospel, without seeing that love is a weapon more potent than the sword?"

WITHDRAWN

THE PROPHETS

Never before in American history had so many Christian leaders equated piety with pacifism. "It may almost be said," writes historian Robert Moats Miller, "that pacifism was the 'party line' of liberal Protestantism."[58] Given their shameful militarism in the First World War, this seemed a moral necessity in the 1920s. Not by 1938. A growing number of thinkers, a group known as the "Christian realists," found the approach utterly unworkable. Like the doves, they'd been chastened by the devastation of Europe's bloodlust. Most had vowed to oppose another war whatever the circumstances. But they hadn't reckoned on a Hitler. "Before the events that followed the invasion of Belgium and Holland I was living in a world of illusion," admitted John Bennett, professor of theology at the Pacific School of Religion at Berkeley. "I did not face the fact that a German victory was the real danger." Reinhold Niebuhr of Union Theological Seminary had announced his opposition to war in 1923. "I am done with this business," he said. Ten years later he upbraided Winston Churchill for his "unyielding imperial ambition." But by the Munich Agreement of 1938, which delivered Czechoslovakia into Nazi hands, Niebuhr reversed course.

Though the realists differed over how America should respond to the crisis—some advocated only U.S. assistance to the Allies, others argued for military intervention—they attacked the peace movement as politically and morally naïve. They called pleas for negotiations with Hitler "a euphemism for surrender and for the abandonment of Germany's present victims to their fate." Widespread disgust for war, they argued, had caused the nation's leaders "to treat peace as an absolute good and to surrender to evil"—a posture exploited by tyrants eager to use treaties as a cover for aggression.

Henry Pitney Van Dusen, a colleague of Niebuhr's at Union Seminary, saw an evasion of reality at work among liberal clergy, what he called a "resolute unwillingness to face known and indisputable facts." Two examples particularly galled him. A peace initiative by *The Christian Century* in May 1940 tried to summon officials from eighteen "neutral" nations to Rome—except that fourteen of the eighteen were already bound to either side in the struggle, making diplomatic action impossible. Two of the remaining states had just been defeated and reduced to servitude by the Axis powers, while the proposed host city was a center of fascist aggression. "The proposal has less meaning than Alice's Wonderland, for the latter had at least symbolic reference to reality; this has none," Van Dusen wrote. "In any Christian, escapism is always pitiable. In one charged with

influence over the views and decisions of others in days like these, it is unforgivable." Later that year, Methodist leader Ernest Tittle proposed that food be sent to prevent starvation in states under Nazi rule and that arrangements be made with Germany to allow free passage of the relief ships. Herbert Hoover's National Committee on Food for the Small Democracies picked up on this idea, but the realists assailed the plan. "Men cry for freedom," Van Dusen thundered, "and are given bread."

Nothing angered these thinkers more, however, than the attempt to soft-pedal the differences between liberal democracies and totalitarian regimes. Though some were committed socialists, they chided those who obsessed over the foibles of democratic states to dismiss the European war as another clash of imperialistic interests. "It is sheer moral perversity," fumed Niebuhr, "to equate the inconsistencies of a democratic civilization with the brutalities which modern tyrannical States practice." Lewis Mumford acknowledged America's various social sins, from class exploitation to the lynching of blacks in the South. Nevertheless, what was happening in Germany was of a different order altogether. "To measure the unbridgeable gulf between fascist barbarism and democratic civilization becomes, therefore, the first duty of every intelligent citizen today."[59] Lynn Harold Hough likewise thrashed the equivocators in an April 1941 article for *Christianity and Crisis*. The doves dredged up every fault of England since the Norman Conquest, but said little about its moral triumphs. The history of parliamentary democracy was ignored, the expanding liberties of the British Empire forgotten. The word *imperial* was used to "black out intelligence" and defame democracy. "We must be honest about its failures," Hough said. "But in God's name we must be honest about its successes." The ultimate problem with equating democracies and tyrannies was that it produced inertia: it allowed leaders to avoid making moral judgments—and thus assuming moral and political responsibilities. "The evil which has been set loose upon the world must be crushed," Hough wrote. "And we cannot wait for perfect men or perfect nations to crush it."[60]

The problem of evil formed the core of the case for intervention. The latest fads in theology, psychology, and economics had flattened the Bible's hard-nosed teaching about evil and its deep link to human personality. The hawks recovered it, at least partially. They didn't ignore political and economic injustices, but they insisted that the origins of the war couldn't be explained by them. Something much darker was at work, and the totalitarian impulse had exposed the depth of the problem.

Indeed, the fatal flaw of liberal intellectuals was what the realists called "the dogma of the natural goodness of man." Mumford, though a well-known and respected humanist, bluntly called this doctrine a heresy in Christian theology. Its advocates mistakenly assumed that sin resided mostly in social and political institutions; once freed from them through reform or revolution, rational man would rise to new humanistic heights. As a result, many clung to "moralistic sentimentality" in their social and ethical philosophies. Editors at *The New Republic*, for example, vowed to resist American intervention because the "evils of a system" could not be cured by "killing the unfortunate individuals who for the moment embody the system."

Reinhold Niebuhr, who emerged as one of America's most important public theologians, assailed this reasoning without mercy. No Bible fundamentalist, Niebuhr nevertheless revived the scriptural meaning of sin as man's rebellion against God and his moral norms for humankind. Social structures might extend its influence, but at its heart sin involved human pride and the corruption of individual conscience. Hitler's rage, he said, was "fed by a pagan religion of tribal self-glorification." His "maniacal fury" against the Jewish race was an essential part of a plan to enslave all the other races of Europe. A fury such as this, Niebuhr argued, could not be tamed through negotiations. Confrontation was inevitable. Yet false dogma about human nature, shared by Americans and Europeans, had produced a "failure to understand the stubbornness and persistence of the tyrannical will." Supported by a modern, militarized state—and aided by the cowardice and prejudices of political leaders—Hitler could extend his will over nearly the entire continent. "Nazi tyranny never could have reached such proportions as to be able to place the whole of Europe under its ban," Niebuhr wrote, "if sentimental illusions about the character of the evil which Europe was facing had not been combined with less noble motives for tolerating Nazi aggression."

Christian thinkers weren't the only ones grappling with the problem of evil. Stephen Wise, president of the World Jewish Congress, was one of the first religious figures to see the implications of Nazi hatreds. Wise reasoned that Hitler's threat to international order must be judged not only by his military strength, but by the viciousness of his anti-Semitism—a campaign that preceded German aggression and now threatened the foundations of every civilized state. "Peoples and churches permitted themselves to be lulled into unawareness, because it was only or chiefly the Jew who at the outset was hurt," Wise observed. "Men heeded not that the Jews were assailed as symbol of that civilization, the values of which Nazism was resolved to destroy." By viewing Hitler's war aims in isolation from his ideology, church leaders persuaded themselves that he could be negotiated with or, at worst, contained. As the Catholic magazine *America* editorialized in the fall of 1938: "It is possible for a Fascist state to sign a Concordat, and even to be faithful to it."[61]

The German dictator advertised himself as the world leader of anticommunism, and many swallowed his sales pitch. Protestants and Catholics both worried that the defeat of Nazism would establish Bolshevism all over Europe; better to downplay Hitler's brutalities.[62] Wise considered that a disastrous foreign policy (as did Winston Churchill). "The world that Hitlerism can save or defend is a world destroyed," he wrote a year before *Kristallnacht*. "Unless free peoples come to understand this truth, the menace is not to the Jew but to mankind." Christian churches also had come under attack in Germany, a fact that got significant attention in the Protestant and Catholic press in America. Moreover, it was widely known that Jews were being arrested, deported, starved, imprisoned, and hunted down without mercy all over Europe. Yet there existed no coalition of church organizations in the West mobilized against Nazi paganism.

As Wise and others suggested, anti-Jewish bigotry was also part of the reason. The 1930s witnessed a surge of anti-Semitism in the United States, often led by members of the clergy. M. E. Dodd, president of the Southern Baptist Convention, rationalized Hitler's policies as necessary to maintain civic stability. Writing in 1934, Dodd claimed that of the 200,000 Jews who had emigrated to Germany since the end of World War I, "most of these were Communist agitators against the government."[63] Father Charles Coughlin, the radio priest, spewed anti-Jewish screeds on his wildly popular *The Hour of Power* (3.5 million weekly listeners), while cultivating Nazi sympathies. From 1933 to 1941, over one hundred anti-Semitic groups appeared in America, many of them with a Christian hue.[64] The overall psychological effect was to shield Hitler from the implications of his crimes. Editors at *The Christian Century*, for example, admitted there was "plenty of extermination" of Jews going on in Europe, yet doubted the numbers being reported. Chief editor Charles Clayton Morrison even questioned whether any good purpose was served by the publication of the charges.[65] Whatever their motives, the isolationists failed to condemn without qualification Hitler's assault on the Jewish people. As Wise argued, their outlook was creating paralysis in the face of a growing international menace. "Jews may yet come to understand that their position in the world is imperiled as never before in history," he wrote in 1938. "The democracies may yet conclude that they will either stay the power of Nazism and Fascism or be destroyed."

THE SWORD OF THE STATE

Compared to the doves, the hawks had a more sharply defined theology of church and state. The church must speak to evil in the human heart, they argued, but secular government had a God-given duty to restrain evil in the world. The pacifists tended to conflate the obligations of the Christian community—or, at least, one aspect of those obligations, the requirement to love thy neighbor—with the duties of government. Indeed, if their foreign policy could be reduced to a single biblical idea, it would be to "turn the other cheek." The Christian realists repudiated that view: the ethic of love expected of Jesus' followers could not be imposed through politics on a sinful world; history had already revealed the folly of that approach. They agreed that the state, like the church, was an institution ordained by God. But it was concerned primarily with promoting justice and opposing wickedness. "It is the function of the state to set a barrier against sin and chaos; to discriminate between right and wrong; and to prevent any revolution of nihilism," wrote Princeton theologian John Mackay in October 1941. The realists had no doubt that the greatest source of chaos and nihilism was now located in Berlin: "While the cause of no nation in this conflict is the cause of God," Mackay said, "it is nevertheless the will of God that evil in the demonic form in which it has appeared should be resisted."[66]

Swiss theologian Karl Barth, who fled Germany after the occupation of the Ruhr, had seen the demons up close. From his teaching post in Switzerland, he exerted a profound influence on American and European theology throughout the 1930s and 1940s. No one explored with more depth and power the biblical themes of sin and divine judgment. Few understood more realistically how the idolatry of fascism might be overcome. It was the God-given role of the state, he wrote, to uphold basic standards of morality. This is why government "bears the sword" of a police force and a military: to prevent human societies from being engulfed by the chaos of lawless men. "The State would lose all meaning and would be failing in its duty as an appointed minister of God . . . if it failed to defend the bounds between Right and Wrong by the threat, and by the actual use, of the sword." Barth denied that the battle against fascism was a crusade or a war of religion; adopting that view only led to "peculiar passions" and "vain expectations." Nevertheless, he said, when Britain declared war on Germany it acted as a just government upholding Christian standards. "The cause which is at stake in this war is our own cause, and we Christians first and foremost must make our own the anxieties, the hardships and the hopes which this war demands of all men," he wrote. "The Christians who do not realize that they must take part unreservedly in this war must have slept over their Bibles as well as over their newspapers."

Ultimately, the Christian realists were driven out of the neutrality camp not only by meditating on scripture, but by contemplating the geopolitical map. They looked beyond the sellout of Czechoslovakia, the blitzkrieg, or even the fall of France. They saw the larger aims of Hitler's Germany, and what a Nazi victory over Britain would mean for Europe and the United States. In this, they followed the logic of the just war tradition: nations must be willing to fight when the failure to do so would unleash grave injustices.

If fascism prevails, wrote Henry Van Dusen in January 1941, the United States will become "an island of democratic ideals and institutions in a world united into a single economic structure and political alliance dominated by antithetic principles." John Bennett envisioned the loss of all political and religious liberties, an omnipresent secret police, and the relentless pursuit and punishment of dissidents. "The alternative to successful resistance to Germany is the extension of the darkest political tyranny imaginable over the whole of Europe, with the prospect that . . . the whole world will be threatened by the Axis powers." Lynn Harold Hough made the same moral calculation: an utterly destructive, even demonic force had appeared on the world stage, and it was winning dangerous victories. Britain might not be a perfect democracy, he admitted, yet it "stands between the rest of the world and incalculable tragedy." Reinhold Niebuhr was candid about the distasteful methods required to fight and win a war against Germany—the undermining of civil liberties on the home front, the economic and human costs, the killing of innocents. But the nature of totalitarianism seemed to leave freedom-loving people no choice. "If we are told that tyranny would destroy itself, if only we would not challenge it, the obvious answer is that tyranny continues to grow if it is not resisted." The cancer of Nazism, he concluded, would not slip quietly into remission.

Yet the interventionists went even further. They argued that failing to challenge this threat meant assisting in its triumph—and betraying the moral principles of Christianity. One such principle, in fact, was the requirement to love thy neighbor. Isolationism offered the beseiged neighbor no practical help. "It is not pleasant to think of the children of Europe robbed for a generation or longer of their freedom," wrote Episcopal Bishop Edward Parsons. "The Christian pacifist, when he thinks of his position as expressing the will of God . . . must remember those children." The United States might be able to survive the fire sweeping Europe, but only by turning a blind eye to its victims—and turning itself into a fortress. "Christians who seek to be responsive to the demands of love," wrote John Bennett, "must recognize their responsibility for saving others from tyranny, for the restraining of violence which is already let loose upon the world." The hawks believed force was necessary not because it could achieve political perfection, but because it was the best hope for securing justice. When all was said and done, the argument for American neutrality amounted to "a preference for tyranny" over liberal democracy. It judged the enslavement of millions to a demonic ideology as a better alternative than the tragedies of war. For the realists, this could not be the responsible Christian position. "Ambiguous methods are required for the ambiguities of history," wrote Niebuhr. "Let those who are revolted by such ambiguities have the decency and consistency to retire to the monastery, where medieval perfectionists found their asylum."

It soon became clear that there could be no safe haven from the Third Reich. Barely a week after the fall of France—a full eighteen months before the attack at Pearl Harbor—the hawks drafted a manifesto urging that American Christians support the Allied cause in the war. Called "America's Responsibility in the Present Crisis," the document laid out in terse moral terms the consequences of an Allied defeat to Germany. Though making clear the ultimate threat to the United States, the signatories explained that much more than national self-interest was at stake. "A German victory which would destroy the liberties of free peoples and subordinate all life under the rule of political totalitarianism would endanger every value embodied in western civilization by the Christian faith and by humanistic culture," they wrote. Despite its ugliness and uncertainties, all-out resistance was the only way to prevent the unthinkable outcome. "When men or nations must choose between two evils, the choice of the lesser evil becomes Christian duty. That is the alternative confronting the American people now."

RESISTING EVIL

The American people again face difficult choices: how to aggressively prosecute a messy war on terrorism abroad without trampling civil liberties at home; whether to use military force against regimes that appear to be collaborating with terrorist organizations; and how to prevent rogue states from acquiring nuclear weapons while respecting national sovereignty. "The [Bush] administration is clearly right that a new arms control cannot rest entirely on the illusory safety of talks and treaties and U.N. resolutions," writes Bill Keller for the *New York Times Magazine*. "The autocrats most likely to be dangerous to us if they get nuclear weapons are the leaders least likely to care about staying in the good graces of the 'international community,' whatever that is."[67]

What can the premier moral argument of the late 1930s teach us about these challenges? And where might we turn for insight into how to apply the lessons of that troubled age?

Spiritual leaders, those charged with the care of men's souls, are expected to understand the contradictions of the human condition—and the need to face them honestly. Having devoted themselves to resisting sin, they're supposed to know the form that sin can take in the human heart and in human societies. Indeed, theirs is a discipline that has implications well outside the sanctuary. Paul Johnson has written that the essence of geopolitics is "to be able to distinguish between different degrees of evil."[68] This ability seemed in short supply in the 1930s, especially among the nation's leading churchmen. Too many could not recognize the moral and spiritual divide separating Nazism from liberal democracy. Though acting as prophets, they failed to see the most obvious signs of Hitler's gathering storm. Though assuming a mantle of public leadership, they offered a politics of pietism that could not possibly check the menace in Berlin. As far as the watching world was concerned, their faith traditions were simply not up to the job. Reinhold Niebuhr distilled their weakness in this way: "The tragic character of contemporary history has not yet persuaded them to take the fact of human sinfulness seriously."

Even secular voices heaped scorn upon the clerical class for its inadequacies and lack of faith. Writing in January of 1940, the editors of *Fortune* noted with some bitterness that numerous ministers had abandoned the fundamental truths of their faith. The resulting lack of spiritual leadership threatened to undermine democratic societies in their moment of testing. "In order for humanity to progress it must believe; it must have faith in certain absolute spiritual values, or at least have faith that absolute spiritual values exist," they wrote. "The Church, as teacher and interpreter of those values, is the guardian of our faith in them. And as laymen we do not feel that that faith is being guarded." *Fortune* had surveyed 137 pastors representing nine major denominations and asked them to explain their attitudes toward the war in Europe. The vast majority of those responding cited their disillusionment with World War I to justify opposition to the current conflict. The magazine's editors were aghast. "The men who urged U.S. soldiers in 1917 to face death against an ordinary emperor, whose chief sin was worldly ambition, now conclude that it would be wrong to fight a virtual Antichrist whose doctrines strike at the base of the civilization which the Church has done so much to build," they wrote. "It is for the flesh to be disillusioned, not for the soul."[69]

That seems a timely warning, especially given the response of many religious thinkers to the events of September 11. Shortly after the terrorist attacks, for example, evangelical leader Tony Campolo offered this assessment of the problem: "There's a swamp out there called poverty and injustice . . . Osama bin Laden is our fault!" Stanley Hauerwas, regarded as one of the nation's most influential theologians, wrote that he felt no need to offer a policy to combat global terrorism. "My only response is I do not have a foreign policy. I have something better—a church constituted by people who would rather die than kill."[70] Echoing many clerics, sociologist Robert Bellah immediately complained that America "has turned out to be a problematic society." Bellah identifies superpower arrogance as the inspiration for further acts of terrorism. "To relapse into the dream of innocence and imagine that evil is the sole possession of our enemies," he concludes, "invites disaster."[71] We expect religious thinkers to draw attention to America's shortcomings and to urge faithfulness to religious ideals, even in a time of crisis. It is an essential part of the freedom they exercise in a democracy. But responsibilities attend this freedom—namely, the obligation to gain a sober view of the gravest threats to democracy. Too many religious voices downplay the unique perversity of militant Islam and its challenge to the norms of civilized nations. They neglect the fact that Osama bin Laden and his allies express a visceral hatred of America and the West. Thus a typical bin Laden judgment of the United States: "You are the worst civilization witnessed by the history of mankind." It's reasonable to wonder what change in U.S. policies could alter that verdict.

One fact is clear in this debate: each terrorist attack, and attempted attack, underscores the truth that the threat of radical Islam is global, relentless, and potentially horrific. Last year alone there were over 200 acts of international terrorism, killing 625 people and injuring over 3,600. Targets ranged from the United Nations headquarters in Baghdad to the International Committee for the Red Cross. Earlier this year, train bombings in Madrid, linked to al-Qaeda, killed 192 people and injured more than 1,900. As Paul Berman summarizes it in *Terror and Liberalism*: "We have all the evidence in the world . . . to conclude that Islamism in its radical version of the present poses every imaginable danger."[72] Indeed, the possibility of weapons of mass destruction falling into the hands of Islamic terrorists seems to be growing. A. Q. Khan, the father of Pakistan's nuclear weapons program, has admitted to selling nuclear technology on the global black market. Libya, though apparently renouncing its illegal weapons programs, had secretly obtained atomic weapon designs from China. North Korea has quit the nuclear Non-Proliferation Treaty and admitted to a clandestine uranium enrichment project. Meanwhile, Iran—a haven of Islamic fundamentalism—appears unwilling to abandon a uranium enrichment program capable of producing material for nuclear weapons.

How should America respond to these dangers?

As the scornful adage goes, generals are always prepared to fight the last war. The Civil War, World War I, Western Europe's collapse before Hitler, the Vietnam War—all are considered textbook examples of military strategies gone bad. *Newsweek*'s Fareed Zakaria believes that the Cold War is back, in the sense that America must wage a battle of ideas as well as covert operations. "The long twilight struggle we face, like that against communism, is both military and political."[73] That seems only partly right. As President Bush has insisted, the fight against terrorism is unlike any previous American war, and understanding why this is so demands a clear-eyed judgment of radical Islam.

To borrow Churchill's phrase, an "armed and resolute wickedness" has openly declared its horrific intentions: to murder massive numbers of civilians in order to rock the foundations of Western democracies. Indeed, in bin Laden's unholy economy, the use of weapons of mass destruction is considered a "religious duty." Islamic scholars such as Bernard Lewis take him at his word. "There is no doubt," he writes, "that the foundation of Al-Qa'ida and the consecutive declarations of war by Osama bin Laden marked the beginning of a new and ominous phase in the history of both Islam and terrorism."[74]

Most ominous is the fact that our enemies have embraced what political scientist Lee Harris calls a *fantasy ideology*. Like the architects of the Third Reich, the leaders of radical Islam see themselves locked in an apocalyptic struggle against the forces of darkness. Their objective is nothing less than the universal implementation of Koranic ideals. Like their Nazi counterparts, they will use any means possible to realize their utopian visions. "We are fighting an enemy who has no strategic purpose in anything he does—whose actions have significance only in terms of his own fantasy ideology," writes Harris. "It matters not how much stronger or more powerful we are than they. What matters is that God will bring them victory."[75] Their method defies the dictum of military strategist Karl von Clausewitz, who saw war as the pursuit of political objectives by other means. There are no political objectives. The terrorists embrace terrorism almost for its own sake, as a sacred act of martyrdom. That such acts might usher in a purified vision of Islam would be a blessed fruit of their faith. As Michael Burleigh argues in *The Third Reich*, the Nazi creed "offered redemption from a national ontological crisis, to which it was attracted like a predatory shark to blood."[76] The predators have returned. The crisis this time is not national and race-based, but supranational and faith-based.

Many derided President Bush when he called the September 11 perpetrators "evildoers." Yet that freighted phrase may be exactly the right one as we continue to hunt them down. After all, the ability of terrorists to use airplanes to assault American cities exposed a profound failure of imagination: secular elites, uncomfortable with religious categories, couldn't foresee the possibilities for wickedness inspired by a perverted religion. The great mistake now is to misread the nature of the threat and heed the Sirens' call to appease it. Political and religious figures alike are in danger of succumbing to an old temptation: allowing their hatred of war to consume all other virtues. But this brand of pacifism is no substitute for empathy, courage, justice, sacrifice, and an iron will to resist evil. "The first Allied response to the Nazi regime had been prompted by the universal loathing among decent men of modern war's senseless slaughter," writes William Manchester. "But revulsion is a frail foundation for a foreign policy."[77]

Frail indeed. Today it would all but guarantee the erosion of freedom and security across entire continents. President Bush, in a visit to the concentration camps in Poland last spring, warned strongly against that course. "The death camps still bear witness," he said. "They remind us that evil is real and must be called by name and must be opposed. All the good that has come to this continent—all the progress, the prosperity, the peace—came because beyond the barbed wire there were people willing to take up arms against evil."[78] If the United States is to successfully lead an international effort against the plague of terrorism, a similar willingness to engage the enemy surely will be required. This should not be confused with hubris or holy wars. Nor must it become a mantra to justify any and all aggression. America's cause demands collaboration with our allies and potential allies. It will require patient persuasion. The military option may be the worst choice in a given situation; it will always be among the most unpredictable in its effects.

The authors represented in this volume lived through a time of comparable challenges and dangers and passionately debated what to do. Their writings reveal how religious leaders sought to become the conscience of a nation on the brink of war. Historians neglect the role of religion in U.S. foreign policy, but the influence of these ministers, and the religious bodies they represented—Protestant, Catholic and Jew—should not be dismissed. They were courted by political leaders, organized massive peace rallies, convened conferences, issued declarations, and published thousands of articles and newspaper op-eds. And they preached: wartime sermons openly addressed the nation's moral responsibilities, and most everyone assumed that the Judeo-Christian tradition was democracy's best bulwark. Though writing more than sixty years ago, the authors clashed over issues now painfully familiar to us: They sought to define America's political, moral, and spiritual obligations to combat an international menace.

French historian Marc Bloch, who fought—and died—in the French resistance, wrote that it's natural and proper to turn to history for insight in times of tumult. "Whenever our exacting Western society . . . begins to doubt itself, it asks itself whether it has done well in trying to learn from the past, and whether it has learned rightly."[79] Have America's political and religious leaders learned rightly from history? Maturity is the product of experience, but experience is no tutor without the discipline of memory: recalling not only the triumphs and failures of statesmen, but the choices that made them possible. Most often, it seems, those choices mean knowing when to embrace the lesser of two evils.

The wisdom and resolve of those who recognized the supreme malevolence of their own day would seem to offer a measure of guidance. Among them, of course, Winston Churchill had no peer. "The whole fury and might of the enemy must very soon be turned upon us," he told his nation on the eve of the Battle of Britain. "If we can stand up to him, all Europe may be free and the life of the world may move forward into broad, sunlit uplands. But if we fail, then the whole world, including the United States, including all that we have known and cared for, will sink into the abyss of a new Dark Age."[80] The United States eventually would join Britain's struggle, but waited until it was almost too late. The ensuing debate over U.S. engagement proved to be one of the most contentious in the history of the American church. Only a handful of religious leaders realized the blackness of the evil that had been let loose in the world. Few could imagine the sacrifices that would be required to meet it. And fewer still dared to predict the consequences of shrinking back from the duties assigned to America, Britain, and their allies. "A penalty is attached to non-action in such a situation," warned Lewis Mumford as most of Europe lay in ruins. "A human society in which men will not help their neighbors to resist evil and struggle for justice, will presently cease to exist as a society, since it will lack even the animal loyalties that are necessary for survival."[81]

Perhaps their example can help us avoid that chilling judgment in the present hour of crisis.

NOTES

1. Winston Churchill, *Memoirs of the Second World War* (Boston: Houghton Mifflin Company, 1959), 1, 87.

2. Bernard Lewis, *The Crisis of Islam* (New York: The Modern Library, 2003).

3. Paul Berman, *Terror and Liberalism* (New York: W.W. Norton & Company, 2003), 26, 60.

4. Charles Krauthammer, "The Enemy Is Not Islam. It Is Nihilism," *The Weekly Standard*, October 22, 2001.

5. Michael Ignatieff, "The Burden," *New York Times Magazine*, January 5, 2003, 50.

6. Bill Keller, "The Thinkable," *New York Times Magazine*, May 4, 2003, 50.

7. "What We're Fighting For," Institute for American Values. Available online: www.Americanvlaues.org. Last accessed April 29, 2004. Some secular and liberal institutions have sounded hawkish as well. "History is asking more of this country than sorrow," argued editors at *The New Republic* two weeks after the attacks. "Above all, we must state clearly as a nation, to ourselves and to the world, that we are preparing to kill anybody who is preparing to kill us." See *The New Republic*, September 24, 2001, 10–11.

8. William L. Langer and S. Everett Gleason, *The Challenge of Isolation, 1937–1940* (New York: Harper & Brothers, 1952), 36.

9. Robert Moats Miller, *How Shall They Hear without a Preacher? The Life of Ernest Fremont Tittle* (Chapel Hill: University of North Carolina Press, 1971), 402.

10. Albert Edward Day, "If America Is Drawn into the War," *The Christian Century*, December 25, 1940.

11. R. Scott Appleby, *The Ambivalence of the Sacred* (Lanham, Md.: Rowman & Littlefield Publishers, 2000), 3.

12. James Turner Johnson, *The Holy War Idea in Western and Islamic Traditions* (University Park: Pennsylvania State University Press, 1997), 111–112.

13. Roland Bainton, *Christian Attitudes toward War and Peace* (Nashville, Tenn.: Abingdon Press, 1990), 14.

14. Donald Meyer, *The Protestant Search for Political Realism* (Middletown, Conn.: Wesleyan University Press, 1988), xviii.

15. Richard H. Pells, *Radical Visions and American Dreams: Culture and Social Thought in the Depression Years* (New York: Harper Torchbooks, 1973), 11.

16. William Manchester, *The Last Lion: Winston Spencer Churchill; Alone: 1932–1940* (New York: Dell Publishing, 1988), 45.

17. Walter M. Horton, *Theism and the Modern Mood* (New York: Harper & Bros., 1930), 6.

18. Justin Wroe Nixon, "The Evangelicals' Dilemma," *The Atlantic Monthly*, July–August, 1925, 368–374.

19. Walter Lippmann, *A Preface to Morals* (New York: Time-Life Books, 1929), 8.

20. Langer and Gleason, *The Challenge of Isolation, 1937–1940*, 16.

21. Ray H. Abrams, *Preachers Present Arms* (New York: Round Table Press, 1933), 246.

22. Abrams, *Preachers Present Arms*, 235.

23. Abrams, *Preachers Present Arms*, 237–238. See Also Gerald L. Sittser's *A Cautious Patriotism: The American Churches and the Second World War* (Chapel Hill: University of North Carolina Press, 1997), 24–25.

24. Sittser, *A Cautious Patriotism*, 18.

25. Dana L. Robert, "The First Globalization: The Internationalization of the Protestant Missionary Movement between the World Wars," *International Bulletin of Missionary Research*, April 2002.

26. Sittser, *A Cautious Patriotism*, 19.

27. Langer and Gleason, *The Challenge of Isolation*, 14.

28. Lewis Mumford, "The Aftermath of Utopianism," *Christianity and Crisis*, March 24, 1941.

29. Meyer, *The Protestant Search for Political Realism*, 174–175.

30. Meyer, *The Protestant Search for Political Realism*, 167.

31. Samuel McCrea Cavert, news release in the *New York Times*, May 22, 1933.

32. "Hitler's Victory," *The Christian Century*, June 26, 1940.

33. Kirby Page, *Jesus or Christianity: A Study in Contrasts* (New York: Doubleday, Doran & Company, 1929), 277, 231.

34. Meyer, *The Protestant Search for Political Realism*, 163.

35. Langer and Gleason, *The Challenge of Isolation*, 51.

36. "Pacifists or Peacemakers? Do Catholics Desire War?" John LaFarge, S.J., *America*, February 18, 1939.

37. John Lukacs, *The Last European War: September 1939–December 1941* (New Haven, Conn.: Yale University Press, 2001), 107–111.

38. Robert W. Ross, *So It Was True: The American Protestant Press and the Nazi Persecution of the Jews* (Minneapolis: University of Minnesota Press, 1980), 263.

39. Paul Johnson, *Modern Times: The World from the Twenties to the Nineties* (New York: HarperCollins Publishers, 2001), 36.

40. Sittser, *A Cautious Patriotism*, 17.

41. Abrams, *Preachers Present Arms*, 236.

42. Paul Johnson, *A History of the American People* (New York: HarperCollins Publishers, 1997), 774.

43. Francis X. Talbot, "The Gains of War," *America*, May 6, 1939.

44. Harold E. Fey, "Defense or Despotism?" *The Christian Century*, January 24, 1940.

30 *Introduction*

45. Meyer, *The Protestant Search for Political Realism*, 377.
46. A. J. Muste, *War Is the Enemy* (New York: Pendle Hill Pamphlet, 1942), 17.
47. Meyer, *The Protestant Search for Political Realism*, 365.
48. Paul L. Blakely, S.J., "Nazi Atrocities and the American War Fever," *America*, December 3, 1938.
49. The "most frequent and direct reporting" of German anti-Semitism among Christian journals was found in evangelical and fundamentalist publications. See Robert W. Ross, *So It Was True*, 145.
50. Ross, *So It Was True*, 158.
51. Georgia Harkness, "What, Then, Should Churches Do?" *The Christian Century*, August 14, 1940.
52. Wayne S. Cole, *America First: The Battle against Intervention, 1940–1941* (Madison: University of Wisconsin Press, 1953), 16.
53. Sittser, *A Cautious Patriotism*, 36.
54. "Peace to Nations," editorial, *America*, December 24, 1938.
55. Sittser, *A Cautious Patriotism*, 21.
56. Meyer, *The Protestant Search for Political Realism*, xv–xvi.
57. Day, "If America Is Drawn into the War."
58. Miller, *How Shall They Hear without a Preacher*, 403.
59. Lewis Mumford, *Men Must Act* (New York: Harcourt, Brace & Company, 1939), 43.
60. Lynn Harold Hough, "Defending Justice Despite Our Own Injustice," *Christianity and Crisis*, April 21, 1941.
61. "Calling the Kettle Black," editorial, *America*, October 8, 1938.
62. Lukacs, *The Last European War*, 469–477.
63. William Lloyd Allen, "How Baptists Assessed Hitler," *The Christian Century*, September 1–8, 1982.
64. Leonard Dinnerstein, "Anti-Semitism in the Depression Era," in *Religion in American History*, ed. Jon Butler and Harry S. Stout (Oxford: Oxford University Press, 1998), 419.
65. Ross, *So It Was True*, 157.
66. Karl Barth, *This Christian Cause* (New York: The Macmillan Company, 1941); see the introduction by John A. Mackay.
67. Keller, "The Thinkable," 94.
68. Johnson, *Modern Times*, 351.
69. "War and Peace: The Failure of the Church to Teach Absolute Spiritual Values Will Undermine Christian Civilization," editorial, *Fortune*, January 1940, volume XXI.
70. Stanley Hauerwas, "September 11, 2001: A Pacifist Response," in *Dissent from the Homeland, Essays after September 11*, ed. Stanley Hauerwas and Frank Lentricchia (Durham, N.C.: Duke University Press, 2002), 430.
71. Robert N. Bellah, "Seventy-Five Years," in *Dissent from the Homeland: Essays After September 11*, ed. Stanley Hauerwas and Frank Lentricchia (Durham, N.C.: Duke University Press, 2002), 263.
72. Berman, *Terror and Liberalism*, 158.
73. Fareed Zakaria, "The End of the End of History," *Newsweek*, September 24, 2001.

74. Lewis, *The Crisis of Islam*, 160, 162.

75. Lee Harris, "Al Qaeda's Fantasy Ideology," *Policy Review*, August 2002.

76. Michael Burleigh, *The Third Reich: A New History* (New York: Hill & Wang, 2000), 12.

77. Manchester, *The Last Lion*, 205.

78. President George W. Bush, "Remarks by the President to the People of Poland," Wawel Royal Castle, Krakow, Poland, May 31, 2003.

79. Marc Bloch, *The Historian's Craft* (New York: Vintage Books, 1953), 6.

80. David Cannadine, *The Speeches of Winston Churchill* (Boston: Houghton Mifflin Company, 1989), 177.

81. Lewis Mumford, "The Aftermath of Utopianism," 5.

I

THE PEACEMAKERS
Keeping America Out of War

1

✢

Albert W. Palmer

President, Chicago Theological Seminary
Pastor, Congregational and Christian Church

A lbert W. Palmer entered Yale Divinity School in the fall of 1901 with
many misgivings. "I expected to have musty and repellant medieval
theological dogmas crammed down my throat willy-nilly," he wrote later.
"I made up my mind to be a martyr if necessary but not to accept anything that did not commend itself to my honest reason." Fortunately, martyrdom would not be necessary: Palmer found himself quite enamored
with the new historical criticism of the Bible being championed at Yale.

One of the dogmas that Palmer discarded early in his ministry was the
doctrine of hell; he couldn't accept a God whose holiness demanded an ultimate judgment of evil. Indeed, his belief in a Deity seeking to reform
mankind seemed to animate his lifelong commitment to social causes. In
this, he embraced the key assumptions of the social gospel movement—
that Jesus preached a social, as well as individual, gospel. "Shall we say
that personal relations come within the range of religious ideals but that
the social and international relations are beyond their influence?" he once
asked. "Shall we say that the Good Samaritan may help the wounded man
but say nothing against corruption that made highway robbery possible?"

The answer for Palmer was obvious, an answer he delivered in countless sermons, books, lectures, and church resolutions. While pastoring a
church in Hawaii, for example, Palmer wrote President Calvin Coolidge
to denounce a 1924 bill restricting Japanese immigration. Soon after becoming pastor at the First Congregational Church in Oak Park, Illinois,
Palmer caught the attention of the *Chicago Tribune* by criticizing the conditions in a Cook County jail from his Sunday pulpit. At a meeting of the
National Council of Congregational Churches in Washington, D.C., he

condemned the racist bigotry of the hotel and restaurant owners who refused to serve the black delegates in attendance. "If we cannot eat with our colored brethren," he said, "we will not eat together at all!" As president of Chicago Theological Seminary from 1930 to 1946, Palmer helped make the "imperative of the social gospel" a defining feature of the school's approach to Christian ethics and theology.

By the late 1930s, Palmer directed his social agenda to the problems in Europe. Shortly after the Munich Agreement of September 1938, in which Hitler demanded and received much of Czechoslovakia, Palmer proposed a world economic conference to stave off war. His peace document garnered signatures from the leaders of twenty-one Protestant bodies and earned him a forty-five-minute interview with President Franklin Roosevelt. Palmer's pacifist message, however, got a cool reception: "My net impression is that, while he saw our view-point, he is also in the grip of the current ideology about the menace of Nazi psychology."

Palmer's theology of evil must have helped him escape that grip: In all his fervent antiwar activity, he never really gave up hope that Hitler and his National Socialists could be reformed. As one of thirty-six delegates at the 1939 Geneva Conference sponsored by the World Council of Churches, he helped draft its signature document, "The Christian Attitude Toward International Affairs." It expressed optimism that a negotiated peace was achievable—even after the Nazis had vanquished Poland, Denmark, Norway, Belgium, Holland, and France. As Palmer wrote at the time: "All the difficulties here seem so entirely capable of reasonable solution and so unnecessary to go to war about."

Nearly two years later, Palmer preached a sermon, carried on CBS Radio, lamenting the conflict in Europe and blaming "the craft of propaganda" for generating support for American entry into the war. "Our own land seems to be staggering blindly, even carelessly down the road that led to war before, and can only lead us into war again." Even as late as April of 1941, as Hitler added Yugoslavia and Greece to his list of fallen states, Palmer wrote to President Roosevelt again imploring him to "offer the world a reasonable alternative to war."

In the first essay included here, "A Road Away from War," Palmer condemns the case for U.S. intervention as "the maddest and most terrible proposal" imaginable. He argues that war only produces atrocities, and that there is no "Christian" way to wage it. Instead, invoking Mahatma Gandhi, Palmer advocates "soul force"—a posture of love and forgiveness—to overcome evil. He then offers a five-point "national peace policy" that includes U.S. neutrality, international trade, and economic reform at home. In the second essay, "Putting Christianity in Cold Storage," he returns to the theme of establishing social and economic justice as the Christian remedy to war. "Is this essentially a war to make democracy secure or is it a clash between two great imperialisms?" he asks. Palmer then explains his own program of Christian pacifism as it would apply to the European conflict. He warns that the heroic acceptance of suffering would be required, but he believes that nonviolent suffering of this sort, on a massive scale, would topple even the Fascist tyranny in Berlin. "If I had a mandate from a people convinced of pacifism and disciplined enough to follow it," he writes, "I would far rather meet Hitler that way than with military force and bluster."

A Road Away from War
The Christian Century, June 19, 1940

Although not advertised as such, this may turn out to be the real war to end war after all! Certainly the present blitzkrieg is giving us a tragic and terrible demonstration of the waste, barbarity and horror of military operations. Is it possible that, after all this fiendish slaughter, the world will not tolerate the war system any longer? Will not the masses of the common people rise up and demand deliverance through some better organization of the world on a non-war basis? And, if the secular community does not, can the Christian church fail to do so if it is true to its historic sense of human values and sensitive to the spirit of Jesus?

Even now, why wait any longer to make definite proposals to stop the war? Obviously it can only go from bad to worse. Nobody, not even in Germany, can gain by its continuation. The end will be a bankrupt world, poisoned by bitterness and chaotic with revolution. Let the United States, therefore, call all the remaining neutrals together at once and outline the main points of a decent postwar order. No man can chart a revolution in advance, but emerging outlines of things to come suggest a pattern somewhat as follows: Local self-government, combined with a universal guarantee of equal access to markets and raw materials for all nations; a world federation controlling tariffs, currency and colonies; a world court and immediate disarmament! Let the United States, as part of its contributions, and an earnest of good will, offer to appropriate for the next five years the four billion dollars a year now contemplated for defense, to be used instead as a rehabilitation fund for Europe and China and to be expended by an international commission. It would be far cheaper than war, would help bind up the wounds of the world and would strike a greatly needed new note of human solidarity and cooperation in the field of international relations.

WOULD HITLER LISTEN?

Would Hitler consider such a proposal? Many will shout, No! But does anyone know until it is put up to him? And to the German people? Would the British accept it? Again nobody knows, but let them vote on it. Would we be willing to do it? There's the first and highest hurdle!

Before we turn down such a proposal, let's consider the alternatives: either a stalemated war of attrition, which seems unlikely now; or an Allied victory, which can be attained, even with our aid, only at frightful cost and after months, perhaps years of slaughter; or a German victory, now seemingly an active possibility, which might lead to terms so severe and cruel as to sow the seeds of future wars and possibly, through aggression in the Western hemisphere, involve us in a titanic battle with Germany and even Japan. Obviously, war offers no solution. In any case its results will be bad. The longer it continues the worse the situation will become. Why not try peace? The airplane has revolutionized modern warfare. Aviators have to learn to think in three dimensions. Isn't it equally necessary to begin to think in new dimensions also concerning peace and tolerable world order?

LET THE CHURCH SPEAK!

In face of the horrible slaughter going on in Europe the Christian religion ought to offer and demand attention to some decent way to stop all this unspeakable cruelty. Let the church speak out, promptly and unequivocally, and denounce this sinful war. Let it propose or demand some alternative, and meanwhile refuse to have any part in so inhuman and terrible a crime. Let the World Council speak! If it cannot, let the Federal Council do so! If it cannot, let the denominations voice their horror of this war and condemn its continuance and let smaller groups of Christians do the same! I ask, in all seriousness and with deep concern for the cause of Christ, will not the Christian religion forfeit all right to the respect of humane men and women in future years if it allows this ghastly war to continue unrebuked, if it takes no steps to propose a reasonable solution to humanity's most tragic problem?

The maddest and most terrible proposal I know of is that we Christian people should now urge our nation to go into this military hurricane. People who suggest such a thing must have forgotten what war is and what it does. No one can wage war without descending to the most awful and diabolical actions. Talk about atrocities, why, war itself is one long atrocity! War isn't just a picturesque contest we can get excited over like a football game. It means drowning, starving, poisoning, shooting, killing, robbing, betraying other people. Shall we jump in and do this too? Terrible as the war in Flanders and France has been, would not the Allies have done much the same thing in Germany if they had got there first? Must we not do the same thing, "right through to Berlin," if we go in and are able to attack the Germans with overwhelming airplanes, tanks, bombs, spies, fifth column traitors and parachute fighters? You can't just fight Hitler, whom you hate as diabolical, you have to kill and destroy the largely innocent German people, nice clean pink-cheeked boys, mothers, grandparents, even babies, with your bombs. There is no such thing as a fair, gentlemanly war, like a well arranged prize fight. There is no such thing as a

Christian military procedure. Let the church and every individual Christian denounce the whole business now before it is too late.

IS IT TOO LATE?

I fear it is too late. We Christians who, out of experience with the last war, know what war really is, have failed to awaken Christian conscience enough to save it from the age-long inherited impulse toward violence and savagery. Bishops and other churchmen, who ought to know better, are already crying out for American participation. The sane and eminently practical proposals at the beginning of this paper will probably be disregarded. The emotions of the country, worked up to feverish intensity by radio and press, will probably hurl millions more young men into the obscene hell of battle. Then, some day, the war will be over. We shall cool off, study the costs and either get ready for a new war twenty years later or else, perhaps, begin to do some of the sensible and constructive things which were suggested. But, oh, if we could only have done the creative and peaceful thing now! "If thou hadst known, in this thy day, the things which belong unto peace!"[1]

Meanwhile, as far as I am personally concerned, I dissociate myself from this war. I have never announced myself as a pacifist but have reserved my right to judge each war as it came along. Well, this one has come, and I now pronounce judgment upon it! I will not shoot, stab, starve, drown, or betray any other human being, if I can help it. If war comes, I will serve in any other way I can in the cause of mercy and in constructive peaceful toil, but I will do nothing hostile or hateful toward any other human being. I legislate for no one else, but as for me I am profoundly convinced that this is the mind of Christ. Will you join me? After war, or even a national emergency, is declared it will be too late. We shall all be silenced. The time to speak is now.

CHOOSING WEAPONS

But that, you say, while it might provide personal emotional release, is not a realistic or practical attitude for all the rest of us. If followed by the British, it would open up England to invasion. It would invite world domination by Hitler. Yes, possibly, but for how long? Can military force do much against soul force which folds its arms and bides its day? With the manhood of America undecimated by war and its womanhood not embittered or shell-shocked, how could any military conquerer rule very long without coming to terms with the population? Has Gandhi lived in vain?

Without military opposition the Hitlers whither away. Time marches on. Ideas have to be met. Contentment and morale have to be developed. Antagonism, violence, coercion give way at last to better understanding and human sympathy. Truth is stronger than falsehood. Faith is more powerful than brutality. Love never faileth, when it is tried persistently and long. Forgiveness heals wounds and prevents new ones from being made. Peace has greater victories than war. If your enemy hunger, feed him—and understand him. Love your enemies and do them good.

It isn't a question of not opposing evil. We must always struggle to overcome evil. We must not blur our moral judgments in the slightest. No red-blooded man can for a moment be supine, cowardly or unconcerned in the face of tragic inhumanity and violence. He can never be indifferent to moral wrong or cruelty. But he may well stop and choose his weapons with care. Confronted by terrible evils he must ask that the means he employs to deal with them give promise of doing good and not more evil. He must not do things that are self-defeating because they involve him in the very same horrible procedures which have aroused his indignations. As clear-eyed realists have we not come to the point where we inevitably recognize the futility of trial by torture? Is there any reasonable hope that cruel military methods will solve any human problem? Are we not, then, driven to the higher ground that evil can never be overcome by another evil but only by good, good will, right reason and a minimum of violence and coercion? I think this would be the mind of Christ facing a threatened modern war. If not, what would it be?

A practical and realistic man, however, will recognize at once that, convinced as he himself may be about the principles set forth, the great majority of the American people have not yet glimpsed them and, in so short a time as is available, cannot be educated up to their full understanding and acceptance. The American people are however, strongly averse to war unless stampeded by mass hysteria and fear. This being so, what national policies should a sane, far-sighted Christian patriot support an advocate today? May I briefly outline five specific points in a possible national peace policy?

A PROPOSED NATIONAL POLICY

1. Not a national policy of immediate unilateral disarmament but rather a definite standing offer, and indeed urgent proposal, of disarmament by international agreement. In the meantime, a holding down of armaments to an obviously defensive basis.
2. Genuine honest neutrality that will stand the test of investigation in all the future years. Let us not be deceived. If we supply munitions

and money to one side on favorable terms while we refuse equal terms to the other we violate our neutrality morally, if not technically. "Means short of war" should not be employed with unfair or hostile intent against either belligerent unless we accept the fact in advance that such a procedure logically leads to war and are prepared to take the consequences. However deep our sympathy with the Allies, we must remember that we see Germany today through a haze of Allied propaganda. Are we sure that when the war is over we shall not regret having signed the Allies' blank check under such pressure?

Menacing things are being said about what the Germans will do to us if they win. But do they represent a calm objective appraisal? Are they not partly born of war hysteria, tinged with fear and promoted by propaganda rather than a reasonable view of our future position if we maintain unquestionable neutrality and fair dealing? Certainly until the Allies openly state their war aims in terms acceptable to neutrals, those neutrals would be incredibly naïve to join up and compromise neutrality—remembering the secret treaties and other skullduggery of the last war.

Economic Defense

3. Cooperation with other neutrals in projecting definite proposals for a just and cooperative world order as the only desirable outcome of the war. In line with this, and preparatory to it, an American policy of economic cooperation rather than economic war toward all other nations.
4. Protection of American life against hysteria by fair and objective analysis and interpretation of the forces which create wars and may produce peace in our modern world order. Rejection of the "devil nation" theory, over-simplified ideological contrasts and short-circuited, adolescent hatred of individual leaders. Realistic recognition of what war inevitably does to all nations that engage in it.
5. Wholehearted devotion to solving the problems of social and economic justice in a democracy. A nation that maintains its civil liberties, overcomes unemployment, repudiates racial prejudice and discrimination, provides decent housing and adequate educational opportunity, will be practically unconquerable. Even though defeated in battle, it would have a social *esprit de corps* that would survive all military disaster.

The editor of *Fortune* recently reproached the church with failure to provide moral leadership or proclaim any "absolutes" in the face of war.[2] He was referring to the last war. The church has learned something in the intervening years and I venture to believe that this article expresses, however inadequately, the profound, though often inarticulate, convictions of a thoughtful, consecrated and deeply determined conscience which is growing up in American Protestantism concerning the war that now is devastating Europe.

Putting Christianity in Cold Storage
The Christian Century, January 8, 1941

If America is drawn into a war, can you, as a Christian, participate in it or support it?

Twenty-five years ago I would have answered, "Yes." It would have seemed to me then that our country could become involved only in a war forced upon it in defense of its own liberty. In that event I, of course, would go along, stupid and anachronistic as I felt war to be. Ten years ago I would have answered, "Perhaps." I had then become aware of the cross-currents of propaganda, economic self-interest, fear and prejudice which draw nations into war. I would therefore have said: "I reserve the right to judge each war as it comes along." Today my answer is a definite and unequivocal "No." I welcome the opportunity to present frankly and plainly in condensed outline form my reasons for dissociating myself, so far as I can, from any participation in or support of any war; and then to make a brief statement of what I propose to do "if and when," in view of the practical difficulties sure to arise in connection with a complete and unflinching commitment to the way of peace.

My decision to use and support only peaceful and nonviolent action, but never war, is due primarily to my religious convictions. War involves such dastardly, cruel and unchristian conduct that I cannot possibly engage to do what it requires. Not only does it carry on the mass murder in battle of trained and supposedly hardened professional soldiers, but, due to modern inventions, it necessitates the impersonal and indiscriminate slaughter and agonizing torture of civilians, women, and children and the aged. Both sides, by airplane attacks by land and mines and submarines by sea, shut the gates of mercy on mankind. Moreover, beyond all the fiendish atrocities perpetrated in the ferocity of battle, war carries on cold-blooded slow murder through starvation caused by food blockades, a cruelty also involving innocent and even neutral, non-combatant populations. Such inhumanity is sure to result in world-devastating epidemics in the near future and a grim harvest of physical degeneration and mental bitterness later on. I am convinced that Jesus would not do these horrible things and that I must not.

War also causes stupendous waste, the destruction of homes, property, churches and the institutions of civilized life, both at once through the fury of bombardment, and later on through the burden of war debts, crushing taxation and economic depressions. This means the abandonment of works of human welfare hopefully begun and the postponement of a nobler civilization which might have been possible if the resources of the race had not been squandered and its powers perverted by war.

Beyond all this there are the mental effects of war: the creation of a psychology of suspicion, fear, and hatred in order to work people up to a fighting mood, and the suppression, distortion or destruction of truth through dishonest and misleading propaganda in order to poison people's minds and regiment them into supporting war.

As a Christian man I cannot commit or condone such acts as these. But they are inevitable in war, along with many other hateful and corroding evils, like ghastly concentration camps, which I have not space even to catalog. And the still more tragic fact is that, once we embark on a war, we ourselves cannot escape the necessity of committing all these abominable outrages against other human beings who, however misled, are in the main just normal, well meaning individuals, remarkably like us and our children. No matter how high-sounding the phrases the orators use back home, no matter how just you feel your cause to be, no matter how noble and inspiring the announced objectives of your government, when once you get caught in the terrible net of war, you have to do these diabolical things.

As soon as you are inducted into military service you will be told, "You're in the army now!" That cynical slogan cancels out all Christian ethics, all mercy, all truthfulness, all sportsmanship, except where these can be indulged in as mere side alleys away from the main street of winning the war. You are like a drunken prize fighter with brass knuckles and a concealed dagger, engaging in a riot which has no rounds, no timekeeper, no referee, no rules. That is war! Christian people need to face these facts. We read about "gridiron battles" or a "political fight" and, by a process of transference, we think of war as just another such contest. Our imagination are so dim and dull that we forget the awful realities of war, and urge help for Britain or promote a frenzy of hatred for Hitler and Mussolini without visualizing where our unneutral deeds will lead us.

I know what one answer will be! Some who think of themselves as hard-boiled realists will say: "Palmer is an impractical idealist. Doesn't he know that this is a demonic world?" Or else: "Bad as war is, and it admits of no Christian whitewashing or justification, nevertheless it is the temporary awful alternative to something worse." This is the position of Reinhold Niebuhr's latest book where he says that, while the ethic of Jesus is "finally and ultimately normative," it is "not immediately applicable to the task of securing justice in a sinful world," and that "the grace of God for man and the Kingdom of God for history are both divine realities and not human possibilities." Niebuhr's idea is that we face a dilemma between tyranny and "the momentary anarchy which is necessary to overcome tyranny." This last phrase is an indirect and polite way of saying "war," with all the horrible and anti-Christian features noted above skillfully glossed over.

Here, then, is my Christian dilemma: Hate war, recognize it as utterly unchristian, inhuman, savage, brutal, but is it not an inescapable alternative to be accepted as a "temporary anarchy" in order that, by it, I may overcome tyranny? In popular language, war is bad but it is the only way to stop Hitler. Once he is stopped we can go back to decency again. Therefore put your Christianity in cold storage and go to war!

Before we thus give up our Christianity, even temporarily, would it not be well to inquire rather searchingly whether war can do the things which this dilemma assumes it will accomplish? In the very significant account of Jesus' temptation in the wilderness, Satan is represented as offering our Lord all the kingdoms of the world. Jesus sharply and absolutely rejected this offer, though it led him to the cross. But suppose he had chosen, at least for a brief period of spiritual anarchy, to worship Satan, could Satan have delivered the goods? Are not hoped-for political and spiritual gains, when purchased at the price of ethical surrender, always deceptive and involved in moral tragedy? Does even a good end justify bad means? Indeed, can bad means really secure a good end? Can you break the vicious circle of evil constantly producing evil, unless, as Fosdick has pointed out, you overcome evil, not with more evil, but with good?

Now look at war. What do its proponents hope from it? What really does it do? War is fought to secure peace. It arrives at an armistice, which may be an opportunity to secure peace. But meanwhile war has sown so much bitterness and propagated so much prejudice and falsehood that it is harder than ever to establish the conditions of real peace. There are three instructive exceptions. The War of 1812, our Civil War and the Boer War were followed by lasting peace. But why? The War of 1812 was stopped in midcareer by a marvelously wise treaty which disarmed the United States-Canadian frontier and never mentioned the alleged objectives of the war. The Civil War ended by taking the southern states back on equal terms into the union. And the Boer War gave South Africa practically everything the defeated Boers were fighting for. Such magnanimity is rare. Things would have been better still if it had been exercised in the beginning. But, in any case, no such termination is contemplated or humanly possible for any war now in progress. Our present wars are an uncanny fulfillment of the prophecy widely attributed to Marshal Foch at the armistice of 1918: "Let the armies stand at ease. The war is postponed for twenty years!"

Wars are alleged to be fought for justice. But, by inflaming hatred and roiling up the wells of truth, they tend to make it psychologically impossible for justice to be done. The Treaty of Versailles was not in all respects a bad treaty. But it contained the dragon's teeth of the present war. And not only the treaty but the deliberate ignoring of Wilson's Fourteen Points, on the basis of which the armistice pledges had been given, and the inhuman blockade of Germany, with the resulting starvation of women and children continuing while the treaty was being drafted—all these things made justice seem a cynical jest in Germany. How much justice is to be expected out of the present war when popular talk quite overlooks the real grievances of Germany and Italy and classes them as "gangsters," "thieves," and "liars" without ever inquiring how they "got that way"?

We are urged to enter this present war to preserve liberty and democracy. But will this action produce that result? War and even thoroughgoing preparedness means embracing fascism, at least for the duration of the war and perhaps indefinitely thereafter. Moreover, is this essentially a war to make democracy secure or is it a clash between two great imperialisms? Is not the basic tension an economic one, in that we have by our inventions made the world an economic unity and left it in control of fifty separate governments, each with its own army and navy, its tariff walls and power to erect trade barriers and block other people's access to the raw materials and markets of the globe? Must not this war, or its successors, continue until either one government dominates the world and establishes a new Pax Romana or the more sensible device of a world federation is substituted for war, guaranteeing to every nation fair and equal access to markets and raw materials? Perhaps a fundamental social and economic revolution is actually taking place in all the warring nations, and ultimately in our own too! Ought we not to seek to understand that revolution, instead of short-circuiting our intelligence by hatred?

Here in America we are also soothingly told that we shall never go to war except for defense. But this means nothing! Every nation is told the same thing by its government. But any real meaning fades out of the word "defense" when military strategy rules that the best defense is an offensive. Our frontier over night becomes the Thames or Singapore or anywhere else the President sees fit to establish it. Once begun, war demands not only defense but victory, and victory demands an offensive. Hating aggressors, we ourselves, by the diabolical alchemy of war, must become aggressors.

Is there no other alternative? Must the Christian inevitably be impaled on either one horn or the other of this dilemma? Is it either tyranny or war? Most dilemmas are false and this one certainly is; for there is a third answer to the problem—a way in following which the Christian can be true to Jesus Christ and, at the same time, feel that he has a reasonable hope of solving the very problems war can never solve but only aggravate. This solution is the way of right reason, non-violence, invincible good will and, if need be, patient, sacrificial suffering—in a word, the way of Christian pacifism.

I feel inadequate to the task of setting forth this solution. I wish some member of the Society of Friends could write these closing paragraphs, for the Friends have been developing this technique for three hundred years and it cannot be mastered in a day. During recent months I feel that

I have become a Quaker—not in dress or language or liturgy or member-
ship, but, I hope, in what is deeper, a certain basic philosophy of life out
of which comes inevitably an attitude toward war and every other kind of
conflict. If the Quakers had a third order, like the Franciscans, I would join
it. Meanwhile, I am still a Congregationalist.

There is, of course, no likelihood that American Christianity, let alone
the American government, will come to the Christian pacifist position in
my day, though I hope my grandchildren may live to see this next great
step in spiritual progress. Meanwhile we are already in the penumbra of
the dread eclipse which we call war and it behooves one to think carefully
what he will do in the darkness of a total eclipse, if such it should turn out
to be. Our international astronomy is very inaccurate and I am no fatalist,
so I recognize and pray that we may even escape the eclipse altogether.
But, if it comes, here is my program:

1. Beginning with the practical concrete situation, I will do all in my
   power to keep the United States from going to war. This does not
   mean that I am an isolationist, except from war. I believe deeply in
   the necessity of world cooperation on a peaceful basis. I am keenly
   aware that before military war breaks out there are preceding stages
   which also ought to be recognized as a kind of war. I mean economic
   antagonism and psychological hostility. I will therefore struggle
   against these preliminary involvements as well.
2. On the positive side I will work for the establishment of some kind
   of world council on conciliation which can formulate and hold up
   before humanity a reasonable plan for world organization which all
   nations could accept without humiliation and to their own ultimate
   benefit. I think our government ought to summon the best brains of
   all the world to come together to form such a council and attack this
   problem. If the government does not do it, the World Council of
   Churches or the Federal Council of Churches of Christ in America
   ought to.
3. Meanwhile, I will seek to relieve the suffering caused by war, especially by cooperating with nonpartisan agencies like the American
   Friends Service Committee. I will give sincere conscientious objectors to military service such aid and counsel as I can regarding their
   rights under law. And I will seek to build a just and brotherly social
   and economic order in American life.
4. At all times I will obey the law and cooperate with the government
   to the utmost limit consistent with my conscientious scruples against
   war. As a Christian pacifist I must do this because government represents the rule of reason and justice rather than of arbitrary violence. It is the precious growing edge of a rational, non-violent social

order. This includes respect for the police force which, as a bulwark against violence, is in no way to be confused with arbitrary military action. Pacifism is the antithesis of anarchy.

5. I will try to practice Christian pacifism first of all in my own personal life by meeting all concrete situations with words, deeds and mental attitudes of non-violence, patience, forgiveness and invincible good will. I will speak gently, avoid coercive policies, be tolerant of other people's opinions and earnestly try to be humble and open-minded, seeking in all things and at all times the promised guidance of the Holy Spirit.

If war comes, the pacifist had better go into silence, so far as the war issues are concerned, and devote himself to helpful loving service, bearing witness to his faith by his life and personal influence rather than by open antagonism to hysterical public opinion. An inflamed, war-minded public is in no mood to be scolded. If petty or larger persecutions come, they must be borne quietly but firmly.

But somebody says: "You are dodging the question! If you had absolute power in the United States today, would you disarm and meet Hitler with bare hands?" My answer is: I could not conceive holding such power except it were by overwhelming vote of the people. If I had a mandate from a people convinced of pacifism and disciplined enough to follow it, I would far rather meet Hitler that way than with military force and bluster. Non-violence combined with Christian good will and the acceptance of suffering rather than the torturing of killing of one's enemies would create a profoundly different atmosphere that that produced by armed resistance.

But put it the other way round. Suppose that, in spite of the most violent warlike opposition and all its resulting bitterness and confusion, Hitler overruns the world. What then? How can he control it or organize it without in the end conforming to those sound and inevitable social, economic and ethical laws and well-known principles of psychology which are the laws of God and are written in the very structure of our universe? Any lasting government must make people contented and reasonably prosperous. Intelligence, loyalty, justice, *esprit de corps* and hope are absolutely essential. No tyranny can permanently disregard them. It will either fall or it will reform. The dictatorship of Napoleon III fell. The dictatorships of George III and of the Yankee reconstruction period in the south reformed.

Let us have faith in God! There is a God indwelling within the universe and operative in all the affairs of men. He is on the side of justice, good will, cooperation, peace. Men may thwart him temporarily by violence and sin. But he cannot by permanently defeated. He has revealed himself in Jesus Christ and his increasing power will work with those who meet life and face its problems in the Christian spirit. That is our faith and, at last, Christian pacifism is essentially a faith, not irrational or unjustifiable, but still a faith!

NOTES

1. Luke 19:42
2. "War and Peace: The Failure of the Church to Teach Absolute Spiritual Values Will Undermine Christian Civilization," *Fortune,* January 1940.

2

✛

Charles Clayton Morrison

Editor, The Christian Century
Ordained Minister, Disciples of Christ

When Charles Clayton Morrison, the young and zealous minister of Chicago's Monroe Street Christian Church, took over the *Christian Century* magazine in 1908, he brought his preaching spirit with him. "I regarded my new work as a genuine extension of my ministry," he wrote. "My desk became my pulpit, and the subscribers were my congregation."

Morrison's new "congregation," though never very large, would include some of the most influential thinkers and activists of Protestant Christianity. Each week in the *Century* he invited them to apply Christian thinking to the political and social issues of the day. Steeped in the humanist philosophy of John Dewey and the sunny theology of the social gospel, Morrison spoke the language of progressive religion with absolute fluency. The Treaty of Versailles, the League of Nations, immigration, the Great Depression, racial injustice, the rise of European fascism—protagonists on all sides found a debating platform in the *Century* under his editorship. (Morrison liked to say that he "discovered" theologian Reinhold Niebuhr, though he spent nearly three decades disagreeing with him.) For much of his thirty-nine-year reign, no publication served as a more important barometer of the intellectual mood of liberal Protestantism.

By the 1930s, that mood had soured on democratic capitalism—and the idea of another war to defend it. During World War I, Morrison managed to justify the Allied cause. "Horrible as Europe now is," he wrote, "more horrible would be the moral degradation and spiritual deadness of a world which would fall to the level of the present Prussian government." He soon abandoned that view. In 1927 Morrison wrote *The Outlawry of War*, a book calling for the codification of "laws of peace" and a world court to resolve international disputes. Its rulings would be enforced not by military action, but by "united public opinion of the world." The 1928 Kellog-Briand Peace Pact (also known as the Pact of Paris), which committed 59 nations to renounce war as a tool of foreign policy, came about in part because of the strength of Morrison's appeal. Throughout the 1920s and 1930s, he opposed rearmament and backed the U.S. Neutrality Acts, which banned American assistance to either side of a European conflict. He used *The Christian Century* to reprint entire chapters of *Preachers Present Arms*, a book by sociologist Ray Abrams exposing the earlier war hysteria of American pastors.

Indeed, as Adolf Hitler began his march on Europe, Morrison made the magazine one of the leading intellectual voices against American intervention. "There is no moral issue, transcending national interest, which would justify the sacrifice of American flesh and blood," he writes in the May 8, 1940, editorial included here. "It is Europe's war." A week later he issued one of the magazine's numerous pleas for a peace conference: It would be led by the United States and bring together the "neutral" states of Europe. Morrison seems to make little distinction, however, between the Axis and Allied powers. As he puts it: "A constructive policy for peace must transcend the mad struggle of the belligerents." The final essay appeared on November 26, 1941. Its title—"A War for Imperialism"—underscores Morrison's conviction that the European conflict is nothing more than a continuation of World War I. As such, even with most of Europe under Nazi control and the fate of European Jews looking increasingly bleak, Morrison opposes an Anglo-American alliance to defeat Germany. "The American people today know that the old rivalries and hatreds of Europe are not dead," he writes. "The clashes of ambition between the various European powers will persist after this conflict is over."

Less than two weeks later came the attack on Pearl Harbor, forcing America to declare war on Japan and the Axis Powers. Yet Morrison clung valiantly to his pacifism: Even in 1942, he wondered whether America was fighting for anything more than the British Empire.

On Saving Civilization
The Christian Century, May 8, 1940

Two paramount objectives command the devotion of the people of the United States in relation to the European war. One is to keep this country out of the conflict, the other is to bring every influence to bear to stop the war. Let us consider at this time the first of these objectives. That there is a fringe of our population which would like to repeat the experience of 1917–18, is no secret; but an overwhelming majority of the nation is convinced that this is not America's war, that our vital interests are not involved in a manner which requires our participation, and that there is no moral issue, transcending national interest, which would justify the sacrifice of American flesh and blood. It is Europe's war, and if it cannot be stopped short of defeat for one side and exhaustion for the other, the policy of America must nevertheless be governed by a determination not to be drawn into it.

This position of impartiality and detachment from the conflict is constantly exposed to influences whose effect is to undermine and weaken it by creating on a national scale the psychology of a divided mind. For one thing, the people have reason to question whether their responsible statesmen share the nation's will against involvement. For another, America's natural sympathies are preponderantly with one side, and it is difficult to subject those feelings to the discipline which national neutrality prescribes.

But the most potent influence tending to break down American neutrality arises from the confusion of the American conscience. It would be wrong to say that the American people are more idealistic or ethical than other peoples, but it is a fact that their moral idealism tends, and notably in international affairs, to operate without the same respect for realities which many other peoples display. This is only a way of saying that Americans are a highly sentimental people. Combine this sentimentalism with the restless activism for which the American temperament is famous, and one has a measure of the susceptibility of this country when the appeal is made to abandon the position to which it had committed itself with increasing purpose during the past two decades.

It is in the region of conscience that American neutrality is being attacked. We are being told that this a war to save civilization, and that one side is really fighting America's battle. If conscience can be confused by the identification of the military struggle with high moral values whose preservation hangs upon the outcome, America's participation is virtually assured. The thesis that this is a war in defense of civilization and democracy is understandable when put forward by governments actually engaged in fighting. It is the nature of war to clothe itself with grandiose moral aims. But a neutral nation should be on its guard against accepting without critical examination an interpretation put forward by belligerents.

In the present war it is well to remind ourselves that there are more than a dozen neutral countries in Europe itself. Many of them possess as high an order of intelligence as America can claim for herself. Certainly, their knowledge of European politics is more accurate and realistic than our own. Their conscience, too, is as keen as ours, molded, as it has been, in many cases, by the same culture and religious faith. Yet they do not identify the military struggle with the cultural and religious issues which have arisen in Europe. They do not believe that this is a war in defense of civilization.

These European neutrals have a larger stake in the preservation of European civilization (and, in most cases, of democracy) than America has. Yet not one of them stands in such fear of the peril to its civilization that it is willing to join the fight to preserve it. Each is striving with all its power to maintain its neutrality. Each is determined not to fight unless it is invaded, or unless—as is probably the case with Italy—it envisages an enormous reward in the outcome. Holland and Belgium and Denmark and Switzerland and Sweden and Finland and Italy and the Balkan countries do not believe that civilization hangs upon the outcome of this war. Why should the United States alone among the neutrals be susceptible to this moralistic interpretation? These European neutrals, if they believed that civilization hung in the balance, could save it by taking sides. Are the people of Holland and Switzerland and Sweden less noble than the people of America? Are they less brave? Less Christian? Who will say so?

Yet the doctrine that the Allies are really fighting America's war, that British and French soldiers are dying to save American soldiers from dying—this doctrine is knocking persistently at the door of America's conscience. It seems odd that the same doctrine finds no favor in the conscience of the people of Holland! It will be time enough for the American conscience to give heed to it when the European neutrals, as neutrals, not as coerced belligerents, call upon the United States to join *them* in saving civilization by taking sides in the conflict.

The best practical cue to neutral America's duty in relation to the war is the attitude of the European neutrals. They hold that it is not their war and they are determined to keep out of it. Against pressure infinitely more acute than any the United States can feel or will feel in any situation which may conceivably develop, they maintain their neutrality. They live in sound of the actual cannonading. Their borders mark the front lines of both belligerents. They know better than we what the war is all about. They have far more to gain or lose in the outcome than we would have. If civilization is at stake in the war they would be engulfed far more quickly and overwhelmingly than we. There might, indeed, be some hope of the survival of a vestige of civilization here. There could be none there. Yet they struggle to maintain their neutrality.

Norway and Sweden were so determined to be neutral that they refused to let Allied troops pass through to the aid of Finland. Would not that have been a bare minimum of reasonable contribution which Finland's neighbors could make to the preservation of civilization? If they were themselves too cowardly to fight for civilization, should they not at least have opened the way for more heroic men to defend civilization? From the standpoint of the doctrine that civilization hangs upon victory for one side in this war, the refusal of Norway and Sweden to let the Allies go through was a contemptible and pusillanimous act. Yet no execrations have been heaped upon them.

Sweden is now leaving Norway to her fate. Not a soldier does she send to her neighbor's defense. Yet her army of more than a half-million, reinforcing the Norwegians and the Allies, could drive the Germans out of Norway in three weeks. Is Sweden willing to have others fight her battles for her? Are Swedes cowards? Who will say so? Is Sweden indifferent to the claims of civilization? Of democracy? It is probable that she has developed the finest type of democracy, especially on its economic side, in the world. All this will be engulfed if the wrong side triumphs in this war for civilization.

No European neutral would accept for itself the thesis formulated by President Roosevelt for the guidance of neutral America when he declared that it is our national duty to do everything within our power "short of war but stronger than words" to beat Hitler. Every neutral in Europe—north, west, south and southeast—is giving a desperate exhibition of walking the tight-rope of neutrality. While the determiners of American foreign policy are edging this country toward participation—psychological, economic, diplomatic, and eventually military—on the ground that it is war to preserve civilization, these other neutrals, whose stake is incomparably greater than our own, seem totally unimpressed with this moralistic appeal.

Who among those loudly declaiming that this is America's war because it is a war to preserve civilization, will affirm that our ideals are higher and our moral convictions more stern and vigorous than those of Protestant, democratic Holland and Switzerland and Scandinavia? Until these and other European neutrals unfurl the banner of civilization and *voluntarily* march forth in its defense, why should America take sides? Why should our neutrality laws have been changed to favor one side, and why should it be assumed that they should be changed again more generously to favor one side? Such a policy, "short of war but stronger than words," is a policy of cowardice. "We will help you fight our war," we say to one side, "by manufacturing military equipment for you, and by selling you food by which you may live while you starve German women and children with your blockade, but you may not use our ships nor our navy, nor will we send our sons to die with your sons for the preservation of civilization."

Such an attitude is utterly ignoble. If this war is America's war, America should fight in it with all its resources, including its flesh and blood. And if it is a war for the preservation of civilization it *is* America's war no less than it is England's and France's and our soldiers ought to be at the fighting front. Whatever else he is, Uncle Sam is no poltroon. And American men are not cowards. Let it once be established in American thought that this war is a war to save civilization, and the American conscience will draw the inexorable conclusion that it is America's war, and our sons will again be on the high seas bound for the slaughter.

But it is *not* a war to preserve civilization! That interpretation is false. It is the war itself that is destroying civilizations—destroying it increasingly with each day that the war lasts, and destroying it definitively if it lasts to the point of victory, no matter which side wins. The European neutrals see this, and they are determined not to be engulfed in the conflict if they can by any means stay out.

For two decades, American intelligence also has lived with this conviction. "Another world war will spell the doom of Western civilization"— who among us has not repeated that ominous thesis over and over again since the first world war? What did we mean by it? Did we leave any place for the hope that one side in such a war would be the champion and defender of civilization and that by its triumph civilization might be preserved? We left no room for any such hope. We meant the exact opposite: We meant that another such war would *itself* be the destruction of civilization; we meant that if civilization rushed into another such war it would *ipso facto* be destroying itself. War *is* the destruction of civilization—that was the insight which crystallized into an all but universal national conviction. The idea that we can preserve civilization by modern war is logically absurd and empirically false. There can be no destruction of civilization comparable to the destruction which this war, if continued, will accomplish.

Perhaps civilization ought to be destroyed. The point is arguable. Perhaps the kind of civilization we have builded contains evils so great and so deeply entrenched that they can be got rid of only by some mighty explosion of irrational action within the body of civilization. War, which pretends to destroy the evils but actually destroys civilization itself, is that explosion. A strong argument can be made for this conception. It has a basis in biblical eschatology and in the Christian doctrine of divine judgment. But if that is what this war is, why should any nation *voluntarily* rush into it on the romantic illusion that it would thereby by contributing to the preservation of civilization? It would only be adding to the destruction of civilization! Every European neutral that is staying out of the war is doing its bit to preserve civilization. And the best the United States can do for the preservation of civilization is to stay out, and to stay as far out as it can.

If America is drawn into the war it will not be because America's vital interests are threatened. It will be because America's conscience is confused by the doctrine that this is a war in defense of civilization. It is a patriotic duty to reject this doctrine before the national emotion crystallizes around it. The doctrine has no standing outside of the belligerent countries (where its acceptance is understandable) and the United States. Why should the United States be susceptible to its appeal when other neutral countries (whose intelligence and conscience quotients are as high as our own) are not? For the United States to make a fateful decision to enter this war on the mistaken and irrational assumption that it is a war for the preservation of anything good in civilization will be the supreme tragedy of our history.

Christian leaders especially should be armed with an understanding of the fallacy in this appeal and be able to confound those who are confounding the American conscience by means of it. As for those in high places who speak unctuous words and initiate national policies on the bland assumption that American intelligence accepts the doctrine that civilization hangs upon a victory for one side in this war, they should be made aware of the presence of an enlightened and determined body of citizens who hold no such view and whose intelligence and patriotism are affronted by the assumption that they do.

America's neutrality and detachment from the conflict are supported by the highest ethical considerations. Her position as a neutral needs no apology. It is not merely, as some say, the expression of a geographic fact. It is also the expression of rational and ethical discernment. To undermine this position, to compromise it, to inculcate in the conscience of our citizenship the feeling that this nation owes a debt to civilization which can be discharged only by taking sides in the war, is to betray both America and civilization.

What Can America Do for Peace?
The Christian Century, May 15, 1940

Besides staying out of the war, what can the United States do for peace and civilization while the war is in progress? The question carries several implications. For one thing, it implies that the primary contribution of the United States to civilization will be made by staying out of the war, not by taking sides in it. This was editorially discussed in these pages last week. Second, the question implies that staying out of the war does not commit this country to isolationism: it implies a national purpose to exercise our full share of responsibility to preserve a civilization that is threatened with destruction. Third, the question implies that whatever the United States undertakes to do for civilization, in relation to this war, must be undertaken in her capacity as a genuine neutral, not as a partisan of one side. Fourth, it, therefore implies that, second only to maintaining our neutrality, the paramount objective of American policy should be to contribute by pacific means toward the bringing of the war to the earliest possible end.

How can America, as the strongest neutral power, contribute to the stopping of the war? Thus far, the government of the United States has done nothing constructive toward the attainment of this objective. Its policies have been dictated by a mixture of neutrality and tacit partisanship. The United States is acting more as a friendly power on the side of the Allies than as a neutral. It has recently made two gestures in the name of peace. Neither of these, however, could be characterized as a constructive effort for peace.

One gesture was the sending of Mr. Sumner Welles to the capitals of the belligerent countries on an exploratory mission: Mr. Welles was to find out from the several belligerents the terms upon which they would make peace.[1] As everyone expected, the reply he received was that victory was the only condition upon which any belligerent was willing at that stage to stop fighting. The Welles mission was merely President Roosevelt's way of saying to the fighting nations that when *they* were ready for peace he would be ready with the good offices of the United States to help them quit fighting in the most graceful and plausible way which the circumstances would allow. The mission was not without value, but it was not a mission of peace*making*.

The other gesture was even less significant, so far as peace*making* was concerned. This was the sending of an ambassador to the Holy See to coordinate, as it was said, the "parallel efforts" of President and pope for peace. The effectiveness of the papacy in the making of peace has been greatly exaggerated. There is no question that its influence in the civil policies of many nations and in their ordinary international relationships is very great. Its influence at a peace conference following a war might be substantial. Its influence as a partisan of one side in any war is, of course, enormous, as was demonstrated in the Franco revolution in Spain. But the influence of the papacy in stopping the war which is now being waged is slight. The ears of the maddened belligerents are as deaf to papal pleadings as to any other cry of humanity, and the papacy, if it is a genuine neutral, has nothing to offer but pleadings. The papacy was genuinely neutral in the First World War, and totally ineffective for peace. The new official liaison between the United States and the Vatican is scarcely more than a diplomatic pantomime serving other interests, no doubt, but hardly significant as a means of stopping the war.

The responsibility which burdens the American conscience will not be discharged by the pantomimic diplomacy of a Colonel House or a Sumner Welles or a Myron Taylor.[2] Such so-called peace activities may prove to be only the logical and psychological preparation for American participation in the war. As these alleged "efforts for peace" prove unfruitful, the popular disappointments will crystallize into the conviction that there is nothing at all the United States can do for peace. This will result in lifting the inhibition which national neutrality lays upon the sympathy which the majority of our citizens cherish for one side. If we cannot do anything for peace, they will say, then let us yield to our heart's desire and make sure that the side we wish to win, does win. Thus our neutral psychology and our peace psychology will pass into war psychology, and we will stand again at April 6, 1917.

If we had a government whose neutrality was heart-whole, whose sense of responsibility for civilization transcended its sympathy for one side in this conflict, such a government would quit the pretension that it was making "herculean efforts" for peace and would seek to coordinate those forces of Europe which are able to implement this peace plea with political power. The European neutrals do not believe the doctrine that civilization hangs on victory for one side in this war—a doctrine to which American susceptibilities too softly yield. They have but one desire, namely, that the war shall stop—shall stop in its tracks, without victory for either side. The European neutrals afford the true field for the operation of an American peace policy.

On the basis of their common neutrality, the United States should long since have been in active contact with these European neutrals for the purpose of common action directed toward the stopping of the war. If our interests in the preservation of civilization were as sincere as the high sounding words of our statesmen claim, and if our neutrality were heart-whole, we would instinctively have taken steps to create a solidarity of neutral peoples for the achievement of peace. There could be no doubt that American initiative would have found a sure and eager response in every neutral capital of Europe—including even Rome, so long as Italy remains non-belligerent.

President Roosevelt sincerely aspires to do something original and creative for peace and civilization. But his thought has run too conventionally in the grooves of precedent made by his great predecessors, notably Theodore Roosevelt and Woodrow Wilson. The former won an easy fame by merely providing a convenient stage setting for negotiating terms of peace *after* Japan had won its decisive victory over Russia. The latter's contribution to peace was by way of taking the United States into the war which he interpreted as a war to end war. Mr. Wilson would unquestionably have been able to take the United States into the League of Nations had he kept the country out of the war. America's profound sense of responsibility for peace will not be satisfied by entering the present war, nor by merely providing its good offices for a settlement of it *after* one side has crushed the other.

A constructive policy for peace must transcend the mad struggle of the belligerents. Civilization cries out today for constructive leadership on the level of neutrality. To this level President Roosevelt is beckoned by the greatest opportunity any statesman has faced in our entire history. Let him abandon the un-American assumption that he must make common cause with either belligerent, and let him make common cause with the European neutrals. They are the custodians of the civilization which the war is destroying. In contrast to the sending of lone diplomats on secret missions to the belligerents, let the President send an impressive deputation of, say, twenty American statesmen on a public mission to the neutral capitals—to Stockholm, Helsingfors, Kaunas, Riga, Tallinn, Dublin, The Hague, Brussels, Bern, Madrid, Lisbon, Rome, Bucharest, Budapest, Belgrade, Athens, Sophia, Ankara (not to mention other Near East capitals). Let this deputation be the bearer of an invitation from himself as President asking each neutral government to join the United States in a peace conference of neutrals, to consist of not less than 150 members, to convene immediately upon the completion of the deputation's itinerary, perhaps in Rome or in Madrid, and to sit uninterruptedly for the duration of the war for no other purpose than to find a way of bringing the war to an end. Dividing itself into four or more sections, the President's deputation could cover the eighteen or more capitals in two or three weeks.

What could such a peace conference of neutrals do? The answer, of course, lies beyond the power of any individual statesman, to say nothing of a citizen bystander, to give. Only the conference itself can provide the answer. But the proposal would hardly have arisen had there not been in mind some line or lines of possibility along which such a conference could act. The proposed conference would first of all confront the brute fact that the belligerents are locked in a life and death struggle in which neither side will yield until it is beaten. This determination has been absolute on the Allied side from the beginning. The Allied war aim has been single and simple: to destroy Hitler and his perfidious regime in Germany. On the German side, the determination to fight to the point of victory or exhaustion is steeled by imperial ambition and by the knowledge that defeat will surely spell dismemberment and national impotence for a long future.

A conference of neutrals, seeking to stop the war, would have also to face the fact that the situation out of which the war emerged could not be revived as a basis of negotiation for peace. Austria, Czechoslovakia, the Polish corridor, Danzig—the issues whose cumulative tension precipitated the Allied declarations of war against Germany—could not now hopefully be brought up for reconsideration. Since war was declared, Germany has taken not only Danzig and the corridor but (with Russia) has crushed and occupied the whole of Poland. In the political and economic framework within which those issues arose neither Germany nor the Allies is willing to negotiate—Germany, for obvious reasons; the Allies, because Hitler's word, solemnly given, has been so repeatedly dishonored that it is now worthless. Peace efforts by a conference of neutrals within that framework would only envisage another, but magnified, Munich.

Thus, such a conference would be confronted directly with the task of projecting a political and economic framework in which the tensions over these pre-war issues would disappear, or at least by greatly relaxed. That is to say, this conference of neutrals would undertake to do, as a means of stopping war, what the belligerent nations and the rest of Europe will have to do after the war is over. It is conceded on all hands, by belligerents and neutrals alike, that a radically new Europe must take shape after the war, if life in Europe (and the world) is to be tolerable. Proposals are now in circulation offering a basis for such a new order. No belligerent is willing to explore these proposals, each having committed himself to the single aim of crushing the enemy. It is unthinkable that a military victory, after a long war, will find the victors in a state of mind to consider any new order within which the tensions of the old order shall be relaxed and ameliorated. Whichever side wins, the peace will be a hard peace.

But a conference of neutrals, each member of which would have a responsible and vital stake in the creation of such an order, could explore its possibilities, sketch however roughly its essential features, proclaim the united determination of non-belligerent Europe to go into it, *and offer it to the fighting peoples as the basis for an armistice.*

In all this the part of the United States could not be that of a paternalistic patron of the conference. We would be integral to it, on a parity with all other neutrals, and implicated in the outcome.

From the moment of the President's announcement of his purpose to project such a conference, the attention of the world would be centered upon it. As the deputation moved from capital to capital, the reports of its successes would be proclaimed in every nation. The bare fact that such a conference was in process of formation would stimulate a new state of mind in Europe. Its effect upon the neutrals themselves would be instantaneous and transforming. The psychology of lonely helplessness and fear and desperation which now possesses them would pass into a psychology of hope and strength, derived from the knowledge that they were united in the common cause of peace. Their neutrality would be changed from a merely negative reaction against desperate danger into a constructive and responsible championship of civilization.

And when the conference meets, its deliberations would divide with the war itself the attention and the anxious hopes of all Europe and the world. No censorship could keep from any belligerent people the peace proposals which the conference would proclaim. No battle on sea or land could eclipse its deliberations. Peace would be at least an equal theme with war. The internal effects upon the populations of even dictator countries would surely weaken their military morale as they contemplated a prospective world order in which the real causes of the war which they are now fighting, and of future war, would at least be on the way to being removed.

A profound effect would be registered in American psychology. Our neutrality would be nothing now to apologize for, or to be juggled with. It would appear no longer as a lucky dispensation of geographical providence which has "isolated" us between two great oceans. We would have found the ethical and religious meaning of this isolation. We should then see it as a gift of divine providence, affording us no excuse for inaction and escape from the struggles of humanity, but laying upon us a unique responsibility for service to mankind. Let America embark upon such a policy of peacemaking, by associating herself with the neutral peoples of Europe in the common cause of stopping the war, and the whole disputatious problem of our relation to the rest of the world, which has vexed us for more than two decades, will be lifted into a new dimension. Peace is America's task, not war. Civilization is America's responsibility, not the destruction of civilization. And the neutral nations of Europe, browbeaten and threatened by warring belligerents, are her natural allies.

A War for Imperialism
The Christian Century, November 26, 1941

Step by step the American people have been led to the brink of a war for world power because they are assured that only by fighting such a war can Germany be prevented from seizing world power. A year ago when Henry R. Luce, the New York publisher, declared that the war offers the United States an opportunity to form a gigantic world empire and make the next hundred years "the American century," there was a general outcry. Who could dream that any such imperialistic motives would gain control of American policy! Yet when the Atlantic Charter was published its resounding silence with regard to any form of post-war international organization caused so experienced an observer as John Foster Dulles to warn that "there would probably result an Anglo-Saxon military and economic hegemony" over the globe. And now what was thus feared to be implicit in the reservations of the document signed by President Roosevelt and Mr. Churchill has been made explicit by an authorized administration spokesman.

In his recent address to the American Bar Association Secretary Knox declared that "for the next hundred years at least" the world's welfare will require a joint Anglo-American naval domination.[3] Lest there be any misunderstanding as to the official nature of this declaration the President's secretary, Stephen Early, has written Mrs. Orris Gravenor Robinson, president of the Women's International League for Peace and Freedom, that "I wish to state emphatically that Secretary Knox's actual speech before the American Bar Association on October 1 does represent the views of the administration." It is thus acknowledged from the White House that the war is expected to result in a globe-encircling Anglo-American policing, which is only another name for the vastest imperialistic enterprise history has ever known.

At the time of the war's outbreak, or even a year ago, it would have been thought impossible that the United States could be enticed again to enter on an imperialistic career. Not only was the belief in this country that imperialism as such had been proved a snare and a delusion, but the reaction from the timid forays into an American colonialism which followed the Spanish War had proved so severe that all ideas of a foreign empire under the stars and stripes were supposed to be dead and buried. The Philippines had been promised their freedom in 1946; the good neighbor policy had been proclaimed to set at rest the fears of Caribbean and Central American peoples. Imperialism, the overwhelming majority of Americans believed, was a form of intoxication from which their nation had sworn off forever. Nevertheless, here the nation stands today, dedicated by its bellicose navy secretary with presidential approval to a hundred-year program of world domination. By what mysterious process has this vital change in national policy, this decision to seek a new imperialistic destiny, come to pass in this brief period of time?

We do not believe that the process has been mysterious. On the contrary, we believe that a sinister logic of events has been operating, so compelling, so nearly inexorable, that no other outcome than this embracing of an imperialistic future could have been expected. Once the administration had begun to look forward to American participation in the war, some justification had to be sought for the enormous sacrifices which would be involved. Entrance into the First World War had required sacrifices which most Americans held were not justified by its outcome. A review of the steps by which the nation has been brought to the eve of conflict will disclose the logic that has led to the Knox avowal.

The administration's first appeals for abandonment of neutrality and adoption of a partisan course in the war were based on warnings which failed to frighten more than a small minority of the American people. It was said that this country was in danger of immediate invasion; Secretary Stimson even spoke darkly of "sixty or ninety days." Then it was said that South America was in danger of invasion, and that bases seized there would later be used to launch an attack against the United States. When both these prophecies failed to alarm, it was said that Hitler in his own person constituted such a megalomaniacal threat to the peace of the whole world that only his destruction could insure our national safety. Not only was it impossible to do business with Hitler; we could not live at peace in the same world with him.

Most Americans remained cold to all such efforts to scare them into the war. Omaha and St. Louis were not convinced that the danger of immediate invasion was a reality, and as for the menace of Hitler, as an individual despot, memories of the charges leveled against the Kaiser remained too vivid for that to provoke more than a few minor tremors. The voice of experience constantly offered a reminder that, after incurring the enormous sacrifices required to overthrow a European tyrant, the nation might still find at the end of another twenty years that it had the same tragic task to do all over again. So there came the appeal to the four freedoms. The American people were exhorted to move toward war as a means of establishing "everywhere in the world" the same liberties which are their own most prized possession and expectation.

Somehow, this appeal to a crusade for freedom also left the nation in a skeptical frame of mind. Instead of rising in a great outpouring of passionate dedication, as Americans did when Woodrow Wilson announced his noble slogans for the last war, the people began to ask questions. How seriously was the proclamation of the four freedoms to be taken? How widely were they to be established? What limitations must realism impose on President Roosevelt's lofty dream? Few slogans can withstand such scrutiny. It soon became clear that the attempt to stir up again the revivalistic mood which carried the American people into the First World War was doomed to failure. When the call came to prepare for another war to make the world safe for democracy, disguised this time as a call to plant the four freedoms throughout the earth, there was no answering response. The American people were in no crusading mood.

Why did the American people fail to rise to the Roosevelt challenge as they had a quarter of a century ago to that of Wilson? The answer is right there in the question: they remembered all too clearly what happened after they rose to the Wilsonian slogans. They remembered not only the sacrifices of the war but the brutal realities of Versailles, the internecine strife which made impossible any healing of Europe, the economic disaster which followed in the wake of the war, "Uncle Shylock"—in other words, they remembered all the bitter experiences which had destroyed the illusions that carried them into the crusade of 1917.[4] Moreover, they looked on today's Europe with experienced eyes. The American people today know that the old rivalries and hatreds of Europe are not dead, that the seeds of new wars are being sowed at this moment all over that unhappy continent, that the clashes of ambition between the various European powers will persist after this conflict is over. Accordingly they listen with apathy to talk of a "new Europe," for from this blood-drenched cockpit of warring nationalities they expect nothing but recurrent slaughter.

That is the reason why the framers of the Atlantic Charter were wholly silent on any proposal to revive the League of Nations or to make the future peace and order of the world dependent on the operations of any association, general alliance or other grouping of the nations. That is why the document signed by the President and the British prime minister contains no whisper of a world court or any future appeal to the rule of international law. The men who wrote that declaration had in view one dominant purpose—to persuade the American people to enter the war. They knew that the American people could not be roused by forecasts of a resurrected league or a revived court; they knew that they must reckon with a widespread belief that as these failed once, so they would fail again, and the structure of peace founding upon them would again dissolve. They knew that in seeking an outcome for the war which would justify entrance to the majority of Americans they must take into account the psychology of a people who perfectly illustrate the truth of the adage, "Once burned; twice shy."

We thus discover the logic by which those now in power in Washington and London have been brought to their proclamation of a coming Anglo-American world hegemony. If the American people will not rise to idealistic slogans, what conception of a future world order may make them ready to undergo the sacrifices of another war? That is the problem which has brought forth Colonel Knox's officially inspired answer. All nonsense about leagues or inclusive alliances or courts or any other sort of collaboration with strange and unreliable—that is to say, "foreign"!—nations is thrown overboard. Instead, the American citizen, with his boundless belief in his own capacities, is asked to prepare to fight a war so that he and his kind can take over the control of the world. The world is in a mess; now let the omnicompetent Anglo-Saxon step in to straighten it out!

Instead of "fancy ideas" sure to be wrecked by the machinations of nations which he already distrusts, the American citizen is asked to make possible a simple concentration of such overwhelming power in Anglo-American hands as shall overawe all the rest of mankind. We are to go to war to force the world to place its fate in our hands! Here will be a reward for sacrifice and suffering which no future Versailles, no future maneuvering behind the scenes at Geneva, can betray! And, lest there linger in any American's mind a fear that even in collaboration with Britain there may be danger that the control of the post-war world will slip out of our hands, Colonel Knox has taken care to affirm that in this new partnership to rule mankind the United States will "provide both the major power and the dominant leadership."

Most of the public want to have the intricate problems of international life presented to them in simple pictures. Here is a simple picture which anyone can understand—the business of running the world taken out of the untrustworthy or inefficient hands of all other nations and entrusted to the sole care of the freedom-loving, justice-serving, God-fearing, English-speaking white peoples of Britain and America! But how many Americans stop to realize that behind this simple picture there waits the prospect of the most ambitious imperialism ever projected, an imperialism which will gradually but inevitably bring to focus against itself the jealousies and hatreds of all the other nations and races on earth? How many stop to realize that in the very hour when they declare that mankind must be saved from a world imperialism based on German land power they are being asked to acquiesce in the establishment of a world imperialism based on Anglo-American sea power?

Many Christians who have finally brought themselves to consent to American entrance into the war as a means of destroying Hitler have not yet grasped the potency of this dark logic which will turn victory into the proclamation of a new imperialism. Some of them in their absorption with the present hour may even go as far as Karl Barth, who in a little quoted passage in his *Letter to Great Britain*, upbraids those who bother themselves with such matters as peace aims.[5] So obsessed are they with the demand that Hitler shall be destroyed, that they never stop to ask what is to follow this destruction. Such Christians will be horrified, and will profess to be completely overtaken by surprise, if victory in the war leads to the erection of a world-wide Anglo-Saxon hegemony. Yet this is the prospect, by implication in the silences of the Atlantic Charter and by forthright avowal in the words of Colonel Knox to which has been given the White House imprimatur. Is it possible for such Christians, in the light of this prospect, to echo Barth's complacent application to the peace terms of the words, "Be not anxious for tomorrow"?

NOTES

1. Sumner Welles was Franklin Roosevelt's Undersecretary of State and a trusted advisor on U.S. foreign policy. In 1941, he helped draft the Atlantic Charter, an Anglo-American joint declaration of principles.

2. Edward Mandell House (nicknamed "Colonel") served as President Woodrow Wilson's closest advisor during the First World War, and helped draft Wilson's Fourteen Points. Myron Taylor was appointed in 1939 as President Roosevelt's Personal Representative to the Vatican.

3. William Franklin Knox served as Secretary of the Navy from 1940 until his death in 1944. Though a Republican and an opponent of the New Deal, Roosevelt chose him in an effort to help build national unity as the nation prepared for war.

4. Shylock is the name of the Jewish userer in Shakespeare's *The Merchant of Venice*, applied as an epithet against the United States (Uncle Sam) for being unwilling to cancel Europe's war debts after World War I.

5. See Karl Barth, "Letter to Great Britain," pages 169–75 in this book.

3

John Haynes Holmes

Pastor, Unitarian Community Church
Chairman, American Civil Liberties Union

On the eve of U.S. entry into World War I, John Haynes Holmes preached a sermon that would not have been well received in many congregations in America. "So long as I am your minister, this Church will answer no military summons. Other pulpits may preach recruiting sermons; mine will not. . . . Other clergymen may pray to God for victory for our arms; I will not." It was too much even for the American Unitarian Association, to which Holmes belonged. Such talk was branded as treason, and he withdrew his fellowship as a Unitarian minister.

Nevertheless, Holmes successfully converted his Community Church in New York to his radical vision of social and political activism—and set a standard for interfaith, interracial fellowship. Few ministers could match his pedigree in reform movements. He joined with Jewish leader Stephen Wise, for example, to form the City Affairs Committee, which waged a nine-year crusade against Mayor Jimmie Walker and his corrupt political machine. He helped found the American Civil Liberties Union, with Roger Baldwin; the League of Industrial Democracy, with Harry Laidler; Planned Parenthood, with Margaret Sanger; and the National Association for the Advancement of Colored People, with W.E.U. Du Bois. (In words reminiscent of Martin Luther King Jr. Holmes said the stamp of manhood depended "not on the color of a man's skin, but the texture of his spirit.")

No issue engaged Holmes more, however, than the burgeoning peace movement between the two world wars. His 1916 pacifist tract, *New Wars for Old*, went through thirteen printings and helped establish him as a towering voice of Western pacifism. Holmes was captivated by the nonviolent philosophy of India's Mahatma Gandhi—sermonizing him in 1921 as "the greatest man in the world"—and became Gandhi's primary champion in America. In the aftermath of World War I, Holmes flung himself into a flurry of peace activism: disarmament rallies, petition drives, and international conferences. In 1935 he led a group assembled in Judson Memorial Baptist Church in reciting an antiwar litany ("If war comes I will not fight; if war comes I will not enlist; if war comes I will not be conscripted. . . . So help me God!"). He chaired the War Resisters League and helped found the Fellowship of Reconciliation, which worked to secure legal recognition for conscientious objectors during World War II. He regularly expounded pacifist principles as editor of *Unity*, a weekly religious journal, and in articles for *The Nation*, *The New Republic*, and *The World Tomorrow*.

Holmes became alarmed by the growing anti-Semitism in Germany and joined Stephen Wise in anti-Hitler protests in the 1930s. He criticized Hitler's advances in Europe, but strenuously opposed U.S. rearmament or assistance to the Allies. The first essay included here appeared in December of 1940, when much of Europe had fallen to Nazism and Britain had barely survived two months of air attacks. Without a whisper of doubt, Holmes condemns any participation in the war as "an open and utter violation of Christianity." He repeats his lifelong conviction that the only way to defeat tyranny is with "compassion, mercy, brotherhood, love." The second essay is drawn from Holmes' book *Out of Darkness*, completed in October of 1941. In it he recycles familiar arguments about the causes of German aggression—that it was merely a continuation of the previous war brought on by an unjust Treaty of Versailles. Thus, the impulse to fault Adolf Hitler for the conflict, he argues, is a mistaken form of moralizing. "Blaming Hitler for this war . . . satisfies the scapegoat instinct of human nature," he writes. "In war there is no absolute division between good and bad, innocence and guilt."

The Same Old War
The Christian Century, December 11, 1940

It is recorded of the First World War that on a certain day Lytton Strachey, the famous English essayist and biographer, was summoned before a draft board to give account of his conscientious objections to war. Mr. Strachey was a long, lean mean, with legs that stretched out, like Abraham Lincoln's, to all corners of the room. He had owlish eyes peering through prodigious spectacles, a scraggly beard, a high, squeaky voice, and an utterly imperturbable mien. After Mr. Strachey had seated himself in the witness chair, the following colloquy took place:

> *Chairman:* We understand, Mr. Strachey, that you a conscientious objector
> to war.
> *Strachey:* O, no! O, no! I'm not a conscientious objector to war.
> *Chairman:* You're not! Then why in heaven's name are you refusing to fight?
> *Strachey:* Well, you see, I'm a conscientious objector to *this* war!

This episode is amusing and important as pointing to a distinction between war in general and war in the particular instance which plays a large part in the history of pacifism. Only it puts this distinction in an extraordinary "reverse"! Mr. Strachey was not opposed to war on any basis of moral principle or Christian idealism. There might be some good wars that were worthy the support of gentlemen and scholars. He was not convinced, however, that the First World War was one of them. So he objected to "*this* war," and refused to have part in it. But the average pacifist who makes distinction puts it the other way around. This pacifist in strenuously opposed to war in general; but whenever any particular war comes along, especially one in which his own country is involved, he finds this war for some reason entitled to his support. War is still evil. But "*this* war" is good—or at least not so much an evil as no war at all in the concrete circumstance.

Just how an evil thing can be good, or something less than bad, I have never been able to make out. We do not outlaw slavery in general, and then say that there are times, especially this present time, when slavery may rightly be acclaimed and practiced. We do not denounce adultery, and then argue that with *this* woman, in *this* place, and at *this* time, it is right for a husband to break his marriage vows. But we agree to condemn war as a principle of action or a program of statesmanship, and then find reason to approve each and every especial war that comes along. It is as though, like John Milton's Satan, we cried, "Evil, be thou my good." And the irony of it is that it is only the war that now is, this current war, which

ever challenges us to action, and thus tests our faith by our works to see
whether it is dead. The last war, which no longer concerns us, was of
course bad—no doubt about that. The next war, which does not yet concern us, will equally be bad—no doubt about that. But *this* war, which very
terribly concerns us now as a veritable trial by fire, *this* war, like an Ed
Wynn joke, is "different," and therefore not bad at all. Which means that
pacifism is a program for periods between wars, but never for the present
crisis! Like Christianity, with which it is supposed to have some connection, pacifism is a gospel effective only at the time when it is not needed.

This distinction between war and *"this* war" is abominable—the bank-
ruptcy of morals and the betrayal of religion. But as the patron of so much
of our thinking these days, I use it as the framework of my reply to the editor's question.

First, then, as regards this present war. If America goes in will I support
my country? No!—because, like Lytton Strachey in the last war, I don't believe in this war, which is only the latest of a long series of European conflicts rooted in the age-old struggle for military predominance and imperialistic rule.[1] It was begun, years ago, in a rivalry between the old British
empire and the new German Reich which threatened for a time to resolve
itself into an armed alliance between London and Berlin for the division of
the world instead of into the present conflict for its universal mastery. It will
end either in an improbable early peace in which Britain and Germany will
share the globe between them and perhaps make war on Russia, or in a remote collapse dictated by mutual exhaustion, in which as in the case of the
Peloponnesian War between Athens, the great sea-power of its day, and
Sparta, the great land-power, the light of civilization will be extinguished.

If America goes into the war, it will be not for idealistic reasons but to
serve her own imperialistic interests so closely identified with those of
Britain, and to no result other than that of prolonging the duration and extending the range of a struggle in which her ruin will be added to the sum
total of the ruin of mankind. There are elements of better and worse in this
war as in all human affairs. I prefer Churchill to Hitler, to put it mildly,
just as in the Peloponnesian War I trust I would have preferred Pericles to
Archidamus.[2] But no one of these moral elements today in Europe, any
more than in Greece yesterday, alters the nature of the event, which is the
fundamentally immoral clash of competing imperialisms. In such an
event, as Muriel Lester has reminded us, "it is not worse to cover empire
than to cleave empire."[3]

I made up my mind about these wars of our time as long ago as 1914–5,
when I stated that the war against the Kaiser had "grown from the dragons'
teeth of secret diplomacy, imperialistic ambition, dynastic pride, greedy
commercialism, economic exploitation at home and abroad." Again, in April
1917, just on the eve of our entrance into the war, I said that "our participa-

tion in war, like the war itself, is political and economic, not ethical, in character. Any honor, dignity or beauty which there may be in our impending action is to be found in the impulses which are actuating many patriotic hearts today, and not at all in the real facts of the situation. The war itself is wrong. Its prosecution will be a crime. There is not a question raised, an issue involved, a cause at stake, which is worth the life of one bluejacket on the sea, or one khaki-coat in the trenches." Continuing, I said, "I question the sincerity of no man who supports this war. I salute the devotion of every man who proposes to sustain it with his money or his blood. But I say to you that when, years hence, the whole of this story has been told, it will be found that we have been tragically deceived, and all our sacrifices been made in vain."

Everything that has happened since 1917 has confirmed the truth of these words, spoken in the furious climax of a war which was glorified in the same idealistic terms as this present war. The Allies were fighting in that 1914–18 conflict, so it was said, for democracy, civilization, an end of war, against an enemy who had raped Belgium, occupied and ravaged northern France, plundered Romania, bombarded Paris, bombed London from the night-flying Zeppelins, and sunk passenger ships without notice or trace.

But that war, won by the Allies, was followed by the revival of the secret treaties, the blockade of Germany, the writing of the Versailles treaty, the Allied invasions of Russia, the French alliances for military predominance on the Continent, the British manipulation of the League of Nations for imperial aggrandizement and power, the looting of the Weimar republic, the humiliation and ruin of the German people, the scuttling of disarmament, economic and conciliation conferences—all of which showed what the war was really about. Indeed, the 1914–18 war never came to an end at all. The armistice was only a "halt," and the Versailles treaty only a truce. The essential struggle went right straight on in the field of power politics, and now has again brought to the same battlefield the same belligerents to fight out the same issues of imperial rivalry to the same ends of imperial dominion.

This present war, in other words, is only a continuation of the last war. There is nothing new in it or strange, except the intensification of forces taut with desperation and the deepening of horror wrought in a final combat to the death. In everything that history will deign to notice and claim to judge, this war of Churchill against Hitler is the same old war of Lloyd George against the Kaiser, just as in the Thirty Years' War Richelieu's struggle against Maximilian in 1647 was the same old war that the Emperor Ferdinand began against Frederick of Bohemia in 1618.[4] Even the advocates of this war see it as only a resumption of the last war, and ask that we support it today as we did yesterday.

Thus, the *New York Herald Tribune*, an ardent pro-war paper, said on June 23 last that it was becoming "clearer than ever that the present war is only a continuation of the war which was started on that fateful August morning in 1914." Just one month later, on August 28, Sonia Tomara, European correspondent of the *Herald Tribune,* wrote in that paper: "The war that struck Europe so soon after the other war was not a war between ideologies, but only one more struggle of the fittest, the push of German imperialism, anxious to expand and dominate"—and, we might add, of British imperialism, anxious to *hold* and dominate! And just a week earlier, on August 21, in a speech to the House of Commons, Prime Minister Winston Churchill, who ought to know, used these words,". . . this war is, in fact, only a continuation of the last."

Why should I change my mind about this war? If I denounce its first chapter, why should I not denounce its second? And if America plunges again into the same old fight, to repeat in 1940 the folly and futility of 1917–18, why should I give my country a support now which I refused a generation ago? I will have nothing to do with this war which was bred in the chaos of a hundred years of diplomatic chicanery, commercial rivalry and imperialistic ambition, to which all the great powers made their respective contributions. I will not take sides in a struggle in which no good cause can survive the ruin which may in the end sweep our civilization into another and more impenetrable dark age.

Unless and until America goes into it, I will labor to keep this country, the melting-pot of nations, outside of and above the battle, that she may use her compassionate and insistent influence as the pope declared, on the first anniversary of the war, he had used the influence of the Vatican, "for the reconciliation of peoples, to limit the extent of the conflict, to safeguard those who are in danger of being dragged in, and to alleviate the suffering that every war brings with it." If and when my country enters the war, I will join neither hand nor heart to the hostilities of the hour, but toil still for brotherhood, in love of friends and enemies alike, and for that peace which can alone save mankind from death.

Yes—and let Hitler run roughshod over the earth to triumph?

I should be the more disturbed by this easy challenge if I saw Hitler with the eyes of so many of my contemporaries—as a unique embodiment of wickedness, a monster intruded upon the earth like Satan come from hell. But I do not see him in this guise. I think it unscientific to isolate a man from the time and place which have together spawned him. To me Hitler is all that is horrible, but as such he is the produce of our world, the veritable incarnation of our nationalistic, capitalistic and militaristic era. Whatever is worst in our civilization seems to have come to a vile head in him. He is our sins sprung to life, to confound us, scourge us and perhaps destroy us.

It is remarkable that Hitler has done nothing not already familiar to us from direful example. Thus, he did not begin the persecution of the Jews, which has been a Christian practice for well-nigh two millennia. He did not originate the myth of race superiority, which has flourished for generations in this country in the relations of whites with blacks. He did not inaugurate the concentration camp, which the Spaniards imposed upon the Cubans, the English upon the Boers, and the Americans upon the Filipinos. He did not initiate the totalitarian state, which is only an extremity of tyranny as transmitted to our time by the Hapsburgs and the Romanovs. He did not invent the idea of the subjection of helpless people, as witness Britain in India, France in Morocco, and Belgium in the Congo. He did not even build his own military machine.

The very weapons that Hitler has developed so formidably and used so fearfully have come from other nations—the tank from Britain, the bomber from America and France, the machine gun and submarine from America. This man, so cruel, so ruthless, so revengeful, is not alien to ourselves. He is the perversion of our lusts, the poisoned distillation of our crimes. We would not be so aghast at his appearance did we not see in him, as in a glass darkly, the image of the world that we have made. Our sins have found us, that's all. If Hitler triumphs, it will be as the punishment of our transgressions.

But will he triumph? He may, if we have no better manner of meeting him that with the weapons which he has so terribly turned against us. The resort to arms is no guarantee of victory. Even a predominance of arms in this struggle against the reich can insure only a prolonged process of mutual destruction, in which, to quote St. Augustine in his *The City of God*, "the conquerors are ever more like to the conquered than otherwise." This is what Mahatma Gandhi has in mind when he declares that he does "not want Britain to be defeated," nor yet "to be victorious in a trial of brute strength." "You want to kill Nazism?" he asks. "You will never kill it by its indifferent adoption. You will have to be more ruthless that the nazis. To win this war, the British must adopt with greater thoroughness the same work of destruction as the Germans."

This would mark the real triumph of the nazis—the transformation of their foes into their own likeness by the sheer necessity of adopting nazi weapons, and nazi methods in the use of these weapons, as a means to victory. This is not the way to solve our problem, meet our danger, save our world. There must be a better way if all that is precious in human living is not by our own frenzy of fear to be doomed to the destruction now impending. Even though I could not find, or follow, this better way, I would not turn to what I know is as evil as it is disastrous.

This brings us to the second and more fundamental aspect of our problem—the challenge not of this war but of war itself.

If America goes to war against Germany or Japan I will not support the war for the simple reason that, like the early Christians and the later Quakers, I am opposed to war—to all war, to war as an acceptable method of settling disputes between nations, to war as an established institution and practice of arms, to war as a weapon either of aggression or defense. Though this war were as righteous as King Arthur's war against Modred, which incidentally killed Arthur as well as Mordred and wrecked "the fair order of the Table Round," I would still be against it. Though this war, as Professor Ralph Perry of Harvard has declared, is the most holy war since the war in heaven between God and Lucifer, which incidentally populated hell and consigned mankind to the reign of sin and death, I would still be against it. Though this war were one more battle in the divine war between Ormuzd and Ahriman, which incidentally dooms the cosmos to eternal strife, I would still be against it.(5)[5] For I am against war—for the simple and all-sufficient reason that it is *war*.

What is war?

War, said Voltaire, is "murder." War, said Edward Gibbon, who describes a thousand years of it in his *Decline and Fall of the Roman Empire*, is "the art of destroying the human species." War, said William Ellery Channing, is "the consensus of all crimes"—the greatest, therefore, of crimes, since it is the combination of all crimes. War, said the House of Bishops of the Episcopal Church in November 1939, "is a hideous denial of God and his condemnation rests upon it. It is rationally unjustifiable, morally indefensible, and religiously irreconcilable with the love of God and our neighbor. And it is wholly incompatible with the teaching and example of our Lord Jesus Christ."

How can I have part in such a monstrous thing as this? War, in its very nature, is wrong. Not even as a bad means to a good end can it be justified, since this principle would justify any certainly bad means to any fancifully good end, and is thus immoral. As long ago as March 7, 1915 I stated my conviction that "war is never justifiable at any time or under any circumstance. No man is wise enough, no nation is important enough, no human interest is precious enough, to justify the wholesale destruction and murder which constitute the essence of war."

These words I solemnly reaffirmed on April 1, 1917 and would as solemnly reaffirm today. I do not deny that war, like polygamy, slavery, cannibalism, may have been inseparable from early stages of social life. I do not deny that war, like famine, pestilence, earthquake, has contributed to some progress of the race, for thus does God make the wrath as well as the agony of men to praise him. I do not even deny that there have been times when war like a storm at sea, has seemed to be unavoidable. What I do deny is that these facts touch the judgment that war is wrong, or should turn the free will of men from its repudiation.

War is an open and utter violation of Christianity. If war is right, then Christianity is wrong, false, a lie. If Christianity is right, then war is wrong, false, a lie. The God revealed by Jesus, and by every great spiritual Jesus of the race from Jeremiah to Gandhi, works not his will by driving men to wanton slaughter. God is the universal Father. His spirit is love, his rule is peace, his method of persuasion is forgiveness. His law, as interpreted and promulgated not alone by the Nazarene, is "love one another," "resist not evil with evil," "forgive seventy times seven," "overcome evil with good," "love your enemies." Such a God and such a law others may reconcile with war, if they can. I cannot. And what I cannot do, I will not profess to do.

Though this resolve stripped me naked, and left me defenseless before my enemies, I would still stick to it. I had rather die than kill, and see my country conquered than a conqueror. But, as every statement of the pacifist ideal implies, we are not defenseless. Can anyone read Jesus' gospel, and study his life in fulfillment of that gospel, without seeing that love is a weapon more potent than the sword? Is it possible that Christians can accept Jesus' voluntary sacrifice on the cross in atonement for the violence and lust of men, and not understand that this is the way of victory? What is our religion but an affirmation that there are spiritual forces in the world, and under our control, which are potent to achieve our ends?

Love, generosity, compassion, forgiveness—these are powers which *do* things among men. We call them imponderables because they cannot be weighed, intangibles because they cannot be touched. But we feel their presence as we feel the presence of the sun; we see their operation as we see the operation of the wind; we know their power as we know the power of gravitation. They are the spirit of man, mightier far than iron or steel, electricity or dynamite. What this spirit is we do not know, but of its reality we are sure. Religion calls it God—the divine within us, God's life within our lives, his omnipotence to clothe us and engird us.

How shall we protect ourselves, and save the things that are precious to our lives? How shall we confront tyranny and confound terror? Not by force and violence, arms and blood, but by compassion, mercy, brotherhood, love. Not by fighting and killing but by serving and dying. The prophet has spoken the word, echoed by every religion of mankind: "Not by power, nor by might, but by my spirit, saith the Lord"!

So my resolve is fixed, as it has been fixed for years. If America enters this war, I will not. As far as the law may allow, or my spirit dictate, I will oppose the war. And my comfort will be as the comfort of those early Christians for whom St. Augustine spoke in that dark day when Rome fell and the empire was overrun and ravaged by the barbarians:

"Christ's children are commanded to endure with patience the calamities that are brought upon them by the ministers of a wicked commonwealth. Be they kings, princes, judges, soldiers and governors, rich or poor, bound or free, of what sex or sort soever, they must bear all with patience; being by their sufferance here to attain that happier commonwealth where the will of Almighty God is their only law, and his law their only will."

The Causes of the War—Hitler
Out of Darkness, 1941

It is easy to blame this war on one man, Adolf Hitler. But we have had wars before Hitler. Wars have been fought since the beginning of time, and many of them have had no Hitlers in them at all. Wars are a constant fact in history, as they are a constant factor in human nature. But it is easy to blame a man, one man, for this horror of our age.

Thus, it fits in with our almost inescapable propensity to dramatize history in terms of conspicuous personalities. For centuries we have told time, and thus classified events, by the reigns of kings, and in our country by the administration of presidents. Many royal rulers have had less to do with the events of their days than infants in a nursery have had to do with the affairs of a household; a succession of American presidents, from Jackson to Lincoln, the most stirring epoch in our annals, were hardly more than chips whirling amid the turmoil of rushing mountain streams. But their names mark the generations as figures mark the hours on the face of a clock, and thus create the illusion of importance. Next to kings and presidents rank conquerors and soldiers. We divide the epochs, as we explain what happened in these epochs, by reference to Alexander, Caesar, Constantine, Charlemagne, Cromwell, Marlborough, Napoleon, Bismarck. We assume that we have interpreted the course of history when we have set one of these mighty men in the midst of events, just as we assume that we have interpreted reality when we speak some mysterious and quite meaningless words like electron, relativity, thermodynamics.

In recent years, however, which have formed a scientific era dominated by the concept of cause and consequence, a change has come over our way of thinking. Slowly but surely we have learned that great men, even rulers like Charlemagne and soldiers like Napoleon, have no exclusive nor even necessarily central influence in controlling the course of human events. Impersonal forces, economic and social, representing masses rather than men, conspire with personal forces, psychological and spiritual, to determine destiny. Names, therefore, even the names of kings, are dropping out of our textbooks. Soldiers and armies and wars are yielding place to machines and crops and money. The elevation of Hitler to the position of decisive importance in this age is a reversion to an outgrown and now discarded philosophy of experience. It is a substitution of mythology for history, and of drama for science.

Blaming Hitler for this war also satisfies the scapegoat instinct of human nature. A scapegoat is necessary to any happy and complacent life. To blame ourselves for anything is painful, but to blame someone else is blissful. The Jews are not the only people who have exalted into a religious rite the demand for a scapegoat to relieve men of their sins. This is a performance to which all of us resort when disaster presses hard upon us, and suffering and death become our lot. Who is to blame for all this present ill? Are *we* to blame? Impossible! Are we partially to blame? Why, not at all— for have not our intentions always been worthy and our ideals high? Then we must look elsewhere for the guilty party. To find him will prove our innocence. And there he is—this Austrian painter who is such a silly upstart, such a crass and cruel leader, a ruler so persistent in rejecting our way of life and so wicked in establishing his own. Hitler is responsible for this dreadful war. Had it not been for his perversity, his madness, it never would have come. *We* certainly wanted peace—everybody wanted peace except the Fuehrer and his accomplices. Of course, it was peace on our own terms; but they were good terms, wise terms. Were they not entirely satisfactory to us? But Hitler would not accept them. He chose war—i.e., dictated his own terms of peace which were utterly impossible to us. And so *we* had to choose war too. Which means, obviously, that he is guilty and we are guiltless! If there is any more satisfying conviction than this, I do not chance to know what it is. Hence the ease with which we make Hitler our scapegoat, and whip him into the wilderness of hate.

It all comes down to what may be called the Satanic theory of history. This is the theory which at bottom pervades the opinions of every mind and dominates the policies of every nation. It is the one universal moral philosophy of mankind. Humanity consists of two parts—the people who are good and the people who are bad. Indeed, the whole cosmos is divided into these two parts—God and his angels on the one side and Satan and his demons on the other. This division extends into the future world, which contains the "saved" who dwell in heaven and the "lost" who are consigned to hell. Now we, of course, are the good—we and our allies, or associates! Other people, especially our competitors and enemies, are the bad. In controversy and conflict, God is with us, since we are serving his wish and will. By the same token, Satan is leading our foes, since they are resisting our high purposes and thus frustrating the divine intention. Satan, in other words, is engaged in the same business here that he was in heaven when he made war upon God—the same war that he has renewed here in all ages, and now again in this our time. What he failed to do in heaven, Satan is proposing to do on earth—to confound God and establish the dominion of evil.

It is all so simple, especially in time of war! This nation is the good nation, since we would not serve Satan. The other nation, the foe, is the bad nation, since they could not serve God. We must win, as they must lose, since God is no more to be defeated here than he was in heaven. This means that everything precious to us, and therefore to God—our culture, our civilization, our religion, everything that makes life precious—must be preserved from the destruction that Satan's minions are striving to bring upon it. The war, therefore, is a war for culture, and civilization, and religion—a war for God and for his Kingdom. That is, it is a holy war! This is what justifies war—certainly the wars fought by our own century. It is in the light of this Satanic theory of events that we can say, without a tremor of doubt, that America has never fought an unjust or unholy war. Our cause has always been a good cause, and our belligerent action therefore righteous action. This is God's country; and when we fight we fight for him.

It is all so simple. At least until we unexpectedly get the enemy's point of view, and see that they also are thinking in terms of the Satanic theory, and are turning its tables straight against us! For, from *their* point of view, *they* are the servants of good and *we* the servants of evil. Satan is *our* leader; and, horror of horrors, God is declared to be *their* leader. When they go into battle they pray to God, just as we do. Each side, that is, invokes the divine aid against the other, and thus God is set defiantly against God. It seems ridiculous, as it is blasphemous. Yet it would seem, in our mutual ignorance of absolutes, that the one side had quite as much right to its point of view as the other. Who is going to decide between them? There is comfort, to be sure, in the thought that, with this dual point of view at work, God is sure to be triumphant in the fray. Whichever side wins, God is championing his cause. But it is true that, by the same logic, Satan is certain victor. Whichever side wins, the black archangel wins as well, since the losing nation sees clearly the victory of evil on the other side. Perhaps this is why there is no end to wars. God wins, and Satan wins; as God loses, and Satan loses. Sooner or later, there must be another fight. The essence of the situation is contradiction, and contradiction must be resolved if the world is not to crack.

No, it is not simple at all, this Satanic theory. On the contrary, it is very confusing. Take England, for example! One hundred and fifty years ago, in the American Revolution, England was a Satanic nation. Were not the redcoats pictured as devils, with hoofs and horns? But today, in this present war, as in the last war, England has apparently been redeemed. The Empire is now on the side of good; and her enemy, Germany, is on the side of evil, with Satan (Hitler) marching hideously in the van. This is an amazing change. But not so amazing as some other changes! Russia, for example! In 1914, when the tyrannical Tsar was on the throne and Russia's government was described as the most Satanic upon earth, we suddenly found the Muscovites fighting with England against the Kaiser, and therefore on the side of God. All our reprobation was suddenly dropped, and we welcomed the Tsar to the radiant company of the angels. Then, in 1917, the Tsar was overthrown, and the revolutionists were not so eager about the war. Before we knew it, Russia was out of the war, and the Russians were no longer angels but demons, fighting on the side of Satan.

Twenty years went by, and Russia, still in revolutionary hands, but now necessary to encircle and confine Hitler, was getting angelic again. Then, without warning, Stalin wrote his non-aggression pact with Hitler, and was straightway cast out of heaven. But this was not the end! For Hitler, in due course, turned against his fellow conspirator; and, Stalin, forced into a war against the Nazis, signed an alliance with Britain; and lo, he was straightaway acclaimed as the latest emissary of God on earth.

The case of civil wars is particularly confusing. Americans, as we know, are always on God's side. They fight only when moral issues are involved and mankind must be saved from the hosts of darkness. But in 1861–1865 Americans fought against each other. Did this mean that God was warring against God? Oh, no! We who live north of Mason and Dixon's line know that Satan got hold of eleven states south of that line, and led them against the Union, to destroy it. But south of Mason and Dixon's line our fellow countrymen believe just otherwise. It was the "damned Yankees" who were bewitched of Satan and the Confederates who were fighting and dying for the holy cause of liberty. Out of such confusion there emerges the sane and compassionate conclusion of Abraham Lincoln, as suggested in his Second Inaugural Address, that both could not be right. There is a possibile alternative, to be sure, that both might have been wrong. In either case, the Satanic theory of history, under the impact of such an experience, cracks up and drops to pieces.

It is not only confusion, but nonsense—this easy doctrine of God with us (*Gott mit uns!*) and Satan with our enemies! Clear as crystal, to any sane and open mind, is the simple fact that there is no such thing in this world as a monopoly of evil. No men anywhere, in any social group, are wholly good and always right. No men anywhere, in any social group, are wholly bad and always wrong. In war there is no absolute division between good and bad, innocence and guilt. Not in this present war, as certainly not in the last war, is all the good on one side and all the evil on the other; nor all the innocence on one side and all the guilt on the other. We are troubled in the economic field because there is no general distribution of the fruits of earth and the products of industry. In the human field, we need have no trouble as to the general distribution of virtue and vice. We all have our share of both. "There is so much good in the worst of us, and so much bad in the best of us, that it hardly becomes any of us to talk about the rest of us"—a saying which has become so familiar only because it is so true! Before so simple a statement of human nature and human affairs as this, the Satanic theory of history melts away like an obscuring mist before the bright rays of the sun. Not a wisp of its miasmic vapor should cloud the minds of men.

Adolf Hitler is not so much a cause as a case. He is beset by psychopathic manias, obsessed by delusions of grandeur, tortured by inward strains and stresses of agonizing intensity. He finds comfort in the exercise of power, and compensation for his own suffering in visiting suffering on others. He is passionate, bigoted, fanatical, cruel. His qualities combine into a form of madness which, as in so many men of this extravagant type, turns again and again into genius. In the sheer energy and sure direction of his spirit, the world has seen few more formidable men than Hitler. In his ruthless exercise of force and violence, he takes on the proportions of a monster. But he is no more responsible as a single cause for this war than Genghis Khan was responsible as a single cause for the armed migrations of his hordes of horsemen, or Napoleon for the flooding of Europe by the surging tides of the French Revolution. Hitler has put a personal stamp on this war, as Ghengis Khan put a personal stamp on his invasions. Hitler has seized upon the forces loosed into the world by this stupendous era and used them to his own terrific purpose, as Napoleon seized upon the forces loosed by the Revolution and used them to similar purpose. But these vast upheavals remain what they are—phenomena of human destiny which far surpass the immediate scope and control of military and political leaders, even the greatest among them. Had Ghengis Khan never lived, the Tartar horsemen, like prairie fire, would still have consumed the earth. Had Napoleon never appeared, the armies of liberated France would still have consumed dynastic Europe. Had Hitler never been born, it would have been necessary to invent him.

NOTES

1. Lytton Strachey was a British writer and biographer, best known for his 1918 work, *Eminent Victorians*, an attack on Victorian morality.

2. Archidamus II, king of Sparta, launched the Peloponnesian War against Athens, defended by Pericles, its greatest statesman and ardent lover of democracy.

3. Muriel Lester was a Christian socialist and a zealous pacifist based in Britain. She served as traveling secretary of the International Fellowship of Reconciliation.

4. Note from John Holmes: "This Thirty Years' War, be it noted, was fought as between Catholics and Protestants for allegedly sacred issues of freedom, civilization and religion, and yes stands utterly condemned today in the judgment of historians. "As there was no compulsion towards a conflict which, in despite of the apparent bitterness of the parties, took so long to engage . . . so no right was vindicated by its ragged end. The war solved no problem . . . morally subversive, economically destructive, socially degrading, confused in its causes, devious in its course, futile in its results, it is the outstanding example in European history of a meaningless conflict . . . Those who, one by one, let themselves be drawn into this conflict . . . wanted peace, and they fought thirty years to be sure of it. They did not learn, and have not since, that war breeds only war" (Professor C. V. Wedgewood in *The Thirty Years' War*). Professor Wedgewood may be taken as representative of the voice of history."

5. The clashing spirits of Evil and Good in Zoroastrianism.

4

+

Paul L. Blakely

Editor, America

Jesuit Priest

American Catholics during the 1930s found themselves in an awkward position. Many of their fellow citizens, especially Protestants, viewed Catholics as a potential threat to democracy. Official Catholic teaching appeared to bless the idea of a Catholic Commonwealth in the United States, a contradiction of the nation's commitment to the separation of church and state. Thus, President Franklin Roosevelt's decision to appoint a personal representative at the Vatican—even for the purpose of negotiating peace in Europe—set off alarms. Many feared a papal power grab across the Atlantic. Numerous editorials in the religious press condemned the appointment, while denominations produced resolutions denouncing it.

It was in this climate of anti-Catholicism that Paul Blakely guided the editorial pages of *America*, a Jesuit weekly and one of the most influential Catholic publications of the era. Over the course of his long career, Blakely wrote nearly 7,000 editorials for the magazine, and another 1,200 articles for a variety of journals. Trained as a Jesuit priest, he was intensely interested in economic issues and the application of papal encyclicals to American-style capitalism. Though a political progressive, Blakely had strong Jeffersonian instincts: He viewed much of Roosevelt's "New Deal" as an assault on local initiative and personal responsibility. As one editorial put it: "One more Federalized plan will kill all that is left of what used to be known as American initiative and self-reliance."

Blakely consistently argued that Catholicism was the strongest foundation upon which to build a stable democracy, and that Catholics were among the most loyal Americans. Nevertheless, he pleaded for an aggressive affirmation of Church doctrine among the laity. He called for

government support of Catholic schools because "education is not education unless its soul is religion." He condemned the birth control movement as "against the law of God" and "morally evil and physically harm-
ful" to women and families.

With the rise of fascism in Europe, Blakely followed the Catholic
Church position as voiced from Rome. When Francisco Franco rebelled
against Spain's left-wing government to ignite the Spanish Civil War, the
Church (along with Nazi Germany) supported the fascist rebels. As Germany began to threaten its European neighbors, Blakely dismissed any
notion of a "holy war against totalitarianism" by reminding his readers
that only Pope Pius XII—"the one supreme spiritual authority"—could
call a crusade to defend Christian civilization. Religious journals in general were wary of circulating atrocity stories, since many accounts during
the previous war proved false. Thus, reports of Nazi crimes against Jews
were met with skepticism, though assaults against Catholics elicited fiery
denunciations. When Germany occupied Poland, Blakely called the widespread killing of Catholic priests and nuns "a reign of terror . . . such as
history has never before recorded." Yet he made no mention of the deportation of Jews to concentration camps. After accounts of mass murders
became undeniable, the magazine's editors admitted that an ominous figure had arisen in Berlin, one who ruled by principles "forged in hell."
Nevertheless, Blakely kept his editorial gaze steadfastly on the course of
neutrality. Germany was a German problem, he argued, and of concern to
European states only.

The first editorial included here, "Nazi Atrocities and the American
War Fever," appeared in December of 1938, just weeks after Hitler staged
Kristallnacht. Church leaders were gathering in major American cities to
denounce Hitler's anti-Semitic violence, but Blakely wonders why examples of atrocities occurring in other nations are being ignored. He suggests
a propaganda campaign is underfoot to drag America into war. In the second editorial, written in June 1940, Blakely assails President Roosevelt's
University of Virginia speech in which he pledged material assistance to
Britain and France, both then at war with Germany (France would fall
within the week). Like many advocates of U.S. neutrality, he opposed
American aid to the Allies as a declaration of hostilities against Germany
and Italy: "We have no moral justification for making war against these
nations," he wrote. "We can gain nothing for Europe, or for ourselves, and
we risk all."

Nazi Atrocities
and the American War Fever
America, December 3, 1938

ARE WE PREPARING FOR WAR WITH GERMANY?

During the last few weeks meetings have been held all over the country to protest the inhuman treatment which the Jews have received from a criminal or insane Nazi Germany. Perhaps it would be more correct to write that these meetings have been "promoted." What is back of this movement which, at the moment, begins to look like a fit of national hysteria?

I should like to think that it springs from our love of freedom, and that it is fanned into flame by our indignation when we see a helpless people put at the mercy of godless tyrants. I am sure that it does, at least in part. We Americans are a soft-hearted people. When a volcano blows up in Sicily, or a river overflows its banks in China, we at once begin to pass the hat. It is our most familiar international gesture. *Quae regio in terris nostri non plena laboris* may be freely translated: "What part of the world is not full of American relief cash?" But we have never had much trouble trying to reduce foreign money to familiar dollars before applying it to the relief of Ohio or Mississippi River flood victims, or of hungry people in the dust-bowl areas. We never got any.

To bolster up an economic theory, we slay shoats by the million, and burn our surplus grain, while thousands in the great cities go hungry. But we always have plenty of meat and bread for hungry people abroad. Perhaps, then, nothing is back of these protest meetings except that ingrained benevolence which, used by skillful propagandists, has more than once made us the world's prize international saps.

But this "benevolence and nothing else theory" does not satisfy.

Thousands of men, women and children have been put to death south of the Rio Grande in a bloody persecution that has lasted many years. That fact has never caused us a sleepless moment. When the Ambassador from the United States publicly praised an alleged educational system which could have no other outcome than the moral debasement of Mexican school children, no one thought of calling him back to Washington for an explanation.

In Spain, more than 14,000 priests and nuns have been slain. They were deliberately butchered by a Government which has outlawed political and religious liberty—butchered in horrible ways which Germany, and even Soviet Russia, have not dared to employ.[1] Our reaction to this carnage has been the promotion of public meetings of approval. We have taken up money collections, even in the Government buildings in Washington, so that this abominable Government could embark on new and bloodier campaigns. Religious groups, reputedly Christian, have pleaded that the "Loyalists" should be permitted to purchase larger supplies of munitions in the United States, and thus establish on a firm basis a Communistic regime to which the Name of God is anathema. Of these groups, many are now taking a leading part in organizing public meetings to protest the infamous conduct of the Nazi Government.

But the American people, it will be said, never had a chance to know much about these Mexican and Spanish outrages. To a large extent, that is true, although it is not true of all American groups which have supported the uncivilized rulers in Mexico and Spain. Many knew that the Governments in these countries were as anti-religious as that of Hitler. That is why they supported them. But it is true that the American press did what it could to hide or to gloss over the outrages in Spain and Mexico. It could hardly have succeeded better had all the newspapers entered into a formal conspiracy of secrecy.

We now observe the contrast in broadcasting reports of Jewish persecution in Germany. The contrast is undeniable, and we are entitled to ask why.

A lead to the answer is supplied, it seems to me, in a letter received some days ago from a well-known historian in the Middle West. "In my opinion," he writes, "much of this stir is propaganda to prepare us for war with Germany. We shall not be asked to go in as an ally, although that is not improbable. Our part will be to act as the financial agent—under some other title, of course—of Germany's European enemies."

Is that opinion far-fetched? Let a few facts be considered. At least two European nations are preparing for war against Germany. Under existing legislation, neither can borrow money in the United States, which means that they cannot borrow it in any country. A campaign for "humanity" (do you remember 1914–17?) can be used to create a demand for the repeal of the Johnson Act.[2] That repeal, whatever else it might do, would make war fairly safe for Germany's enemies.

In persecuting Jews and Catholics, Germany has been guilty of frightful cruelty. But that is no reason for going to war with Germany, or for supporting any war movement. We once set out to make the world safe for democracy, and the sad results are still with us. One result is the rise of totalitarian governments in Europe. As AMERICA advised last week: "Let's keep our hearts warm, and our heads cool." Otherwise we may find ourselves forced into a war which can only bring the world new woes.

All Will Be Lost by War
America, June 29, 1940

That the President of the United States declared war on Italy and Germany in his address at the University of Virginia, is a thesis that cannot be sustained. He merely declared his intention of furnishing the enemies of Italy and Germany with all possible material aid at the earliest possible moment.

What material aid the President has in mind is not clear. Nor is it clear how we can build up an adequate national defense if the material resources of this country are to be turned over to Great Britain.

Is the affair at Charlottesville simply another instance in which the President has allowed his emotions to run away with him?

That would seem to be the charitable interpretation. If it is true, we may well ask for ourselves whether the country will be safe for the next four years under the administration of an emotional leader.

Other interpretations have been made. Some of them are borne out by the letter of former Premier Reynaud to the President. It would appear that France was led to expect immediate military aid. In this, as in other matter nearer home, the Government of France was grievously in error. For what guns could we send, or motorized cavalry, or what aircraft? As for men, only Congress can raise and equip an army. As for guns, we have none.

Those facts France should have known. Apparently, however, the French Government was in ignorance both of our resources, or, more accurately, our lack of resources, and of what the Administration was authorized to do with what it had.

Again, from the last Reynaud letter, the inference that France saw in the President a disposition to bring this country into war, supporting the Allies, seems justified. The Premier did not understand that the President meant every aid short of military commitments.

Yet in what other light could the French regard the promise of material to aid them in war? To aid one side in a war is generally considered an act of war. Declarations of war are apparently not needed. Neither China nor Japan has yet published any such declaration. Is it the fixed purpose of the President to disregard the authority of Congress, and to bring this country into an undeclared war against Germany and Italy?

Hitler and Mussolini probably answer that question in the affirmative. Within a week, after promising material aid to the Allies, the President characterizes the Duce as an assassin, and refers to the Fuhrer as a liar. These can hardly be considered friendly acts by the heads of two countries with which the United States is at peace.

Yet, if we are to begin arming, against whom are we arming? At the moment, we can fight no one. As Colonel Lindbergh has said, we are gesturing with empty guns; a palpable understatement, since we have no guns that can use ammunition, and no ammunition. Our gestures are with wooden guns, pop-guns.

Today the United States is at peace with all the world. Our uneasy consciences make us fear that war may be declared against us. In any case, the world is topsy-turvy today, and we must begin to get together that protection for which billions of dollars have been spent in the last few years, with no visible results.

But we must not prepare to make war. No policy merits national support except a policy for adequate protection against attack.

To say that our first line of defense is to come to the aid of Great Britain, is to say that we are justified in attacking Germany and Italy. I do not think that claim can be sustained. As the Archbishop of Cincinnati has said, we have no moral justification for making war against these nations. We did not help Europe to settle her affairs when we went to war in 1917, nor could we help her by entering the war now. It is our duty to prepare to defend this country, in the unlikely, but possible, event of attack. It is no part of our duty, morally, or because of legitimate commitments, to prepare armaments to be used in England's aid. To quote again the Archbishop of Cincinnati: "Come what may, America must resolve to have no part in the war. There can be no moral justification for our entering a war because of the international crises in Europe." We can gain nothing for Europe, or for ourselves, and we risk all.

In preparing an adequate defense for the United States, every political interest should be excluded. If we are Democrats or Republicans, or anything but Americans, it will not be possible to prepare that defense. Democrats and Republicans should unite on an anti-war program. If they do not, then it should be possible for a third-party candidate to win the election on the pledge to spend what is necessary for national defense, but not one penny for American participation in a war in Europe.

In the moment that this country goes to war, the guarantees of the American Constitution will be swept aside by a dictatorship. We fight best for this Government by not fighting in Europe. If we go to war, we are bound to lose, for before the first contingent of American boys could be disembarked at some foreign port, government under the Constitution, the American Government of our fathers, would have ceased to be.

NOTES

1. Spain's left-wing government openly persecuted the Catholic Church in the 1930s, helping to set the stage for the Spanish Civil War.

2. The Johnson Act, passed by Congress In 1934, prohibited loans to nations behind on World War I debt repayment.

5

Ernest Fremont Tittle

Methodist World Peace Commission
Minister, First Methodist Church,
Evanston, Illinois

If Methodist minister Ernest Fremont Tittle held any opinions about war as a legitimate tool of foreign policy, he likely dispensed with them by September of 1918. Tittle had volunteered to serve as a chaplain to American troops in France, and his letters home were filled with gloom. One historian says, "he was shaken by all that he had seen."

The carnage of World War I may have altered Tittle's views about armed conflict, but it apparently changed little else. Throughout his thirty-one-year pastorate at First United Church in Evanston, Illinois, Tittle retained a robust optimism in human nature and in the possibilities for social transformation. His theology was a blend of Methodist perfectionism (with its emphasis on personal piety) and the social gospel activism of Washington Gladden and Walter Rauchenbusch (with its attention on economic and political institutions).

Located in an affluent Chicago suburb, First United Church was one of American Protestantism's most prestigious pulpits. It was supported by some of the richest and most powerful figures in the Midwest, and was a vital force in the life of Northwestern University, Garrett Biblical Institute, and the larger Chicago area. *Christian Century* editor Charles Clayton Morrison once claimed that among Protestant ministers, "there is no man regarded with more respect, listened to with more attention, or followed with more hope than Ernest Fremont Tittle." An exaggeration, to be sure, but the members of First United Church adored Tittle the preacher, even if they disagreed with his platforms for social reform.

The heavily Republican congregation got an earful of Tittle's politics and his piety. He rejected the importance of doctrinal Christianity. He attacked anti-Catholicism, excessive patriotism, and capitalism. He declared himself a socialist and spoke approvingly of the Soviet Union's large-scale experiment in "human perfectionism." He denounced racism and supported the National Association for the Advancement of Colored People. Tittle even persuaded northern Methodism's General Conference to adopt a provision requiring that it meet only in cities that provided equal accommodations for both black and white delegates.

Tittle exerted his most important influence, however, as the leading voice for absolute pacifism within the Methodist Church. In 1930 he preached a sermon called "An Adequate National Defense," in which he argued that the existence of large armies made war inevitable. "The militarist believes that the way to get peace is to become so physically strong that nobody will dare to attack you," he said. "The pacifist believes the way to get peace is to become so just and so friendly that nobody will desire to attack you." This represented the classic pacifist view of the 1930s, a position that Tittle promoted feverishly throughout the decade. He became a charter member of numerous groups working for world peace, including the War Resisters League, the Fellowship of Reconciliation, the League for Industrial Democracy, the Committee on Militarism in Education, the National Council for Prevention of War, the Ministers' No War Committee, and the Methodist World Peace Commission. He was deeply involved in the Emergency Peace Campaign of 1936–37, perhaps the most significant effort in the history of the American peace movement. By 1940, Tittle had played a decisive role in winning the adoption of several pacifist resolutions in the Methodist Church.

Far from being an isolationist, Tittle recognized the need for international engagement and campaigned aggressively for the World Court and League of Nations (he once called the League "the one last hope of civilization"). He saw economic disparities as the central causes of war: The only way to resolve such differences was by promoting "economic justice" through international trade and aid. As the Nazi shadow spread across Europe, Tittle maintained his belief that military solutions violate Christ's dictums and gain nothing. Blaming Hitler on the Treaty of Versailles, he proposed that the German leader be given an opportunity to explain his grievances in a public forum so he might be understood and conciliated.

In this February 1941 essay from *The Christian Century*, Tittle sees in the current conflict only one outcome: destruction, starvation, disease, and death. Rather than defeating evil, war sanctions an "orgy of indiscriminate killing." Tittle agrees that Hitler poses a serious threat to all of humanity, more serious than the German kaiser in the previous war. But armed conflict, he argues, will not eliminate Hitlerism. "Christian pacifists do not proclaim that tyranny is better than war; they proclaim that tyranny cannot be overcome by war." The only way to overcome dictators like Hitler, he says, is by imitating Christ on the cross: by doing good, showing love, engaging in nonviolent resistance. This is the method of Jesus, a policy of charity and reconciliation, "which appeals to the best in the aggressor and calls for the best in his victim." Even after America entered the war, Tittle refused to pray for an Allied victory—a position rejected even by the liberal Methodist General Conference.

A Clash of Imperialisms
The Christian Century, February 5, 1941

In 1917, I believed that war was the only means of preserving a humane and civilized culture. In that conviction, I left a wife and three children and went to France. I undertook to promote a fighting morale. I did what little I could, at a first aid dressing station, to relieve the suffering of wounded men. On the way to the front, I came upon a poem that deeply moved me. It was found on the body of a dead and unidentifiable Australian, who had written:

> Rejoice, whatever anguish rend the heart,
>   That God has given you a priceless dower
> To live in these great times and have your part
>   In freedom's crowning hour,
> That ye may tell your sons, who see the light
>   High in the heavens, their heritage to take,
> I saw the powers of darkness put to flight,
>   I saw the morning break.

But the powers of darkness were not put to flight. Men were killed, millions of them, including promising young writers and artists and musicians and scientists and philosophers. Women were left desolate, multitudes of them. Wealth was destroyed. Hunger stalked and pestilence raged over vast areas of the earth. Thirty million civilians were liquidated. The world was set on the road to an economic debacle. But justice was not achieved. Liberty was not secured. The rights and liberties of small nations were not guaranteed. Brute force was not banished from international affairs. The world was not made safe for democracy or for morality or for Christianity or for anything else that decent men care for and would be glad to die for. A heritage there was for the sons of men who died in the First World War, but it was not light "high in the heavens" or anywhere else. It was the descending darkness of the present war.

I am now convinced that war, being, as the Oxford Conference said, "a defiance of the righteousness of God as revealed in Jesus Christ and him crucified," cannot serve the ends of freedom and justice but is certain to defeat them. So, if the United States becomes a belligerent in Europe or Asia, I shall undertake to contribute in some way to the good, of my country, but I shall not "support" the war.

The present war in Europe is not only a clash of imperialisms; it is also a conflict of ideologies and ways of life. There is now far more at stake than there was in 1917. Prussianism threatened the world with whips;

Hitlerism threatens it with scorpions. It is now all-essential to the welfare and progress of humanity that Hitlerism be overcome. On this point American Christians are agreed. The point on which they are not agreed is the means by which Hitlerism *can be* overcome. Christian pacifists do not proclaim that tyranny is better than war; they proclaim that tyranny cannot be overcome by war. They believe with the late Lord Lothian that "the triumph of Hitler grew out of the despair that settled on central Europe in the years of war, defeat, inflation and revolutionary propaganda."[1] And they believe that this war is now producing political, economic and psychological conditions that make for the survival and spread of Hitlerism.

1. I believe that war as we now know it cannot pave the way for the doing of good. When the fighting ends, who makes the peace? Not the man who actually fought the war, nor the parsons who blessed it, nor the professors who glorified it. When the fighting ends, the people who make the peace are the same people whose ambitions and practices created the situation which bred the war. It is they who, behind the scenes if not at the peace table, decide what is to be done. It is their interests that are considered, their ideas that prevail. Idealists may fight or bless a war, but they, when the fighting ends, have little voice in the making of peace. This is inevitable; for war, being what it is, plays into the hands of unreason and reaction. It provides a field day for the munitions industry, for the jingoistic press, for every kind of industry that is anti-social and reckless in the pursuit of private gain. It provides a sounding board for politicians and other persons who have the deadly gifts of the demagogue. Inevitably, war strengthens the forces of darkness and destruction.

The makers of the peace settlement, even if they were well intentioned (as they sometimes are), and if their hands were not tied by secret treaties, would almost certainly be helpless against the tide of popular emotion created by propaganda, terror and suffering. In total war not only must soldiers be made to go on fighting, but civilians must be made to go on suffering and steeling themselves against terror by day and by night. Total war cannot be waged without the aid of organized propaganda that seeks not to inform but only to inflame. And a propaganda that serves war is bound to betray peace. The hatred it has aroused blocks the way to justice, as does also the belief it has fostered that the enemy, being completely devoid of reason and virtue, cannot be treated as a man but only as a mad dog. Nor can human beings for years go on bombing and being bombed without being overcome by terror, suffering and bitterness. In its issue of December 4, 1940, the *Christian News-Letter*, an English publication edited by Dr. J. H. Oldham, has this to say: "Some sections of the press are clamoring for recourse to unrestrained frightfulness. This is sheer nazism. In the early days of the *News-Letter* I called attention to the danger that under the strain of war the spirit of nazism might subtly enter into us, so that, even if we gained victory on the battlefield the evil which we took up arms to resist would have won its hellish triumph. This danger has become a serious reality."

It has been said of the pacifist that he has "a confidence in human nature that human nature cannot support." As a matter of fact, it is the non-pacifist, not the pacifist, who believes that after a long-drawn-out orgy of indiscriminate killing and wholesale destruction people may be expected to think rationally and act justly. The pacifist has no such confidence in human nature.

2. I believe that war as we now know it cannot even hold evil in check. Total war is itself a most active and destructive evil. It knows no distinction of guilty and innocent or even of combatant and non-combatant. It has no "reverence for personality." It treats human beings as if they were things. It demands the distortion of truth. It knows no distinction of right and wrong but only military necessity. It requires men to believe that the end for which they are fighting is so important that it justifies the use of any means. It is now persuading men that food blockade, although it may bring starvation, disease and death to innocent aged persons and women and children, is justified on the ground that it is essential to the preservation of civilization!

Can war, nevertheless, be made to hold evil in check? I have no confidence in attempts to preserve civilization by means that are themselves a denial and betrayal of everything that is essential to a humane and civilized culture. When men do evil that good may come, what they get is not the good they seek but the evil they do. History joins the New Testament in saying, "Be not deceived; God is not mocked: for whatsoever a man soweth, that shall he also reap."

It is the Christian faith that the cross of Christ is the supreme revelation of God's method of dealing with evil. The Son of God goes about doing good. He encounters opposition, but when he is reviled he reviles not again. He does not try to overcome evil with more evil. He undertakes to overcome evil with good. He resists evil but never with its own weapons. Condemning it unsparingly, he resists it with truth and love even unto death—his own death on a cross. That, Christianity maintains, is God's way of dealing with evil. That, St. Paul declares, is the power of God and the wisdom of God. That, pacifists believe, is the only way out of the world's misery.

I am convinced that the doing of good is the only way to put an end to aggression. Under present conditions, aggression may not be wholly unprovoked. It may be provoked by fear of future aggression on the part of some other nation. It may be provoked by bitter belief, not wholly unwarranted, that there is now no peaceful way of solving a desperate economic problem. It may be provoked by a stinging sense of inferiority in a world where certain other nations are now in a position to gather wealth from the ends of the earth and to lord it over others. To say this is by no means to condone aggression, which in any case is an infamous thing; it is only to face the fact that, rooted in historical events and psychological situations, aggression is seldom unprovoked. Nations that benefit from a world situation which denies equality of opportunity may view with abhorrence an attempt to change it by force. But if they themselves refuse to consent to peaceful change through discussion and negotiation, their refusal may be as immoral as the aggression it provokes.

In a world that is suffering from injustice piled upon injustice, the immediate overcoming of evil may be impossible. There may be no escape from the wages of sin. The question then is, What course, if faithfully followed, would eventually lead to a better state of affairs? War, I am convinced, is not the answer. War can overcome a dictator, it cannot rid the world of dictatorship. It can stop an aggressor; it cannot put an end to aggression. On the contrary, it can only provide new soil for the growth of dictatorship and aggression. The answer, I believe, is the persistent doing of good. Injustice breeds injustice. Hatred breeds hatred. Cruelty breeds cruelty. War breeds war. And no less surely does good beget good.

If the United States were invaded I should feel called upon to resist the invader by refusing to become his accomplice in the doing of evil. Both in South Africa and in India this kind of resistance has produced notable results. (To say that it can be effective only when the aggressor is an Anglo-Saxon is to invite the charge of dogmatism, if not of self-righteousness.) It produces a situation which the aggressor is unprepared to handle. Air raid for air raid, blockade for blockade, evil for evil—this he has been taught to expect, and when it occurs he knows what to do. But what is he to do when the pastors of all the Protestant churches of the Netherlands read from their pulpits a vigorous protest, in the name of Christ, against any attempt to force upon their country an anti-Jewish program? Non-violent resistance forces the aggressor to think, which he can hardly do without a disastrous loss of military morale. It forces him to think because, although it refuses to become his accomplice, it does not seek to hurt him.

Pacifists do not suppose that non-violent resistance can be offered without risk of arrest, imprisonment and death. There would doubtless be many casualties, just as in war. Yet the end result, pacifists believe, would be far different; for war produces in victor and vanquished alike a state of mind that forbids the making of a just and durable peace, whereas non-violent resistance, which appeals to the best in the aggressor and calls forth the best in his victim, may hope to be redemptive. Of course, non-violent resistance to evil is not enough. It must be accompanied by a positive program of good which seeks long-range objectives.

I believe that Christian pacifism has relevance to the relations between nations as well as to the relations of the individual to his fellows. The doing of good is not only the way of life for the individual; it is also the way of life for society. This way the pacifist is obligated both to take for himself and to advocate for his nation.

What would pacifism as our national policy require? The space given to this article does not permit of a complete answer, to say nothing of my own limitations! But I shall make bold to state a few personal convictions. As a national policy, pacifism would require the United States to set its own house in order. It would seek a real solution (which peacetime conscription is not) for the problem of unemployment and equality of opportunity for all Americans, including Negroes. It would require the repeal of the Oriental exclusion act and the placing of Orientals on the quota basis which now governs immigration from other countries. It would call upon the United States to abrogate its present unequal treaties with China and to establish its relations with China on a basis of complete equality and reciprocity. It would require the United States, in the formation of its domestic policies, to have a lively and continuing regard for the welfare of the rest of mankind. This would forbid such selfish—and shortsighted—conduct as the Smoot-Hawley tariff act and the Silver Purchase Act of 1934. It would lead the United States to become indeed a good neighbor, concerned that all nations should have equal access to raw materials and needed markets for their industrial goods.

In the present crisis, pacifism as a national policy would constrain the United States to announce to the world (1) its readiness to associate itself with other nations in the building of a new world order; (2) its determination in any case to order its own life with a sensitive regard for the well-being of other peoples; (3) its desire to contribute to the relief of human suffering in war-stricken regions, through gifts of food, clothing and medical supplies; and (4) its readiness at the war's end to make loans for economic rehabilitation, if convinced of the desirability of the projects for which the money was sought. This foundation of justice being laid, pacifism would constrain the United States to appeal for an armistice and for an earnest attempt through discussion and negotiation to find a fundamental solution of world problems in a just peace.

The pacifist well knows the objections which are now being offered to the idea of a negotiated peace. He also knows that the same objections were offered when Woodrow Wilson, in his address to the Senate (and to the people of the warring nations) on January 22, 1917, made his earnest plea for "a peace without victory." With high purpose and political realism he declared that "upon a triumph which overwhelms and humiliates cannot be laid the foundations of peace and equality and good will"; that a dictated peace would "leave a sting, a resentment, a bitter memory upon which terms of peace would rest not permanently but only as upon quicksand." These words were not heeded. There could be no hope, it was then said, of a just and durable peace until Germany was brought to her knees. The idea of a negotiated peace was scorned and rejected; the result was Versailles—and the present war. What reason is there to believe that the result would be greatly different if the present conflict should be decided by slow attrition and ultimate exhaustion or by a knockout blow?

Pacifism as a national strategy would pursue a policy not of appeasement but of reconciliation. Between these policies there is a vast range of difference. Appeasement is concerned only to safeguard individual and national self-interest at whatever cost to others; reconciliation seeks to promote fellowship through justice and good will. Pacifism finds the surest grounds of security not in concession or in conquest but in confidence. "Good will" is a recognized asset in business; it is equally crucial in the affairs of nations. To seek good will is not impractical idealism; it is the most hard-headed realism.

But would it not be an act of insanity to trust Hitler? Yes, under present conditions. It is a fact, however, that Hitler has power only so long as the German army chooses to support him. And it is *not* a fact that the German people are wholly devoid of human decency or that they have no appreciation of the things which make for peace. To say that the Germans have ceased to be a civilized people is to reveal oneself a victim of war-born bitterness and confusion. It would not, in my judgment, be an act of insanity to seek an official statement of peace aims, a reasonable basis for the cessation of hostilities, an opportunity through discussion and negotiation to find a fundamental solution of world problems in a just peace. On the contrary, it would be an act of high statesmanship, which would indicate that the responsible leadership of the United States had decided to trust in God and in the power of justice and good will, not merely in human cunning and brute force.

War is an attempted short cut to the solution of terrific social problems, which it does not solve but only makes more difficult of solution. It is thought to be, but never is, a relatively quick way out of an intolerable situation. I can see only ruin ahead if the United States becomes a belligerent in Europe or in Asia—ruin for us and for all mankind. The only way out of the world's misery is, I believe, the doing of good. That way I feel bound to take and to advocate for my country.

NOTE

1. Phillip Henry Kerr, otherwise known as Lord Lothian, was the British ambassador in Washington when the Second World War broke out. Contrary to Tittle's suggestion, Lothian was no pacifist and actively sought the assistance of neutral nations in the fight against Fascism. In a speech to the St. Louis Chamber of Commerce in 1940, he argued that "the menace of Nazi international gangsterdom must be defeated" and even quoted a previous U.S. president who, in another season of crisis, remarked that "we stand at Armageddon and battle for the Lord."

6

Georgia Harkness
Garrett Biblical Institute

In January of 1939, editors at *The Christian Century* launched a series of essays in which America's leading religious figures were asked to explain "How My Mind Has Changed in the Past Ten Years." For Georgia Harkness, the first woman theologian of American Christianity and one of its most gifted, the answer was that it hadn't changed much. "I was a pacifist and socialist ten years ago," she wrote, "and still am."

Like many others of her generation, Harkness arrived at her socialism by coming under the influence of the social gospel during her college days at Cornell and Boston University. And, like other Protestant thinkers, her pacifism was largely a response to what she'd seen in Europe after the First World War. Harkness had joined a group of thirty-five ministers and educators who toured European capitals in 1924, and the lingering waste of war—the half-destroyed cities and widespread hunger—shocked her. "My trip to Rheims and the battlefields . . . have made me a pacifist, I think, forevermore." She was more or less right: Harkness joined the Fellowship of Reconciliation, a leading antiwar group, and upheld pacifist principles until her death.

If Harkness fit a predictable pattern of Christian clergy in the 1920s, she nonetheless displayed a complexity of thought not always evident in her peers. A Methodist by temperament as well as theological training, Harkness was a centrist and a negotiator. Her works reflect an attempt to balance competing ideas: orthodox Christianity and philosophical idealism, personal faith in Christ and social justice. Though a defender of the social gospel and its leftist political agenda, she was drawn to neo-orthodox views of sin. From that mixture came a bracing call to the church: to live

99

out Christian unity by transcending national, racial, and class differences. Though never a militant feminist, she also spoke out vigorously against what she regarded as sexism in the church. "The Christian gospel has done more than any other agency for the emancipation of women," she wrote, "yet the church itself is the most impregnable stronghold of male dominance." Harkness broke through that stronghold by being the first woman admitted to the American Theological Society, and the first to join Henry Van Dusen's Theological Discussion Group, a regular gathering of the nation's most prominent theologians.

During the war years Harkness taught theology at Garrett Biblical Institute, a Methodist seminary in Evanston, Illinois. Though a systematic theologian, she also wrote hymns, poetry, and works on Christian spirituality for the laity. The author of thirty-six books, Harkness returned again and again to the theme of social justice: It belonged at the center of the church's witness in the world. As Europe edged toward war, no issue of social justice engaged her more than the need to establish "economic security" to address international grievances. The lack of economic justice, she said, is "the corrupt core from which has spread most of the present anguish of the world." Her involvement in the world ecumenical movement, including the 1937 Oxford Conference and the 1939 Geneva Conference of the World Council of Churches, nurtured a triumphalist hope in the power of the church to instigate global economic changes.

The ultimate enemy was war, Harkness said, the greatest obstacle to advancing the Kingdom of God on earth. She acknowledged that some governments were patently more wicked than others, and that every war involved a measure of heroism and sacrifice. Yet these distinctions vanished for her in the horror of conflict. "War destroys every value for which Christianity stands," she said, "and to oppose war by more war is only to deepen the morass into which humanity has fallen." The first essay included here, "What Can Christians Do?" was written in May of 1940, while Britain and France were fighting Germany and news of the latest Nazi blitzkrieg was in the air. Harkness denies that the pacifist position means the "self-righteous acquiescence in evil." Yet she also takes pains to explain—and evidently endorse—the hawkish view that force is required to maintain an ordered society. Where Harkness parts company with the interventionists is the kind of force they have in mind. She prefers economic force, the force of public opinion, and "the spiritual force of moral idealism." The second essay, "What, Then, Should Churches Do?" appeared after the defeat of France and when the fate of Great Britain was seriously in doubt. Harkness avoids discussing the practical implications of a German victory, insisting only that "America's supreme duty is to remain out of war." She suggests several themes to shape the preaching and public messages of the Christian churches, including absolute loyalty to

God alone, not the American flag; repentance for intolerance and prejudice "which are the breeders of unjust treaties, economic confusion and
war"; and love for one's enemies, even the dictator in Berlin. "Unless
churches can inculcate good will toward those within and those without
the Christian fellowship . . . then the churches had better stop talking
about love as the basic Christian virtue."

What Can Christians Do?
The Christian Century, May 29, 1940

News of the blitzkrieg which has swept across Norway, Denmark and the low countries has generated in Americans a mounting sense of horror, anger and dismay. Fear of our own implication in the war has caused the public temperature to rise several degrees, and feverish demands for stronger armaments are the natural result. But perhaps more corroding to morale than either horror or fear is the sense of futility that such events generate.

"Why don't we do something about it?" "What can anybody do?" These are questions asked more often than answered. The futility of the First World War has been so many times demonstrated that most of us, at least in our saner moments, are unwilling to launch America upon a repetition of its processes. Yet the futility of diplomatic maneuvering seems equally demonstrated. To even the most courageous and sensitive spirits, the present impasse looks like a choice between the collapse of civilization through war on the one hand and through submission to aggression on the other.

I am not writing this article because I know the way out. I do not. I am sure that some courses are better than others. Some are so obviously wrong in their motivation and disastrous in their consequences that we ought to avoid them at all costs. Such distinctions we must make. Yet, past events being what they are and the world situation what it is, there is now no perfect solution. Whatever course is taken that can be taken in the present political setting, some persons will be hurt and some values jeopardized.

Nevertheless, there are still some constructive things that Christians can do. Because we can do them, we ought to do them. This is a time to be serious; it is no time to surrender to futility. What, then, can Christians do?

First, Christian pacifists and non-pacifists can stop fighting each other. One of the most distressing developments since the outbreak of the war has been the amount of energy expended by Christians, all of whom want peace, in acrimonious dispute because we do not agree with one another as to how to get it.

I do not wish to minimize the importance of a difference in strategy. Means and ends are so intertwined that wrong means will corrupt the best of ends. We ought to recognize that some means head toward peace and some toward war. We ought each to decide for ourselves, and not hesitate to state to others, what means we sanction as steps toward the just and peaceful world all Christians desire. Nevertheless, for pacifist and non-pacifist Christians in the present juncture to waste our energies and destroy by dispute the impact of a common front is worse than fiddling while Rome burns, for such dissension fans the flames. Most of what I shall say hereafter will elaborate this point.

It is time to declare a moratorium on the calling of names and the setting up of straw men to knock down. As a pacifist I have frequently been disturbed by the implications that pacifism means "passivism"—a do-nothing policy. It is amazing that so many intelligent and otherwise informed persons can talk about Christian pacifism as if it were solely a negative approach, or as if it were identical with a selfish and supine isolationism. There is also the stock charge that pacifists adopt a "holier than thou" attitude, assuming themselves to be morally superior. Perhaps some do, but I have known hundreds of pacifists and have encountered only one or two to whom I thought this charge applicable. To equate Christian pacifism with self-righteous acquiescence in evil does nobody any good except to help the pacifist discipline his soul in patience.

But the setting up of straw men as scarecrows and punching-bags is not all on one side. Pacifists do not often say (or believe) that non-pacifists are not *Christians*. But too often we have said or implied that our opponents are in this respect not *Christian*. Without surrender of conviction all Christians need to recognize that in such a moot issue no one position has a monopoly on Christian insight. Furthermore, to judge positions is one thing and to judge individuals is another. As there is diversity of gifts among Christians, so there is room within the Christian fellowship for difference of opinion. But not for suspicion. Non-pacifist Christians, for the most part, hate war and loathe killing as much as any pacifist does, and to charge a supporter of one's government in war with being a "fire-eater" or a "war-monger" is as far off the track of Christian courtesy as to call a pacifist "pro-German" or a "slacker."

Second, we can appreciate and appropriate what is constructive in alternative positions. It is not enough to refrain from the use of epithets, though to do this would be much. It is important to discern that both the Christian pacifist and the Christian non-pacifist prize values which are distinctive and essential, but which are not the exclusive prerogative of either.

The primary emphases of Christian pacifism are (1) the redemptive power of love, of forgiveness, of reconciliation, and (2) the refusal to let conscience be regulated by an edict of the state. The first of these appears in the attempts, however halting, that pacifists have made to cultivate sympathetic understanding and good will towards all persons, regardless of national boundaries and including even those persons whose acts one is morally bound to condemn. No one has the right to call himself a Christian pacifist unless he believes that Hitler, too, is a child of God—a man to be pitied and not a devil to be hated. Inevitably such a judgment must seem to many as sheer romanticism. How realistic it is depends on what one believes about Christian love. Note carefully that the pacifist does not say, if he is wise, that redemptive love is a substitute for political action. What he does say is that without such love as its foundation, political action degenerates into mass brutality and mutual destruction.

The pacifist's emphasis on the supremacy of the Christian conscience makes of him a conscientious objector. But the emphasis belongs on conscience and not on objection. Nothing is to be gained by courting martyrdom; much is to be lost by refusing to stand by a conviction. Nobody has the right to call himself a pacifist unless he is willing to suffer for conscience' sake when his conviction runs counter to the mores or the law. To be a pacifist means the willingness to suffer *now* in undramatic ways, not the enjoyment of a vicarious martyrdom by imagining oneself in jail at some time in the future.

Both of these emphases—the refusal to hate and the refusal to bow the knee to Caesar—are vital to the Christian outlook whether we are pacifists or not. Like the way of the cross to which they lead, they are not the exclusive possession of any group. Upon these principles Christians ought to find a larger meeting ground.

The primary emphases of the Christian non-pacifist position are (1) the necessity of force for the maintenance of an ordered society, and (2) the moral obligation not to condone evil. Both of these emphases are valid, and for any Christian to disregard them is neither wise nor ethical.

Every social group needs good will for the maintenance of order; no complex social group can be kept in order wholly by good will. Where the pacifist parts company with the non-pacifist is not upon the need of force, but upon the kind of force to be used. There is no term in our vocabulary that has greater need of precise definition. Force may mean military force, or economic force, or domestic police force, or the force of public opinion, or the psychological force of the consent of the governed, or the spiritual force of moral idealism. It may mean the force let loose by an enemy state to secure *Lebensraum* or other alleged rights (and condemned by us as diabolical), or it may mean the force used on our side for the protection of rights (glorified by us but condemned by the enemy as diabolical). It may mean the force exercised by constitutional government in a sovereign state; or the force employed without deference to either moral or international law by one state upon another; or (theoretically) international police force in a world federation of states.

All of these types of force except the last are now operative in the world, and it is this last, involving some surrender of national sovereignty and much economic reorganization, that we must have if international anarchy is to be checked. Without such surrender of sovereignty, collective security is a utopian dream and the use of military force to check aggression means simply war with all that goes with it. Christians have a right to disagree as to whether this is the proper course to take. But no one has a right to talk about force as if its meaning were unambiguous and its moral implications clear. It would be no slight contribution to the cause of world peace if we could resolve never to mention force without saying what kind of force we mean!

The second main emphasis of the non-pacifist—that we must not condone evil—has as its correlate the obligation not to run all evils into one "devil's brew" and call them equally black. There are not many things in international relations that are pure white. But there certainly are shades of gray.

To recognize this fact is likewise the obligation of us all. The Christian faith is rooted in paradox, and not the least of the paradoxes is the moral obligation to judge and at the same time to "judge not." That Japan is presenting the world with a late edition of Western imperialism, that Germany has exploded because of the dynamite latent in an unjust treaty, that Great Britain is trying to drive tandem the "noble and ignoble steeds" of world democracy and British imperialism—these and many other facts need to be faced with as much historical perspective as we can bring to bear upon them. Knowledge should breed charity. But knowledge must never obliterate moral distinctions. To forgive and to approve are not synonymous.

From two perils we Christians must keep our hearts with all diligence, for the issues are those of life and death for the world. These are the perils of emotional antipathy and of moral dullness. It will not do to condemn the acts of Germany, Russia, or Japan without knowing what has made these nations what they are. Neither will any good cause be served by condoning the action of these states toward innocent neutrals whose chief offense is geographical propinquity. If Christians cannot maintain sanity in such judgments, who else will? But Christians can if they will. It is the essence of the Christian imperative resting on us all that we bring our relative human judgments under divine judgment, and thus find power to condemn without hate and to love without compromise.

Third, Christians can discover, interpret, correct and extend the function of the church in relation to the international situation. We must do all of these things together, and do them all the time.

Since the Oxford Conference the shibboleth, "Let the church be the church!" has resounded around the world. To many who have heard it (and perhaps to some who have quoted it!) I suspect that this phrase has seemed about as meaningful as, "We're here because we're here." What I think it means is what I think the author of the much discussed editorial

in the January *Fortune* means, namely, that it is the business of the church
to speak a distinctive, incisive, prophetic message grounded in "absolute
spiritual values."

To discover what this message is is so much the total problem of Christianity that I shall attempt no summary here. But one aspect of it is so
crystal-clear that no Christian need miss it. This is that we worship a God
who is above all nations and races, and that to be brothers in Christ is to
refuse to set any earthly boundaries to our fellowship. The church can be
international because it is supranational. Because of this simple but profound conviction the Christian evangel has gone around the world, the
missionary and the ecumenical movements have come into being, and in
spite of all that may be truly said of the capitulation of the church to nationalism it has labored more zealously and more persistently than has
any other body for the promotion of world peace.

What all Christians can do is to see, and then say without arrogance or
apology, that in the Christian church and its gospel are the stable and enduring foundations of peace. While everything else totters, the church
grows daily in unity and power. The machinery of international justice
has broken down; the universities have capitulated to the dictators; the
church continues to educate, to heal and to unite. We read of the flights of
political officials from invaded areas, of the heroism of missionaries who
stay at their posts. Each of the great ecumenical conferences has vividly
demonstrated the capacity of Christians to love one another across national frontiers that bristle with hostility. The world Christian community
is not a dream but a fact—and because it is a fact Christians everywhere
ought to thank God and take courage.

This is not to say that we ought to laud the church beyond what the facts
will bear. The reading of *Preachers Present Arms* is a sobering pursuit, and
while I doubt whether it tells the whole story I believe we ought to face its
record as a call to repentance for the past and a warning for the future.[1]
Most congregations, even under the most enlightened preaching, are still
more nationalistic than Christian in their fundamental attitudes toward
the state. Ministers who have not yet discovered this fact will soon find it
out. It will not do to assume that because Christians (whether laity or
clergy) hate war they are willing to pay the price of peace. Nevertheless,
the church has within its keeping the only principle that can shatter nationalistic prejudices to lay the foundations of an international ethos. This
is the principle, rooted in the Christian gospel, of the supreme worth of all
persons as sons of God . . .

Finally, Christians can refuse to despair. Nothing is more needed, in
these desperate days, than the courage born of the conviction that above
all nations is humanity and above all humanity is God. Our supreme duty
and our supreme opportunity is, as the Geneva report puts it, to "preach

and pray like Christians." Much that Christians have striven for through the ages is now in peril and only the wisest human effort in conjunction with divine resources can save it. Yet we know, if we are Christians, that whatever may befall our temporal fortunes "God's truth abideth still."

To preach and pray like Christians in the difficult days that lie ahead will take courage and faith. Whether we shall be able to do so depends on how radically we take to ourselves the words of assurance, "Lo, I am with you always, even unto the end of the world."

NOTE

1. The 1933 book, *Preachers Present Arms* (New York: Round Table Press), by Ray H. Abrams, was a much-discussed critique of the war fever that gripped numerous ministers during the First World War.

What, Then, Should Churches Do?
The Christian Century, August 14, 1940

The article by Henry P. Van Dusen, entitled "Irresponsible Idealism," in
The Christian Century requires further elaboration (See pp. 201–204 in this
book). After affirming that a promise of American assistance to the democratic powers was the only thing that could have averted war he says: "It
is not for one moment suggested that the American churches should have
advocated such a national policy." To leave no room for doubt he says
later, "Again, it cannot be too strongly stressed that the advocacy of such
a course [the enlistment of our full national resources in assistance to
Great Britain] is no task of the churches."

If not, why not? There is logic in the position that America ought to
send not only moral and material but military aid to Europe, and that because it is right and Christian to do so, the churches should bend every effort to support this policy. This was the course largely followed by the
churches in the last war, and it is a being consistently pursued by some
churchmen in the present. There is logic also in the position that it is both
unchristian and futile to try to fight fire with fire, to cast out Satan by Satan, and that because America's entering the war would destroy more values than it would conserve, the churches should do everything in their
power to prevent it. This is the position of hundreds of churchmen who
are "intelligent students of world affairs." But the statement that America
ought to intervene to save Great Britain and democracy, yet the churches
ought not to advocate such a course, is a baffling one the logic of which is
not clear to me.

If churches ought not to advocate a national policy of intervention (as
many readers will agree who dissent from other aspects of Dr. Van Dusen's
statement), what, then, should churches do? There is no more vital question at the moment, for if civilization is to be saved the church is the only
institution which has the truth needed for its salvation. In an article published in *The Christian Century* of May 29, 1940, I tried to suggest some procedures under the title, "What Can Christians Do?" Though it is, of course,
impossible to draw any sharp distinction between what Christians can do
and what churches can do, I wish now to put the emphasis mainly on what
churches can do as congregations and as corporate bodies.

Churches through preaching and public affirmations can maintain their
distinctively prophetic functions. This does not mean that the churches
should retreat from the world and make "protestations, pronouncements,
the calling of the conferences, talk" a substitute for action. It does mean
that the primary function of the church is to speak, and by its speech lead

the people to worship, to love one another, to act responsibly in the light of Christian ideals.

What in time of war should be the primary notes in our preaching? Exactly the same notes as in time of peace, but with our message intensified and chastened. I venture to suggest four of these preaching notes which have especial relevance to a world in travail.

1. We must declare the reality of the living God and the summons to faith in God. This is no time for false optimism. But neither is it a time to surrender to hysteria and panic. If preachers and congregations cannot find any surer sounds of stability than the multitude who get their attitudes mainly from the radio, the secular press, the movies, and their own biological impulses to fear and to hate, then quite legitimately the question may be put to the churches, "What do ye more than others?" But if the Christian gospel means anything, the churches have something to say that is not being said elsewhere. This is that there runs through history a living pattern of enduring spiritual values because God lives in history; that men may have confidence in God's ultimate triumph whatever the temporal outcome; that not security but the cross is the center of our faith. Repeatedly we have sung:

   > In the cross of Christ I glory
   > Towering o'er the wrecks of time.

   The wrecks of time are here. Now is the time to decide whether we believe what we have sung!

2. A second vital note is that of absolute loyalty to God alone. This is easy to say, and is constantly being said. It is not easy to put into action, especially when the test comes, as it does, in so many subtle forms. Whether one will participate in the use of military force when his country goes to war is a crucial and difficult decision. It is probably both less crucial and less difficult, because more clear-cut, than the decisions that must continually be made about everyday acts and attitudes. How should one feel—what should one say in conversation or from the pulpit, about the news from Europe, about national defense, about compulsory military training, about the fifth column, about the finger-printing of aliens, about alien refugees, about Jehovah's Witnesses, about the Dies committee?[1]

   Which is our symbol of supreme loyalty, the flag or the cross? Most Christians think it is the cross and act as if it were the flag. It is not the business of any preacher to make decisions for his congregation in these matters; it is every preacher's business to throw the searchlight of the gospel on all issues where nationalism and the infringement of civil liberties make encroachments on the supremacy of loyalty which the Christian owes to God before all gods.

3. A third prophetic note is that of repentance. It receives more honor in words than in deeds. As the bulletin I saw outside one church truly admitted, "We love to confess their sins." Repentance for other people's sins readily runs into the escapism which Christians must ever guard against. There has been enough public repentance for the treaty of Versailles in the past twenty years to have made the world over. There has been far less recognition of, or repentance for, those personal sins of self-interest, arrogance, intolerance and prejudice which are the breeders of unjust treaties, economic confusion and war. There are both worthy and unworthy motives now prompting Americans to want this country to stay out of the European conflict, and one of the major perversities of the present situation is the degree to which these motives are mixed without recognition of the mixture. Churches have the difficult but crucial task of stripping off the camouflage and of calling the people, not only to repentance, but to fruits meet for repentance.

4. A fourth note, commonplace in expression but not too common in practice, is the Christian obligation of good will toward all persons. If "love your enemies" means anything, it means the maintenance of sympathy and Christian understanding even toward those whose cruelty and brutality one is morally bound to condemn. It means the maintenance of charity and good will not only toward the German people, but toward the leader of that people. That Hitler, too, is a child of God, a man to be pitied and prayed for, not a devil to be hated, is an assertion so foreign to the prevailing mood that to make it is to precipitate the suspicion that one is either pro-German or mentally unbalanced. Yet I do not myself see what else to make of "Love your enemies; pray for them that persecute you."

In a recent address I quoted the words of a Czechoslovakian girl who said to me at Amsterdam last summer: "We thought we could love our enemies while we had none. Then we found that all we could do was to lift ourselves and our enemies up to God." I suggested that we, too, should remember Hitler in our prayers—with the result that I received a number of protests from those who thought I was asking a prayer for Hitler's victory! To avoid misunderstanding, let me say that I was not. But unless churches can inculcate good will toward those within and those without the Christian fellowship, toward those who espouse Christian democracy and those who thwart it, toward those whose acts accord with the Christian ideal and those whose deeds leave us sick with dismay and apprehension for the future, then the churches had better stop talking about love as the basic Christian virtue.

These four emphases—the reality of the living God, absolute loyalty to God, repentance, good will—are not the only elements in a Christian message for these times. But they are indispensable emphases. If churches can maintain them, they can serve a war-torn world as no other institution can. If not, preachers will again "present arms."[2]

Churches must maintain fellowship. There is not much use talking about loving one's enemy or one's neighbor in the abstract unless we can love our neighbors and fellow Christians. One of the first (and worst) casualties of war is the suspicion and mistrust which Christian fellowship alone can effectively overcome. There is ground for rejoicing that such fellowship within churches has thus far been maintained far better than it was in the last war. Whether it can still be maintained as tensions mount is a challenge that awaits the churches.

Will the fellowship of Christians in the world church stand the strain? Hard days lie ahead, and there is no use evading the fact that a Hitler victory would increase enormously the difficulty of maintaining both the ecumenical movement and the world mission of the church. Whatever the political outcome, America must carry a very much greater financial and spiritual responsibility than in the past. There are those among my friends, both in America and in Europe, who believe that the saving of the world church requires American military intervention. I do not. The church is the carrier of the living gospel of Christ, and whatever may happen to its outer structure it can no more be destroyed in its true life than can Christ himself. In one of our most militant hymns we have affirmed:

> Crowns and thrones may perish,
> Kingdoms rise and wane,
> But the Church of Jesus
> Constant will remain.

Again let me say—this is the time to discover whether we believe what we have sung.

The churches of America must minister to a stricken world. This is a truism. But most American Christians, living still amid scenes of beauty, security and comfort, have no more awakened to the meaning of millions of homeless, ill-clothed, starving refugees and the billions of dollars needed for their care than we have awakened to the meaning of the billions so readily being voted for armaments. It is an index of the length we have yet to go in our Christian sympathy that a staggering outlay for national defense has been accepted with comparatively little protest, while a corresponding amount, if asked by the churches or the Red Cross for the expression of friendship and the alleviation of misery, would have seemed an incredibly unreasonable demand.

Yet the situation demands such giving. "Unprecedented" is a cheap and frequently inaccurate term. The obligation resting upon the members of American churches for generous giving in relief of suffering is truly unprecedented. A graphic but restrained bulletin of the Federal Council of Churches outlines such needs. Civilian relief in China, care of exiled and destitute evangelical Christians in Europe, field relief for millions of European refugees herded into stricken France and for Christian as well as Jewish refugees here and in Europe, aid to stranded missionaries and other emergency Christian services call literally not for millions but for billions from American Christians. If we do not give them, who else will?

Not only the relief of suffering, but the maintenance of missions throughout the world now rests mainly upon the American churches. Heretofore there have been British, Scandinavian, German, French, Dutch, Belgian and Swiss missions. Will there continue to be? No one knows. But it is certain that the burden of war debt and of social dislocation will enfeeble all the European countries, and therefore all the European churches, for a generation. If America does not assume this work, who else will?

I am not an isolationist. But to any American Christian who believes, as I do, that America's supreme duty is to remain out of war, let me say that we have no right to this judgment unless we are willing to try to give to "the last full measure of devotion." Interventionists and non-interventionists alike, let us search our souls!

Finally, let us pray. Let us pray not for security, or for national victory, or for any setting aside of God's eternal moral laws. Let us pray for forgiveness, for humility, for courage, for a strengthening of our feeble impulses to sympathy and service. Let us pray for a purging of our impulses to hate, to retaliate, to think evil of others, to have recourse to military might in those areas where only the curative processes of world cooperation and brotherhood can avail. Let us pray in the mood to do our best and leave the rest to God.

NOTES

1. The "fifth column" refers to infiltrators or collaborators with the enemy. The Dies Committee on Un-American Activities, led by by Texas congressman Martin Dies in the late 1930s, investigated various groups and organizations suspected of anti-American activities.

2. See Ray H. Abrams, *Preachers Present Arms* (New York: Round Table Press, 1933).

7

✛

Harry Emerson Fosdick

Pastor, Riverside Baptist Church

A fundamentalist minister once called Harry Emerson Fosdick "the Jesse James of the theological world"—meaning that the Baptist minister was wreaking havoc on the Christian church with his liberal doctrine denying the inerrancy of the Bible, the virgin birth, and the physical resurrection of Jesus. A 1922 sermon "Shall the Fundamentalists Win?" launched a bitter debate with conservatives and sealed his fate at the First Presbyterian Church in New York City. "They call me a heretic," he said in his farewell address. "I should be ashamed to live in this generation and not be a heretic."

Nevertheless, thousands thronged to hear the silver-tongued preacher. A newspaper headline reported: "Crowds Smash Door: Near Riot to Hear Fosdick." With the help of benefactor John D. Rockefeller, he assumed the pulpit at Riverside Church in New York, where he remained for the next twenty years. His preaching ministry, numerous books and articles, frequent travel, and regular presence on the National Radio Pulpit made Fosdick one of the best-known preachers in America between the two world wars.

Fosdick was tutored at Colgate University by William Newton Clarke, the foremost liberal Baptist theologian at the turn of the century. He then studied at Union Theological Seminary, where he absorbed the writings of social gospel leader Walter Rauchenbusch. Convinced that the precepts of the gospel must be applied to the totality of economic and political life, Fosdick leveraged his immense influence on behalf of numerous social causes. He was an early supporter of Margaret Sanger's planned parenthood campaign. He turned his upscale Riverside Church into a job-placement center for the unemployed (helping about 7,000 people find work between 1930 and 1935). Fosdick supported labor's right to organize. He spoke out against Germany's increasingly hostile treatment of Jews, and pushed to loosen immigration laws to allow more Jewish refugees into the United States. "The ultimate criterion of any civilization's success or failure," he said, "is to be found in what happens to the underdog."

Nevertheless, Fosdick was a staunch pacifist and rejected outright a war to defend democratic values. "A modern war to protect the weak—that is a grim jest," he once told the League of Nations Assembly Service in Geneva. Like many of his religious colleagues, Fosdick had become deeply disillusioned over World War I, and came to regard all armed conflict as "utterly and irremediably unchristian." As tensions mounted in Europe in the 1930s, he joined the Emergency Peace Campaign. The group was composed of educators, lawyers, editors, and political figures, whose stated goal was to "keep a neutral America out of foreign wars." Yet Fosdick and his pacifist peers did not consider themselves isolationists: They supported foreign relief, international trade, the League of Nations, and the World Court.

The following essay appeared in January of 1941, after France and half a dozen European states had fallen into Nazi hands. Fosdick admits that "disarmament can never be unilateral." He acknowledges that a German victory in Europe would be the worse of two evils, and he chides some fellow pacifists as "too complacent" about the battle raging across the Atlantic. Yet Fosdick insists that Jesus would condemn both the aggressor and defender in the European war. Moreover, he sees only catastrophe ahead if America intervenes militarily to help the Allied cause. "I will not prostitute the ministry of Jesus Christ to the sanction and support of war," he writes. "For the United States to become a belligerent in this conflict would be a colossal and futile disaster."

Keeping Christ Above the Strife
The Christian Century, January 22, 1941

In replying to the question proposed by *The Christian Century*, "If America is drawn into war, can you, as a Christian, participate in it or support it?" my answer must be, No!

As I understand the matter, this inquiry is to be taken as intimate and personal. I am not asked to discuss in the abstract "absolute" and "doctrinaire" pacifism, concerning which I should have to be critical. I am not asked what I would do were I a Chinese or an Englishman, although the answer may be implied in what I say. I am not asked what I would do were I a layman of draft age. If I understand myself I should be a conscientious objector, asking for alternative civilian service, the harder the better. The question proposed faces me, a minister of Christ in the United States today, with the practical inquiry: If this nation now becomes an active belligerent, will I support the war?

In answering I propose mainly to present my minimal position, the place where no matter how urgent the national necessities may seem to be, I know I must take my stand. That minimal position seems clear: I can never use my Christian ministry in the support and sanction of war.

During the last war I did so use my ministry. I was ready to declare war, as some of my brethren are today, even before the nation was. I, a minister of Christ, went all out for the backing of the fray, and was proud when, in France, after an address to the troops, an officer told me I was worth a battalion. To be sure, it cost a struggle. The whole business of war, the causes that produce it, the processes that characterize it, the moral consequences that accompany it, are too obviously the denial of everything that Jesus taught, for a minister easily to fit Christ into a military uniform. I twisted and turned every which way to harmonize war and the Christian ethic, preaching against hate, praying for the Germans, and arguing beautifully about the way we could slaughter them in the spirit of love. My rationalizations in trying to make that oil and water mix arouse my wonder at their ingenuity and my shame at their futility, and the crux of my regret is that I so used my Christian ministry, as though such howling after the dogs of war were the function of the church of Christ.

Today when I picture Christ in this warring world I can see him in one place only, not arrayed in the panoply of battle on either side, but on his judgment seat, sitting in condemnation on all of us—aggressor, defender, neutral—who by our joint guilt have involved ourselves in a way of life that denies everything he stood for. The function of the church is to keep

him there, above the strife, representing a manner of living, the utter antithesis of war, to which mankind must return if we are to have any hope.
But the Christian ministry does not keep him there by throwing itself,
generation after generation, into the support and sanction of the nation's
wars. Rather it drags him down, until the people, listening, can feel little
if any difference between what Christ says and what Mars wants. It is not
the function of the Christian church to help win a war. A church that becomes an adjunct to a war department has denied its ministry. The function of the church is to keep Christ where he belongs, upon his judgment
seat, condemner of our joint guilt, chastener of our impenitent pride,
guide to our only hope.

This does not mean that in the present world-wide conflict I am neutral.
These last months I have sometimes thought I lived more in Britain and
China than at home, so keen have been my sympathies, so deep my ap-
prehensions, so desperate my hopes. Obviously it makes a difference to us
which side wins. The Christian minister, maintaining the position for
which I plead, lives in no ivory tower apart from the realistic facts, but under terrific tension, with a warring world on one side, in which his personal emotions and his nation's interests are involved, and with Christ
upon the other; but he accepts the *tension*, and does not try to resolve it by
reducing Christ to the level of the warring world.

This does not mean that I am uncritical of pacifism as it sometimes is
presented. Some pacifists seem to me to drift unwittingly into philosophical anarchism, denying the rightful functions of the state, blind to
the incalculable benefits that arise when private force is supplanted by
public force for the good of all, falsely resting their case on opposition
to all force rather than on a distinction between salutary and diabolical
uses of it, and unrealistic about the necessities of social coercion,
whether through municipal police or through international police
when a world government has been created. Some pacifism seems to
me merely individualistic and negative, as though a few individuals,
refusing the fight, were the solution of the peace problem, when only a
federation of the nations, a unified world order, can present an ultimate
substitute for war.

Some pacifists seem to me far too complacent, as though by refusing
any part in war themselves, they washed their hands of the common guilt
that involves us all, from the burden of whose consequence the conscientious soldier feels he cannot ask exemption. And some pacifism becomes
mere passiveness, as though one who let himself be a doormat for aggressive evil to wipe its feet on were really a peace-maker, whereas to be
that always involves a whole battery of positive moral qualities issuing
from creative good will, and commonly involves obdurate, sacrificial resistance to evil, even if violent means are eschewed.

Yet, while I am neither neutral nor a contented absolutist in my paci- fism, I come back to my position, sure that I must maintain it: I will not prostitute the ministry of Jesus Christ to the sanction and support of war.

In this position a conviction is involved concerning the meaning of Christ's life and teaching. That the spirit, methods, processes, accompani- ments and results of war are the complete denial of Jesus' ethic, that war stands for everything he was against, and against everything he was for, seems to me clear. Surely, the least we can do is to say with the Oxford Conference: "War involves compulsory enmity, diabolical outrage against human personality and wanton distortion of the truth. War is a particular demonstration of the power of sin in this world, and a defiance of the righteousness of God as revealed in Jesus Christ and him crucified."

Whether one studies the texts in detail—read, for example, MacGre- gor's *The New Testament Basis of Pacifism*—or considers the whole bent and meaning of Jesus' teaching and his way of life, the endeavor to harmonize him with war seems to me impossible.[1] If nothing else persuaded me to be a pacifist, I think I should be persuaded by the sophisticated rationali- zations, the wishful twisting of texts out of contexts, the dreadful perver- sions of Jesus' most characteristic teaching, by which the churchly sup- porters of war try to get Christ to be their yes-man.

I can indeed understand one who, seeing no possibility of compromise between Christ's ethic and war, says frankly that Christ's ethic is at pres- ent inapplicable, that it represents an ideal hope, not a program of present action. That, at least, is a clear-headed facing of the issue involved in a Christian's decision about war, and is a candid surrender of Jesus' way of life as a guide to conduct. But it leads to the substitution of theology, ec- clesiasticism or ritualism for the spirit and teaching of Christ, and its out- come Westermarck correctly described in his *Christianity and Morals*: "War is the rock on which Christian principles have suffered the most miserable shipwreck."[2] Full of sympathy, as one must be, with men and nations in this brutal world who see no possibility of being ethically Christian in their desperate emergencies, surely the Christian minister has no right to lower his flag. This agelong conflict, this head-on collision, between war and the ethic of Jesus, will not be resolved by the abject surrender of Christ's representative every time that war comes on.

Involved in this position, along with such conviction regarding Christ's spirit and way of life, is a factual judgment about this present situation. I have said that it makes a difference to us who wins this war, but how much difference it makes has yet to be decided. We, the democracies, with smashing completeness won the last war. We had the world in our hands and could do what we would. As to what we did and did not do, the bill of particulars has often been written, and the all but unanimous judgment seems to be that we, the democracies, are just as responsible for the rise of the dictators as the dictatorships themselves, and perhaps more so. Even President Butler, of Columbia University, says: "That great war, with all its terrible sacrifice of life, of the comfort and happiness of tens of millions of human beings and of the world's savings for generations, was absolutely futile."

In that outcome to war, even when democracies win it, there is nothing unique. When we moderns begin a war we no longer "draw the sword," but rather start a forest fire that stops at nothing, spares nobody, destroys everything, creates naught but havoc. With Europe and Asia devastated, with famine and pestilence awaiting their terrible innings, with economic prostration and social revolution trailing after them, and with Stalin hoping to become the residuary legatee of a ruined continent, it is still an open question what anybody's "winning" of this war may mean. But it is not an open question that if any creative consequence is to be snatched from the havoc, it will come from such spiritual forces as may still be left intact.

Do we Christians really believe that? Does not that fact create the special function of the church? This gospel of Christ, which in wartime we are tempted to compromise, postpone as too ideal for present application, put into cold storage or quite explicitly deny, is really the hope of the world. Should not the Christian ministry keep that fact central? What business has the minister throwing the weight of his influence on the side of war? What place in the Christian economy have sermons entitled "To Arms! To Arms!"?

My personal judgment is that for the United States to become a belligerent in this conflict would be a colossal and futile disaster and, along with millions of others, I should hold that judgment, pacifist or no pacifist. What if, however, the United States were invaded? That, I think, is not a practical possibility and never has been, but it is continually presented as a test case to those who do not propose to use their ministry in support of war. What would we do in case of invasion? My own answer is clear: resist, whether by violent or non-violent means.

The identification of pacifism with mere submissiveness is a familiar misunderstanding. Denmark is used as an example of pacifism. That seems to me a case of mistaken identity. Denmark, under necessity, submitted. Gandhi, however, has never submitted, but has organized tireless, incorrigible, courageous, non-violent resistance. I profoundly admire him, and venture to predict a long and influential future for his ideas and methods. If, however, someone says that, under present circumstances, to rely on America's meeting invasion with a mass movement of non-violent resistance is trusting moonshine, I agree. America is utterly unprepared for such a process. When I hear that plan proposed as a realistic alternative to armed resistance in the United States today, I am entirely incredulous. Even Gandhi, with his long training of his people in his ideas and techniques, would face a brand new problem if, in Winston Churchill's ominous words, Hitler should "stand at the gates of India."

Nevertheless, non-violent resistance—tireless, incorrigible refusal of participation in tyranny and of subjection to it—is today one of the major hopes of Europe in countries like Norway, Holland, Belgium. At least when military resistance breaks down and a nation faces the choice between submission on the one side and, on the other, the pacifist method—obstinate, courageous, non-violent resistance—the latter can determine the course of history, and those who are at work on its basic ideas and practical methods are about important business.

If our country were invaded, therefore, I should say resist, each according to his best conscience, by violent or non-violent means. The pacifists have not been dubious or mealy-mouthed about this matter. Muriel Lester quotes with approval the assertion of Gandhi that it is better to fight than to do nothing. Leyton Richards, one of the leading pacifist ministers of Europe in both the last war and this one, says: "If a man has not seized the significance of the Christian reaction to aggressive evil as seen in the way of Jesus, it is better to react by way of war than not to act at all." And A.J. Muste, who is a pacifist if ever there was one, writes: "Personally, I believe that resistance to evil and oppression, even if it takes a violent form, is on a higher moral plane than cowardly or passive acquiescence."

Nevertheless, even in case of invasion, I should hold to my position. Honoring the consciences of all who resist aggressive evil whether by violent or non-violent means, trying in the church I serve to minister alike to the needs of the conscientious objector and the conscientious soldier, all the more in such a crisis I should try to keep Christ where he belongs—on his judgment seat, above the strife, standing for a way of life that condemns both aggressor and defender, and offers the only hope of salvation from their joint guilt and their insensate brutality. I will not use my Christian ministry to bless war.

To be sure, I distrust the judgment of any man so contented with his attitude in this complicated crisis that he thinks he has escaped inconsistency. We pacifists need humbly to confess that we are deeply involved in the war system and cannot pretend that we purely wash our hands of it. Like a socialist fighting the profit system who is at leisure to do so because he owns stock on whose profits he can live, so, like everyone else, we are inextricably entangled in the very war system we disclaim and are trying to displace.

We say we will not support war, but we do support it in every tax we pay, and we have no intention of imitating Thoreau's inane refusal. We know that vast armaments are essentially anti-Christian, and yet we know too that disarmament can never be unilateral, that when disarmament comes it must come by mutual international agreement, and so we have habitually taken our national army and navy for granted and now take for granted their inevitable enlargement. We see clearly that a war for democracy is a contradiction in terms, that war itself is democracy's chief enemy, and that after every world war, whoever wins it, there is bound to be less democracy than there was before, yet we see too that the military victory of Hitler is the worse of two evils, that American bombing planes going to Britain may give democracy at least a breathing space, and may conceivably save us here from plunging into active belligerency.

Moreover, sure as we are that we stand for convictions which in the long run are the world's hope, we nonetheless recognize that in the immediate emergency were our attitude to become predominant and controlling on one side of the battle line and not on the other, the worse of two evils might temporarily be strengthened by the very stand that so conscientiously we take.

If the pacifist finds himself so involved in difficulty, the Christian who supports war, and especially the Christian minister who throws his influence as Christ's representative into the waging of war, seem to me utterly distraught by self-contradiction. Christ and the bombing of civilians, the Sermon on the Mount and the starving of whole populations, every essential element in the gospel on one side, and on the other every "diabolical outrage against human personality"—it may be difficult to choose between them, but what can one say about trying to amalgamate them?

Let the Christian non-pacifist get this matter down out of the abstract into the concrete, stripped of the sentimental romanticism with which once more the "glory of war" is being clothed, and let him see war as it actually is! In the last war an officer drilling a group of boys in the use of the bayonet said this: "You've got to get down and hook them out with a bayonet; you will enjoy that, I ensure you. Get sympathy out of your head. We go out to kill. We don't care how so long as they are killed . . . And I say to you, if you see a wounded German, shove him out and have no nonsense about it . . . Kill them, every mother's son of them. Remember that your job is to kill them—that is the only way—exterminate the vile creatures." That, along with innumerable things like that, on a scale more terrible than any previous conflict knew, *is* war, and when a minister of Christ supports war, that is what he is supporting.

Well aware of the difficulties of my own position, I watch with deep concern the endeavors of Christian ministers to subsume war under Christian categories. A sermon lies before me in which the preacher urges that because God sends men to hell—an obviously coercive process!—therefore Christians may use violence in war. All the way from *that* the devious arguments range to and fro, and up and down, until I find one eminent and fine-spirited preacher, laboring with the text, "God is love," who concludes that bombing planes can be one expression of the divine compassion and that "men may be forced at times, *in the service of love* [the italics are his], to use weapons which strike down the innocent as well as the guilty." Am I wrong in being horrified at that?

Whichever side a man espouses, let him not suppose he can extricate himself from inconsistency! Humility becomes us all. Nevertheless, facing the choice between the two, I think I see where the clearer ground is and the better hope of maintaining our Christian testimony unimpaired.

Meanwhile, to the limit of our ability, let us keep our Christian fellowship intact! Dr. Tittle is right: "Christian fellowship cannot survive internationally unless it survives locally. It cannot possibly be maintained in the ends of the earth unless it is maintained in the church on the corner." As the crisis thickens this will grow more difficult; in some cases it will doubtless be impossible; some churches will be torn asunder by the war-psychosis and some ministers will lose their pulpits. Hard as it is to discover the truly Christian position in this crisis, it is often harder to maintain it in a Christian spirit when one thinks one has found it. I see letters written by Christian pacifists to their non-pacifist brethren that for bitterness, acrimony, venom and dogmatism pass all decent bounds; and I see statements made by Christian non-pacifists about their pacifist fellows that for scorn, misrepresentation, rancor and contemptuousness are appalling. There is no hope in such a spirit. Unless we Christians can maintain humility, a joint penitence, good will, and a sincere respect for one another's consciences within our churches, we cannot help the world much in maintaining such attitudes, without which we and the world alike are doomed.

Nevertheless, if the issue is drawn, some of us will have to abide by the consequences. We will not use our Christian ministry to support war. As for myself, I am essentially a Quaker, and my convictions belong in what seems to me the great traditions of the Society of Friends.

NOTES

1. Rev. GHC MacGregor was an influential theologian and religious writer of the 1920s and 1930s. His 1936 book, *The New Testament Basis of Pacifism*, was published by the Fellowship of Reconciliation, a leading pacifist organization in the interwar years. MacGregor regarded the teachings of Jesus as "uncompromisingly pacifist."

2. Edward Alexander Westermarck was a Finnish social philosopher and anthropologist. He published *Christianity and Morals* in 1939, though his best-known work is *The History of Human Marriage*, published in 1891.

II

THE PROPHETS
Resisting the Evil of Nazism

8

Reinhold Niebuhr

Editor, Christianity and Crisis
Union Theological Seminary

In the late 1930s, as appeals mounted for America to get involved in the European crisis, the hawks were criticized for allowing the cords of family and friendship with Great Britain to sway their views. Pacifists accused them of exaggerating the misdeeds of Adolf Hitler and his ultimate designs on Europe. Reinhold Niebuhr, who had emerged as a national religious figure and leading critic of Nazism, took offense at that charge. "I am an American of pure German stock. . .[and] I gained most of these convictions in many visits to Hitler's Germany."

Besides his German pedigree, at least two other features of Niebuhr's life made him an unlikely advocate of American support for the war. First, America's economic inequalities led him to embrace socialism, and most socialists feared another European conflict would involve the United States and turn the country into a capitalist dictatorship. (Niebuhr himself ran as a Socialist Party candidate for Congress in 1930.) Second, as the devastation of World War I, and the cynical diplomacy that followed it, became more apparent, Niebuhr converted to pacifism. He once described the Great War thus: "Here was simply a tremendous contest for power." He eventually served as national chairman of the Fellowship of Reconciliation, one of the most important disarmament groups of the interwar period.

Such were the credentials of America's ardent antiwar activists; they defined many, if not most, of the liberal Protestant clergy of the era. But Niebuhr had been charting his own course, politically and spiritually, for quite some time. His pastor's post at Bethel Evangelical Church in a working-class section of Detroit helped discredit the social gospel theology to which he'd been attached. More important, the viciousness of

European Fascism finally demolished any lingering notions about human goodness or perfectability. "I must confess," he said, "that the gradual unfolding of my theological ideas has come not so much through study as through the pressure of world events."

As professor of Applied Christianity at Union Theological Seminary in New York, Niebuhr developed his "Christian realism" to answer the pietism of the right and the utopianism of the left: In his view, fundamentalists obsessed over individual salvation as the world rushed toward disaster, while liberals dismissed the problem of evil as they tried to build the kingdom of heaven on earth. Niebuhr published groundbreaking works such as *Moral Man and Immoral Society* and *The Nature and Destiny of Man*. A driving motif was that the practical goal of politics could not be the realization of the Christian ideal of unconditional love. Instead, the objective was to achieve some measure of justice in a world ravaged by sin. His belief in the tragedy of human nature, in fact, qualified every political choice; social perfectionism was simply out of the question. "Individuals may be saved by repentance, which is the gateway to grace. . . . But the collective life of mankind promises no such hope of salvation."

A preacher more than a theologian, Niebuhr had a gift for offering a theological interpretation of contemporary events and urging practical action, yet doing so in a public grammar that was widely accessible. As European capitals fell one by one to Germany, he used this gift to its fullest. No religious thinker saw more clearly the fundamental nature of the Nazi threat to civilization. None offered a more withering critique of the Christian pacifism that had seized American clergymen in response to it. Few approached him in sheer literary output. In all of it, Niebuhr stopped short of recommending that America declare war on Germany. Yet, as more than one pacifist sympathizer admitted, he "completely demolished the case for pacifism."

The first essay, "An End to Illusions," was written in the spring of 1940, when Britain and France were already at war with Germany. Niebuhr describes the "utopian fog" that still engulfed most of the liberal intelligentsia in their critique of Fascism. He also announces his break with the Socialist Party because of its "dogma that this war is a clash of imperialisms"—and nothing more. In the next essay, "Why the Church Is Not Pacifist," he explains how the pacifism of his day was a betrayal of Christian ethics, what he calls a "secularized and moralistic" counterfeit of the message of Jesus. "The gospel is something more than the law of love," he writes. "The gospel deals with the fact that men violate the law of love."

The final selection, "Christian Faith and the World Crisis," was Niebuhr's opening essay for *Christianity and Crisis*, the magazine he founded in 1941 to counter what he considered the distorted Christianity embodied by the politics of *The Christian Century*. It remains a powerful rebuke to those who would invoke the ethical ideals of Jesus as a way of evading moral obligations to one's neighbor. "American Christianity is all too prone to disavow its responsibilities for the preservation of our civilization against the perils of totalitarian aggression," he writes. "If this task does not engage us, both our repentance and our hope become luxuries in which we indulge while other men save us from an intolerable fate, or while our inaction betrays into disaster a cause to which we owe our allegiance."

An End to Illusions
The Nation, Spring 1940

The morning newspaper brings reports of disaster everywhere. The morning mail acquaints me with the confusion created by these reports. My mail this morning, for example, contains four significant communications. The first is a letter from the Socialist Party informing me that my views on foreign affairs violate the party platform and asking me to give account of my nonconformity. The party position is that this war is a clash of rival imperialisms in which nothing significant is at stake. The second letter asks me to support an organization which will bring peace to the world by establishing "world education" and erecting a "world radio." It fails to explain how its world education is to seep into the totalitarian states and wean them from their mania. The third letter is from a trade union under Communist influence asking me to speak at a union "peace" meeting. The fourth is from a parson who wants me to join in an effort to set "moral force against Hitler's battalions," but it fails to explain just how moral force is to be effective against tanks, flame-throwers, and bombing planes.

This mail increases the melancholy promoted by the morning's news. I answer the Socialist communication by a quick resignation from the party. I inform the trade union that my views would not be acceptable at its peace meeting. The proposal for a world radio is quickly consigned to a file which already contains eighty-two different recipes for world salvation. I start to answer the parson who wants to set "moral force" against Hitler, but overcome with a sense of futility and doubting my ability to penetrate the utopian fog in which the letter was conceived, I throw my reply into the wastebasket. Thus I save some time to meditate upon the perspective which informs this whole morning's mail and upon the vapid character of the culture which Hitler intends to destroy. This culture does not understand historical reality clearly enough to deserve to survive. It has a right to survival only because the alternative is too horrible to contemplate. All four letters are but expressions of the utopianism which has informed our Western world since the eighteenth century.

The Socialists have a dogma that this war is a clash of rival imperialisms. Of course they are right. So is a clash between myself and a gangster a conflict of rival egotisms. There is a perspective from which there is not much difference between my egotism and that of a gangster. But from another perspective there is an important difference. "There is not much difference between people," said a farmer to William James, "but what difference there is is very important." That is a truth which the Socialists in America have not yet learned. The Socialists are right, of course, in insisting that the civilization we are called upon to defend is full of capitalistic and imperialistic injustice. But it is still a civilization. Utopianism creates confusion in politics by measuring all significant historical distinctions against purely ideal perspectives and blinding the eye to differences which may be matters of life and death in a specific instance.

The Socialists rightly call attention to the treason of the capitalistic oligarchy which has brought the cause of democracy to so desperate a state. But we are defending something which transcends the interests of Mr. Chamberlain and the venality of M. Bonnet. Furthermore, the Socialists have forgotten how much they contributed to the capitulation of democracy to tyranny. It was a Socialist Prime Minister, Paul-Henri Spaak who contrived the unrealistic neutrality policy of Belgium which was responsible for the German break-through at Sedan. The policy was unrealistic because it was based upon the quite untrue assumption that Belgium was imperilled equally by rival imperialistic powers. The peril was not equal at all, and history has avenged this lie in a terrible way. The Socialists of the Scandinavian countries were deeply involved in the parasitic pacifism of these small nations which scorned "power politics" and forgot that their security rested upon the British navy and the contingencies of a precarious balance of power. The Socialists of Britain willed to resist Hitler but did not will the means of resistance. As for Munich, I heard American Socialists give thanks that a madman with a gun was met by a man with an umbrella. If there had been two guns, rather than an umbrella and a gun, they said, the world would have plunged into conflict. European Socialists have learned to repent of these errors under the pressure of tragic events, leaving only American Socialists to indulge the luxury of their utopianism.

The proposal for "world radio" and "world education" is merely a particularly fatuous form of the utopian rationalism and universalism which have informed the thought of liberal intellectuals in the whole Western world. These liberals have always imagined that it was a comparatively simple matter for the human mind to transcend the welter of interest and passion which is the very stuff of existence. They have not understood that man's very capacity for freedom creates the imperialist will to dominate, as well as the desire to subordinate life to universal standards. The five hundred American scientists who recently presented a memorial to the President favoring neutrality in the name of scientific impartiality seem not to have the slightest idea that scientific freedom is dependent upon the vicissitudes of political history. Their allusions reveal that modern culture completely misunderstands history precisely because it has learned a great deal about nature and falsely imagines that the harmonies and securities of nature are a safe asylum for man.

There seems to be absolutely no end to the illusions of which intellectuals are capable and no height of unrealistic dreaming to which they cannot rise. Aldous Huxley dreams in Hollywood of a method of making man harmless by subtracting or abstracting the self from selfhood, and stumbles into a pseudo-Buddhistic mysticism as the way of salvation without understanding that this kind of mysticism annuls all history in the process of destroying the self.

When the intellectuals are not given to a vapid form of universalism they elaborate an impossible individualism. Bertrand Russell, who has now repented of his pacifism, wrote in an article recently reprinted in *The Nation* that any political view which made individuals the bearers of ideological forces was outmoded.[1] The fact is that Nazi collectivism with its primitive emphasis upon "blood and soil" is but a cruel and psychopathic emphasis upon organic and collective aspects of life which liberal individualism has outraged. As late as last February the *New Republic* promised to stand resolutely against any moral urge that might carry us into war because it knew so certainly that the "evils of a system" could not be cured by "killing the unfortunate individuals who for a moment embody the system." It failed to tell us that the individuals who for the moment embody a system might possibly fasten a system of slavery upon us which would not be for a moment. When Germany invaded Holland and Belgium and the situation of the western democracies became precarious, the *New Republic* forgot these individualistic scruples and solemnly warned that we could not afford to allow the British navy to be destroyed, though it did not tell us how we were to prevent it without imperilling the lives of unfortunate individual sailors and soldiers "who for the moment embody a system." The real fact is that we have no right to deal with the rough stuff of politics at all if we do not understand that politics always deals with collective action and that collective action invariably involves both guilty and guiltless among the individuals who for the moment embody a system.

The letter from the communistic trade union in my mail can stand as a symbol of the aberrations of those who frantically cling to Russia as their hope of salvation. The fear that a triumphant Germany will invade the Ukraine may bring Russia back on the side of the angels shortly, and then the rest of us will be told how wrong we were in judging Russia prematurely. Fortunately, we have no intellectuals of the standing of George Bernard Shaw and J. B. S. Haldane who, under the influence of the Russian obsession, talk such nonsense as these two men have permitted themselves.

The letter from the parson who wanted to set "moral force" against Hitler's battalions is a nice example of the sentimentalized form of Christianity which has engulfed our churches, particularly in America, and which has prompted them to dream of "spiritualizing life" by abstracting spirit from matter, history, and life. It is significant that this kind of "spiritual" religion identifies religious perfectionism with the morally dubious and politically dangerous dogmas of isolation. If we could only keep free of this European struggle we might still indulge our illusions about the character of human existence, which Christianity at its best illumines.

A survey of our culture gives us the uneasy feeling that Hitler was not quite wrong in his boast that he would destroy the world of the eighteenth century. In its more articulate forms out culture suffers from illusions which weaken its will and its right to survive. One can only be grateful for the common sense of common folk which has not been corrupted by these illusions and which in the hour of peril expresses itself in sound political instincts. But for this common sense we might capitulate to a system of government which declares war to be normal, because we do not believe in war. We might submit to a culture which glorifies force as the final arbiter, because we thought it a simple task to extricate reason from force. We might allow a primitive collectivism to enslave us, because we had false ideas of the relation of the individual to the collective forces of life. We might submit to tyranny and the negation of justice, because we had an uneasy conscience about the injustices which corrupt our system of justice.

Hitler threatens the whole world not merely because the democracies were plutocratic and betrayed by their capitalist oligarchies. His victories thus far are partly due to the fact that the culture of the democracies was vapid. Its political instincts had become vitiated by an idealism which sought to extricate morals from politics to the degree of forgetting that all life remains a contest of power. If Hitler is defeated in the end it will be because the crisis has awakened in us the will to preserve a civilization in which justice and freedom are realities, and given us the knowledge that ambiguous methods are required for the ambiguities of history. Let those who are revolted by such ambiguities have the decency and consistency to retire to the monastery, where medieval perfectionists found their asylum.

Why the Church Is Not Pacifist

Christianity and Power Politics, 1940

WHEN PACIFISM BECOMES HERESY

Whenever the actual historical situation sharpens the issue, the debate whether the Christian Church is, or ought to be, pacifist is carried on with fresh vigor both inside and outside the Christian community. Those who are not pacifists seek to prove that pacifism is a heresy; while the pacifists contend, or at least imply, that the Church's failure to espouse pacifism unanimously can only be interpreted as apostasy, and must be attributed to its lack of courage or to its want of faith.

There may be an advantage in stating the thesis, with which we enter this debate, immediately. The thesis is, that the failure of the Church to espouse pacifism is not apostasy, but is derived from an understanding of the Christian Gospel which refuses simply to equate the Gospel with the "law of love." Christianity is not simply a new law, namely, the law of love. The finality of Christianity cannot be proved by analyses which seek to reveal that the law of love is stated more unambiguously and perfectly in the life and teachings of Christ than anywhere else. Christianity is a religion which measures the total dimension of human existence not only in terms of the final norm of human conduct, which is expressed in the law of love, but also in terms of the fact of sin. It recognizes that the same man who can become his true self only by striving infinitely for self-realization beyond himself is also inevitably involved in the sin of infinitely making his partial and narrow self the true end of existence. It believes, in other words, that though Christ is the true norm (the "second Adam") for every man, every man is also in some sense a crucifier of Christ.

The good news of the gospel is not the law that we ought to love one another. The good news of the gospel is that there is a resource of divine mercy which is able to overcome a contradiction within our own souls, which we cannot ourselves overcome. This contradiction is that, though we know we ought to love our neighbor as ourself, there is a "law in our members which wars against the law that is in our mind," so that, in fact, we love ourselves more than our neighbor.

The grace of God which is revealed in Christ is regarded by Christian faith as, on the one hand, an actual "power of righteousness" which heals the contradiction within our hearts. In that sense Christ defines the actual possibilities of human existence. On the other hand, this grace is conceived as "justification," as pardon rather than power, as the forgiveness of God, which is vouchsafed to man despite the fact that he never achieves the full measure of Christ. In that sense Christ is the "impossible possibility." Loyalty to him means realization in intention, but does not actually mean the full realization of the measure of Christ. In this doctrine of forgiveness and justification, Christianity measures the full seriousness of sin as a permanent factor in human history. Naturally, the doctrine has no meaning for modern secular civilization, nor for the secularized and moralistic versions of Christianity. They cannot understand the doctrine precisely because they believe there is some fairly simple way out of the sinfulness of human history.

It is rather remarkable that so many modern Christians should believe that Christianity is primarily a "challenge" to man to obey the law of Christ; whereas it is, as a matter of fact, a religion which deals realistically with the problem presented by the violation of this law. Far from believing that the ills of the world could be set right "if only" men obeyed the law of Christ, it has always regarded the problem of achieving justice in a sinful world as a very difficult task. In the profounder versions of the Christian faith the very utopian illusions, which are currently equated with Christianity, have been rigorously disavowed.

Nevertheless, it is not possible to regard pacifism simply as a heresy. In one of its aspects modern Christian pacifism is simply a version of Christian perfectionism. It expresses a genuine impulse in the heart of Christianity, the impulse to take the law of Christ seriously and not to allow the political strategies, which the sinful character of man makes necessary, to become final norms. In its profounder forms this Christian perfectionism did not proceed from a simple faith that the "law of love" could be regarded as an alternative to the political strategies by which the world achieves a precarious justice. These strategies invariably involve the balancing of power with power; and they never completely escape the peril of tyranny on the one hand, and the peril of anarchy and warfare on the other.

In medieval ascetic perfectionism and in Protestant sectarian perfectionism (of the type of Meno Simons, for instance) the effort to achieve a standard of perfect love in individual life was not presented as a political alternative.[2] On the contrary, the political problem and task were specifically disavowed. This perfectionism did not give itself to the illusion that it had discovered a method for eliminating the element of conflict from political strategies. On the contrary, it regarded the mystery of evil as beyond its power of solution. It was content to set up the most perfect and unselfish individual life as a symbol of the Kingdom of God. It knew that this could only be done by disavowing the political task and by freeing the individual of all responsibility for social justice.

It is this kind of pacifism which is not a heresy. It is rather a valuable asset for the Christian faith. It is a reminder to the Christian community that the relative norms of social justice, which justify both coercion and resistance to coercion, are not final norms, and that Christians are in constant peril of forgetting their relative and tentative character and of making them too completely normative.

There is thus a Christian pacifism which is not a heresy. Yet most modern forms of Christian pacifism are heretical. Presumably inspired by the Christian gospel, they have really absorbed the Renaissance faith in the goodness of man, have rejected the Christian doctrine of original sin as an outmoded bit of pessimism, have reinterpreted the Cross so that it is made to stand for the absurd idea that perfect love is guaranteed a simple victory over the world, and have rejected all other profound elements of the Christian gospel as "Pauline" accretions which must be stripped from the "simple gospel of Jesus." This form of pacifism is not only heretical when judged by the standards of the total gospel. It is equally heretical when judged by the facts of human existence. There are no historical realities which remotely conform to it. It is important to recognize this lack of conformity to the facts of experience as a criterion of heresy.

All forms of religious faith are principles of interpretation which we use to organize our experience. Some religions may be adequate principles of interpretation at certain levels of experience, but they break down at deeper levels. No religious faith can maintain itself in defiance of the experience which it supposedly interprets. A religious faith which substitutes faith in man for faith in God cannot finally validate itself in experience. If we believe that the only reason men do not love each other perfectly is because the law of love has not been preached persuasively enough, we believe something to which experience does not conform. If we believe that if Britain had only been fortunate enough to have produced 30 per cent instead of 2 per cent of conscientious objectors to military service, Hitler's heart would have been softened and he would not have dared to attack Poland, we hold a faith which no historical reality justifies.

Such a belief has no more justification in the facts of experience than the communist belief that the sole cause of man's sin is the class organization of society and the corollary faith that a "classless" society will be essentially free of human sinfulness. All of these beliefs are pathetic alternatives to the Christian faith. They all come finally to the same thing. They do not believe that man remains a tragic creature who needs the divine mercy as much at the end as at the beginning of his moral endeavors. They believe rather that there is some fairly easy way out of the human situation of "self-alienation." In this connection it is significant that Christian pacifists, rationalists like Bertrand Russell, and mystics like Aldous Huxley, believe essentially the same thing. The Christians make Christ into the symbol of their faith in man. But their faith is really identical with that of Russell or Huxley.

The common element in these various expressions of faith in man is the belief that man is essentially good at some level of his being. They believe that if you can abstract the rational-universal man from what is finite and contingent in human nature, or if you can only cultivate some mystic-universal element in the deeper levels of man's consciousness, you will be able to eliminate human selfishness and the consequent conflict of life with life. These rational or mystical views of man conform neither to the New Testament's view of human nature nor yet to the complex facts of human experience.

In order to elaborate the thesis more fully, that the refusal of the Christian Church to espouse pacifism is not apostasy and that most modern forms of pacifism are heretical, it is necessary first of all to consider the character of the absolute and unqualified demands which Christ makes and to understand the relation of these demands to the gospel.

SECURING JUSTICE

It is very foolish to deny that the ethic of Jesus is an absolute and uncompromising ethic. It is, in the phrase of Ernst Troeltsch, an ethic of "love universalism and love perfectionism." The injunctions "resist not evil," "love your enemies," "if ye love them that love you what thanks have you?" "be not anxious for your life," and "be ye therefore perfect" even as your father in heaven is perfect," are all of one piece and they are all uncompromising and absolute. Nothing is more futile and pathetic than the effort of some Christian theologians who find it necessary to become involved in the relativities of politics, in resistance to tyranny or in social conflict, to justify themselves by seeking to prove that Christ was also involved in some of these relativities, that he used whips to drive the money-changers out of the Temple, or that he came "not to bring peace but a sword," or that he asked the disciples to sell a cloak and buy a sword. What could be more futile than to build a whole ethical structure upon the exegetical issue whether Jesus accepted the sword with the words: "It is enough," or whether he really meant: "Enough of this"?[3]

Those of us who regard the ethic of Jesus as finally and ultimately normative, but not as immediately applicable to the task of securing justice in a sinful world, are very foolish if we try to reduce the ethic so that it will cover and justify our prudential and relative standards and strategies. To do this is to reduce the ethic to a new legalism. The significance of the law of love is precisely that it is not just another law, but a law which transcends all law. Every law and every standard which falls short of the law of love embodies contingent factors and makes concessions to the fact that sinful man must achieve tentative harmonies of life with life which are less than the best. It is dangerous and confusing to give these tentative and relative standards final and absolute religious sanction.

Curiously enough the pacifists are just as guilty as their less absolutist brethren of diluting the ethic of Jesus for the purpose of justifying their position. They are forced to recognize that an ethic of pure non-resistance can have no immediate relevance to any political situation; for in every political situation it is necessary to achieve justice by resisting pride and power. They therefore declare that the ethic of Jesus is not an ethic of non-resistance, but one of non-violent resistance; that it allows one to resist evil provided the resistance does not involve the destruction of life or property.

There is not the slightest support in Scripture for this doctrine of non-violence. Nothing could be plainer than that the ethic uncompromisingly enjoins non-resistance and not non-violent resistance. Furthermore, it is obvious that the distinction between violent and non-violent resistance is not an absolute distinction. If it is made absolute, we arrive at the morally absurd position of giving moral preference to the non-violent power which Doctor Goebbels wields over the type of power wielded by a general.[4] This absurdity is really derived from the modern (and yet probably very ancient and very Platonic) heresy of regarding the "physical" as evil and the "spiritual" as good. The *reductio ad absurdum* of this position is achieved in a book which has become something of a textbook for modern pacifists, Richard Gregg's *The Power of Non-Violence*. In this book non-violent resistance is commended as the best method of defeating your foe, particularly as the best method of breaking his morale. It is suggested that Christ ended his life on the Cross because he had not completely mastered the technique of non-violence, and must for this reason be regarded as a guide who is inferior to Gandhi, but whose significance lies in initiating a movement which culminates in Gandhi.

One may well concede that a wise and decent statesmanship will seek not only to avoid conflict, but to avoid violence in conflict. Parliamentary political controversy is one method of sublimating political struggles in such a way as to avoid violent collisions of interest. But this pragmatic distinction has nothing to do with the more basic distinction between the ethic of the "Kingdom of God," in which no concession is made to human sin, and all relative political strategies which, assuming human sinfulness, seek to secure the highest measure of peace and justice among selfish and sinful men.

A PREFERENCE FOR TYRANNY

If pacifists were less anxious to dilute the ethic of Christ to make it conform to their particular type of non-violent politics, and if they were less obsessed with the obvious contradiction between the ethic of Christ and the fact of war, they might have noticed that the injunction "resist not evil" is only part and parcel of a total ethic which we violate not only in war-time, but every day of our life, and that overt conflict is but a final and vivid revelation of the character of human existence. This total ethic can be summarized most succinctly in the two injunctions "Be not anxious for your life" and "love thy neighbor as thyself."

In the first of these, attention is called to the fact that the root and source of all undue self-assertion lies in the anxiety which all men have in regard to their existence. The ideal possibility is that perfect trust in God's providence ("for your heavenly father knoweth what things ye have need of") and perfect unconcern for the physical life ("fear not them which are able to kill the body") would create a state of serenity in which one life would not seek to take advantage of another life. But the fact is that anxiety is an inevitable concomitant of human freedom, and is the root of the inevitable sin which expresses itself in every human activity and creativity. Not even the most idealistic preacher who admonishes his congregation to obey the law of Christ is free of the sin which arises from anxiety. He may or may not be anxious for his job, but he is certainly anxious about his prestige. Perhaps he is anxious for his reputation as a righteous man. He may be tempted to preach a perfect ethic more vehemently in order to hide an unconscious apprehension of the fact that his own life does not conform to it. There is no one who does not violate the injunction "Be not anxious." That is the tragedy of human sin. It is the tragedy of man who is dependent upon God, but seeks to make himself independent and self-sufficing.

In the same way there is no life which is not involved in a violation of the injunction, "Thou shalt love they neighbor as thyself." No one is so blind as the idealist who tells us that war would be unnecessary "if only" nations obeyed the law of Christ, but who remains unconscious of the fact that even the most saintly life is involved in some measure of contradiction to this law. Have we not all known loving fathers and mothers who, despite a very genuine love for their children, had to be resisted if justice and freedom were to be gained for the children? Do we not know that the sinful will-to-power may be compounded with the most ideal motives and may use the latter as its instruments and vehicles? The collective life of man undoubtedly stands on a lower moral plane than the life of individuals; yet nothing revealed in the life of races and nations is unknown in individual life. The sins of pride and of lust for power and the consequent tyranny and injustice are all present, at least in an inchoate form, in individual life. Even as I write my little five-year-old boy comes to me with the tale of an attack made upon him by his year-old sister. This tale is concocted to escape paternal judgment for being too rough in playing with his sister. One is reminded of Germany's claim that Poland was the aggressor and the similar Russian charge against Finland.

The pacifists do not know human nature well enough to be concerned about the contradictions between the law of love and the sin of man, until sin has conceived and brought forth death. They do not see that sin introduces an element of conflict into the world and that even the most loving relationships are not free of it. They are, consequently, unable to appreciate the complexity of the problem of justice. They merely assert that if only men had loved one another, all the complex, and sometimes horrible realities of the political order could be dispensed with. They do not see that their "if" begs the most basic problem of human history. It is because men are sinners that justice can be achieved only by a certain degree of coercion on the one hand, and the resistance to coercion and tyranny on the other hand. The political life of man must constantly steer between the Scylla of anarchy and the Charybdis of tyranny.

Human egotism makes large-scale co-operation upon a purely voluntary basis impossible. Governments must coerce. Yet there is an element of evil in this coercion. It is always in danger of serving the purposes of the coercing power rather than the general weal. We cannot fully trust the motives of any ruling class or power. That is why it is important to maintain democratic checks upon the centers of power. It may also be necessary to resist a ruling class, nation or race, if it violates the standards of relative justice which have been set up for it. Such resistance means war. It need not mean overt conflict or violence. But if those who resist tyranny publish their scruples against violence too publicly the tyrannical power need only threaten the use of violence against non-violent pressure to persuade the resisters to quiescence. (The relation of pacifism to the abortive effort to apply non-violent sanctions against Italy in the Ethiopian dispute is instructive at this point.)

The refusal to recognize that sin introduces an element of conflict into the world invariably means that a morally perverse preference is given to tyranny over anarchy (war). If we are told that tyranny would destroy itself, if only we would not challenge it, the obvious answer is that tyranny continues to grow if it is not resisted. If it is to be resisted, the risk of overt conflict must be taken. The thesis that German tyranny must not be challenged by other nations because Germany will throw off this yoke in due time, merely means that an unjustified moral preference is given to civil war over international war, for internal resistance runs the risk of conflict as much as external resistance. Furthermore, no consideration is given to the fact that a tyrannical State may grow too powerful to be successfully resisted by purely internal pressure, and that the injustices which it does to other than its own nationals may rightfully lay the problem of the tyranny upon other nations.

It is not unfair to assert that most pacifists who seek to present their religious absolutism as a political alternative to the claims and counterclaims, the pressures and counter-pressures of the political order invariably betray themselves into this preference for tyranny. Tyranny is not war. It is peace, but it is peace which has nothing to do with the peace of the Kingdom of God. It is a peace which results from one will establishing a complete dominion over other wills and reducing them to acquiescence.

One of the most terrible consequences of a confused religious absolutism is that it is forced to condone such tyranny as that of Germany in the nations which it has conquered and now cruelly oppresses. It usually does this by insisting that the tyranny is no worse than that which is practised in the so-called democratic nations. Whatever may be the moral ambiguities of the so-called democratic nations, and however serious may be their failure to conform perfectly to the democratic ideals, it is a sheer moral perversity to equate the inconsistencies of a democratic civilization with the brutalities which modern tyrannical States practise. If we cannot make a distinction here, there are no historical distinctions which have any value. All the distinctions upon which the fate of civilization has turned in the history of mankind have been just such relative distinctions.

One is persuaded to thank God in such times as these that the common people maintain a degree of "common sense," that they preserve an uncorrupted ability to react against injustice and the cruelty of racial bigotry. This ability has been lost among some Christian idealists who preach the law of love but forget that they, as well as all other men, are involved in the violation of that law; and who must (in order to obscure this glaring defect in their theory) eliminate all relative distinctions in history and praise the peace of tyranny as if it were nearer to the peace of the Kingdom of God than war. The overt conflicts of human history are periods of judgment when what has been hidden becomes revealed. It is the business of Christian prophecy to anticipate these judgments to some degree at least, to call attention to the fact that when men say "peace and quiet" "destruction will come upon them unaware," and reveal to what degree this overt destruction is a vivid portrayal of the constant factor of sin in human life. A theology which fails to come to grips with this tragic factor of sin is heretical, both from the standpoint of the gospel and in terms of its blindness to obvious facts of human experience in every realm and on every level of moral goodness.

THE RENAISSANCE SPIRIT

The gospel is something more than the law of love. The gospel deals with the fact that men violate the law of love. The gospel presents Christ as the pledge and revelation of God's mercy which finds man in his rebellion and overcomes his sin.

The question is whether the grace of Christ is primarily a power of righteousness which so heals the sinful heart that henceforth it is able to fulfill the law of love; or whether it is primarily the assurance of divine mercy for a persistent sinfulness which man never overcomes completely. When St. Paul declared: "I am crucified with Christ; nevertheless I live, yet it is no more I that live but Christ that dwelleth in me," did he mean that the new life in Christ was not his own by reason of the fact that grace, rather than his own power, enabled him to live on the new level of righteousness? Or did he mean that the new life was his only in intention and by reason of God's willingness to accept intention for achievement? Was the emphasis upon sanctification or justification?

This is the issue upon which the Protestant Reformation separated itself from classical Catholicism, believing that Thomistic interpretations of grace lent themselves to new forms of self-righteousness in place of the Judaistic-legalistic self-righteousness which St. Paul condemned. If one studies the whole thought of St. Paul, one is almost forced to the conclusion that he was not himself quite certain whether the peace which he had found in Christ was a moral peace, the peace of having become what man truly is; or whether it was primarily a religious peace, the peace of being "completely known and all forgiven," of being accepted by God despite the continued sinfulness of the heart. Perhaps St. Paul could not be quite sure about where the emphasis was to be placed, for the simple reason that no one can be quite certain about the character of his ultimate peace. There must be, and there is, moral content in it, a fact which Reformation theology tends to deny and which Catholic and sectarian theology emphasizes. But there is never such perfect moral content in it that any man could find perfect peace through his moral achievements, not even the achievements which he attributes to grace rather than the power of his own will. This is the truth which the Reformation emphasized and which modern Protestant Christianity has almost completely forgotten.

We are, therefore, living in a state of sorry moral and religious confusion. In the very moment of world history in which every contemporary historical event justifies the Reformation emphasis upon the persistence of sin on every level of moral achievement, we not only identify Protestant faith with a moralistic sentimentality which neglects and obscures truths in the Christian gospel (which it was the mission of the Reformation to rescue from obscurity), but we even neglect those reservations and qualifications upon the theory of sanctification upon which classical Catholicism wisely insisted.

We have, in other words, reinterpreted the Christian gospel in terms of the Renaissance faith in man. Modern pacifism is merely a final fruit of this Renaissance spirit, which has pervaded the whole of modern Protestantism. We have interpreted world history as a gradual ascent to the

Kingdom of God which waits for the final triumph only upon the willingness of Christians to "take Christ seriously." There is nothing in Christ's own teachings, except dubious interpretations of the parable of the leaven and the mustard seed, to justify this interpretation of world history. In the whole of the New Testament, Gospels and Epistles alike, there is only one interpretation of world history. That pictures history as moving toward a climax in which both Christ and anti-Christ are revealed.

The New Testament does not, in other words, envisage a simple triumph of good over evil in history. It sees human history involved in the contradiction of sin to the end. That is why it sees no simple resolution of the problem of history. It believes that the Kingdom of God will finally resolve the contradictions of history; but for it the Kingdom of God is no simple historical possibility. The grace of God for man and the Kingdom of God for history are both divine realities and not human possibilities.

The Christian faith believes that the Atonement reveals God's mercy as an ultimate resource by which God alone overcomes the judgment which sin deserves. If this final truth of the Christian religion has no meaning to modern men, including modern Christians, that is because even the tragic character of contemporary history has not yet persuaded them to take the fact of human sinfulness seriously.

THE LAW OF LOVE

The contradiction between the law of love and the sinfulness of man raises not only the ultimate religious problem how men are to have peace if they do not overcome the contradiction, and how history will culminate if the contradiction remains on every level of historic achievement; it also raises the immediate problem how men are to achieve a tolerable harmony of life with life, if human pride and selfishness prevent the realization of the law of love.

The pacifists are quite right in one emphasis. They are right in asserting that love is really the law of life. It is not some ultimate possibility which has nothing to do with human history. The freedom of man, his transcendence over the limitations of nature and over all historic and traditional social situations, makes any form of human community which falls short of the law of love less than the best. Only by a voluntary giving of life to life and a free interpenetration of personalities could man do justice both to the freedom of other personalities and the necessity of community between personalities. The law of love therefore remains a principle of criticism over all forms of community in which elements of coercion and conflict destroy the highest type of fellowship.

To look at human communities from the perspective of the Kingdom of God is to know that there is a sinful element in all the expedients which the political order uses to establish justice. That is why even the seemingly most stable justice degenerates periodically into either tyranny or anarchy. But it must also be recognized that it is not possible to eliminate the sinful element in the political expedients. They are, in the words of St. Augustine, both the consequence of, and the remedy for, sin. If they are the remedy for sin, the ideal of love is not merely a principle of indiscriminate criticism upon all approximations of justice. It is also a principle of discriminate criticism between forms of justice.

As a principle of indiscriminate criticism upon all forms of justice, the law of love reminds us that the injustice and tyranny against which we contend in the foe is partially the consequence of our own injustice, that the pathology of modern Germans is partially a consequence of the vindictiveness of the peace of Versailles, and that the ambition of a tyrannical imperialism is different only in degree and not in kind from the imperial impulse which characterizes all human life.

The Christian faith ought to persuade us that political controversies are always conflicts between sinners and not between righteous men and sinners. It ought to mitigate the self-righteousness which is an inevitable concomitant of all human conflict. The spirit of contrition is an important ingredient in the sense of justice. If it is powerful enough it may be able to restrain the impulse of vengeance sufficiently to allow a decent justice to emerge. This is an important issue facing Europe in anticipation of the conclusion of the present war. It cannot be denied that the Christian conscience failed terribly in restraining vengeance after the last war. It is also quite obvious that the natural inclination to self-righteousness was the primary force of this vengeance (expressed particularly in the war guilt clause of the peace treaty). The pacifists draw the conclusion from the fact that justice is never free from vindictiveness, that we ought not for this reason ever to contend against a foe. This argument leaves out of account that capitulation to the foe might well subject us to a worse vindictiveness. It is as foolish to imagine that the foe is free of the sin which we deplore in ourselves as it is to regard ourselves as free of the sin which we deplore in the foe.

The fact that our own sin is always partly the cause of the sins against which we must contend is regarded by simple moral purists as proof that we have no right to contend against this foe. They regard the injunction "Let him who is without sin cast the first stone" as a simple alternative to the schemes of justice which society has devised and whereby it prevents the worst forms of anti-social conduct. This injunction of Christ ought to remind every judge and every juridical tribunal that the crime of the criminal is partly the consequence of the sins of society. But if pacifists are to be consistent they ought to advocate the abolition of the whole judicial process in society. It is perfectly true that national societies have more impartial instruments of justice than international society possesses to date. Nevertheless, no impartial court is as impartial as it pretends to be, and there is no judicial process which is completely free of vindictiveness. Yet we cannot dispense with it; and we will have to continue to put criminals into jail. There is a point where the final cause of the criminal's anti-social conduct becomes a fairly irrelevant issue in comparison with the task of preventing his conduct from injuring innocent fellows.

The ultimate principles of the Kingdom of God are never irrelevant to any problem of justice, and they hover over every social situation as an ideal possibility; but that does not mean that they can be made into simple alternatives for the present schemes of relative justice. The thesis that the so-called democratic nations have no right to resist overt forms of tyranny, because their own history betrays imperialistic motives, would have meaning only if it were possible to achieve a perfect form of justice in any nation and to free national life completely of the imperialistic motive. This is impossible; for imperialism is the collective expression of the sinful will-to-power which characterizes all human existence. The pacifist argument on this issue betrays how completely pacifism gives itself to illusions about the stuff with which it is dealing in human nature. These illusions deserve particular censure, because no one who knows his own heart very well ought to be given to such illusions.

The recognition of the law of love as an indiscriminate principle of criticism over all attempts at social and international justice is actually a resource of justice, for it prevents the pride, self-righteousness and vindictiveness of men from corrupting their efforts at justice. But it must be recognized that love is also a principle of discriminate criticism between various forms of community and various attempts at justice. The closest approximation to a love in which life supports life in voluntary community is a justice in which life is prevented from destroying life and the interests of the one are guarded against unjust claims by the other. Such justice is achieved when impartial tribunals of society prevent men "from being judges in their own cases," in the words of John Locke. But the tribunals of justice merely codify certain equilibria of power. Justice is basically dependent upon a balance of power. Whenever an individual or a group or a nation possesses undue power, and whenever this power is not checked by the possibility of criticizing and resisting it, it grows inordinate. The equilibrium of power upon which every structure of justice rests would degenerate into anarchy but for the organizing center which controls it. One reason why the balances of power, which prevent injustice in international relations, periodically degenerate into overt anarchy is because no way has yet been found to establish an adequate organizing center, a stable international judicatory, for this balance of power.

A balance of power is something different from, and inferior to, the harmony of love. It is a basic condition of justice, given the sinfulness of man. Such a balance of power does not exclude love. In fact, without love the frictions and tensions of a balance of power would become intolerable. But without the balance of power even the most loving relations may degenerate into unjust relations, and love may become the screen which hides the injustice. Family relations are instructive at this point. Women did not gain justice from men, despite the intimacy of family relations, until they secured sufficient economic power to challenge male autocracy. There are Christian "idealists" today who speak sentimentally of love as the only way to justice, whose family life might benefit from a more delicate "balance of power."

Naturally the tensions of such a balance may become overt; and overt tensions may degenerate into conflict. The center of power, which has the function of preventing this anarchy of conflict, may also degenerate into tyranny. There is no perfectly adequate method of preventing either anarchy or tyranny. But obviously the justice established in the so-called democratic nations represents a high degree of achievement; and the achievement becomes the more impressive when it is compared with the tyranny into which alternative forms of society have fallen. The obvious evils of tyranny, however, will not inevitably persuade the victims of economic anarchy in democratic society to eschew tyranny. When men suffer from anarchy they may foolishly regard the evils of tyranny as the lesser evils. Yet the evils of tyranny in fascist and communist nations are so patent, that we may dare to hope that what is still left of democratic civilizations will not lightly sacrifice the virtues of democracy for the sake of escaping its defects.

We have a very vivid and conclusive evidence about the probable consequences of a tyrannical unification of Europe. The nature of the German rule in the conquered nations of Europe gives us the evidence. There are too many contingent factors in various national and international schemes of justice to justify any unqualified endorsement of even the most democratic structure of justice as "Christian." Yet it must be obvious that any social structure in which power has been made responsible, and in which anarchy has been overcome by methods of mutual accommodation, is preferable to either anarchy or tyranny. If it is not possible to express a moral preference for the justice achieved in democratic societies, in comparison with tyrannical societies, no historical preference has any meaning. This kind of justice approximates the harmony of love more than either anarchy or tyranny.

If we do not make discriminate judgments between social systems we weaken the resolution to defend and extend civilization. Pacifism either tempts us to make no judgments at all, or to give an undue preference to tyranny in comparison with the momentary anarchy which is necessary to overcome tyranny. It must be admitted that the anarchy of war which results from resistance to tyranny is not always creative; that, at given periods of history, civilization may lack the resource to fashion a new and higher form of unity out of momentary anarchy. The defeat of Germany and the frustration of the Nazi effort to unify Europe in tyrannical terms is a negative task. It does not guarantee the emergence of a new Europe with a higher level of international cohesion and new organs of international justice. But it is a negative task which cannot be avoided. All schemes for avoiding this negative task rest upon illusions about human nature. Specifically, these illusions express themselves in the failure to understand the stubbornness and persistence of the tyrannical will, once it is fully conceived. It would not require great argumentative skill to prove that Nazi tyranny never could have reached such proportions as to be able to place the whole of Europe under its ban, if sentimental illusions about the character of evil which Europe was facing had not been combined with less noble motives for tolerating Nazi aggression.

A simple Christian moralism is senseless and confusing. It is senseless when, as in the World War, it seeks uncritically to identify the cause of Christ with the cause of democracy without a religious reservation. It is just as senseless when it seeks to purge itself of this error by an uncritical refusal to make any distinctions between relative values in history. The fact is that we might as well dispense with the Christian faith entirely if it is our conviction that we can act in history only if we are guiltless. This means that we must either prove our guiltlessness in order to be able to act; or refuse to act because we cannot achieve guiltlessness. Self-righteousness or inaction are the alternatives of secular moralism. If they are also the only alternatives of Christian moralism, one rightly suspects that Christian faith has become diluted with secular perspectives.

In its profoundest insights the Christian faith sees the whole of human history as involved in guilt, and finds no release from guilt except in the grace of God. The Christian is freed by that grace to act in history; to give his devotion to the highest values he knows; to defend those citadels of civilization of which necessity and historic destiny have made him the defender; and he is persuaded by that grace to remember the ambiguity of even his best actions. If the providence of God does not enter the affairs of men to bring good out of evil, the evil in our good may easily destroy our most ambitious efforts and frustrate our highest hopes.

FACING UP TO SIN

Despite our conviction that most modern pacifism is too filled with secular and moralistic illusions to be of the highest value to the Christian community, we may be grateful for the fact that the Christian Church has learned, since the last war, to protect its pacifists and to appreciate their testimony. Even when this testimony is marred by self-righteousness, because it does not proceed from a sufficiently profound understanding of the tragedy of human history, it has its value.

It is a terrible thing to take human life. The conflict between man and man and nation and nation is tragic. If there are men who declare that, no matter what the consequences, they cannot bring themselves to participate in this slaughter, the Church ought to be able to say to the general community: We quite understand this scruple and we respect it. It proceeds from the conviction that the true end of man is brotherhood, and that love is the law of life. We who allow ourselves to become engaged in war need this testimony of the absolutist against us, lest we accept the warfare of the world as normative, lest we become callous to the horror of war, and lest we forget the ambiguity of our own actions and motives and the risk we run of achieving no permanent good from this momentary anarchy in which we are involved.

But we have a right to remind the absolutists that their testimony against us would be more effective if it were not corrupted by self-righteousness and were not accompanied by the implicit or explicit accusation of apostasy. A pacifism which really springs from the Christian faith, without secular accretions and corruptions, could not be as certain as modern pacifism is that it possesses an alternative for the conflicts and tensions from which and through which the world must rescue a precarious justice.

A truly Christian pacifism would set each heart under the judgment of God to such a degree that even the pacifist idealist would know that knowledge of the will of God is no guarantee of his ability or willingness to obey it. The idealist would recognize to what degree he is himself involved in rebellion against God, and would know that this rebellion is too serious to be overcome by just one more sermon on love, and one more challenge to man to obey the law of Christ.

Christian Faith
and the World Crisis
Christianity and Crisis, February 10, 1941

It is our purpose to devote this modest journal to an exposition of our Christian faith in its relation to world events. This first article will seek, therefore, to offer a general introduction to the faith that is in us. We believe that many current interpretations have obscured important elements in that faith and have thereby confused the Christian conscience. This confusion has been brought into sharp relief by the world crisis; but it existed before the crisis, and it may well continue after the crisis is over. We therefore regard our task as one that transcends the urgent problems of the hour, though we do not deny that these problems are the immediate occasion for our enterprise.

At the present moment a basic difference of conviction with regard to what Christianity is and what it demands runs through the whole of American Protestantism and cuts across all the traditional denominational distinctions. There is, on the one hand, a school of Christian thought that believes war could be eliminated if only Christians and other men of good will refused resolutely enough to have anything to do with conflict. Another school of thought, while conceding that war is one of the most vivid revelations of sin in human history, does not find the disavowal of war so simple a matter. The proponents of the latter position believe that there are historic situations in which refusal to defend the inheritance of a civilization, however imperfect, against tyranny and aggression may result in consequences even worse than war.

This journal intends to express and, if possible, to clarify this second viewpoint. We do not believe that the Christian faith as expressed in the New Testament and as interpreted in historic Christianity, both Catholic and Protestant, implies the confidence that evil and injustice in history can be overcome by such simple methods as are currently equated with Christianity. We believe that modern Christian perfectionism is tinctured with utopianism derived from a secular culture. In our opinion this utopianism contributed to the tardiness of the democracies in defending themselves against the perils of a new barbarism, and (in America at least) it is easily compounded with an irresponsible and selfish nationalism.

We intend this journal to be both polemic and irenic, as far as human frailty will permit the combination of these two qualities. It will be polemic in the sense that we shall combat what seem to us false interpretations of our faith, and consequent false analyses of our world and of our duties in it. It will be irenic in the sense that we shall seek to appreciate the extent to which perfectionist and pacifist interpretations of Christianity are derived from genuine and important elements in our common faith.

Perfectionists are right in their conviction that our civilization stands under the judgment of God; no one can have an easy conscience about the social and political anarchy out of which the horrible tyranny that now threatens us arose. But they are wrong in assuming that we have no right or duty to defend a civilization, despite its imperfections, against worse alternatives. They are right in insisting that love is the ultimate law of life. But they have failed to realize to what degree the sinfulness of all men, even the best, makes justice between competing interests and conflicting wills a perennial necessity of history.

The perfectionists rightly recognize that it may be very noble for an individual to sacrifice his life or interests rather than participate in the claims and counterclaims of the struggle for justice (of which war may always be the *ultima ratio*). They are wrong in making no distinction between an individual act of self-abnegation and a political policy of submission to injustice, whereby lives and interests other than our own are defrauded or destroyed. They seek erroneously to build a political platform upon individual perfection. Medieval perfectionism, whatever its limitations, wisely avoided these errors. It excluded even the family from the possible consequences of an individual's absolute ethic, and it was profoundly aware of the impossibility of making its rigorous standards universal.

We believe that there are many Christians whose moral inclinations might persuade them to take the same view of current problems as our own, except for the fact that they are inhibited by religious presuppositions that they regard as more "purely" Christian than those represented by the consensus of the Church through all the ages. Therefore we will begin with an analysis of these religious presuppositions.

Christians are agreed that the God who is revealed in Christ is source and end of our existence and that therefore his character and will are the norm and standard of our conduct. It is only in recent decades, however, that it has been believed that the "gentleness" of Jesus was a sufficient and final revelation of the character of God, that this character was one of pure love and mercy, and that this revelation stood in contradiction to an alleged portrayal of a God of wrath in the Old Testament.

Both the Old and the New Testament take the wrath of God as well as the mercy of God seriously. The divine mercy, apprehended by Christian faith in the life and death of Christ, is not some simple kindness indifferent to good and evil. The whole point of the Christian doctrine of Atonement is that God cannot be merciful without fulfilling within himself, and on man's behalf, the requirements of divine justice. However difficult it may be to give a fully rational account of what Christ's atoning death upon the Cross means to Christian faith, this mystery, never fully comprehended by and yet not wholly incomprehensible to faith, speaks to us of a mercy that transcends but also satisfies the demands of Justice.

The biblical answer to the problem of evil in human history is a radical answer, precisely because human evil is recognized as a much more stubborn fact than is realized in some modern versions of the Christian faith. These versions do not take the problem of justice in history seriously, because they have obscured what the Bible has to say about the relation of justice to mercy in the very heart of God. Every sensitive Christian must feel a sense of unworthiness when he is compelled by historic destiny to act as an instrument of God's justice. Recognition of the common guilt that makes him and his enemy kin must persuade him to imitate the mercy of God, even while he seeks to fulfill the demands of justice. But he will seek to elude such responsibilities only if he believes, as many modern Christians do, that he might, if he tried a little harder, achieve an individual or collective vantage point of guiltlessness from which to proceed against evil doers. There is no such vantage point.

Christians are agreed that Christ must be the norm of our human life as well as the revelation of the character of God. But many modern versions of Christianity have forgotten to what degree the perfect love of Christ was recognized both in the Bible and in the Christian ages as finally transcending all historic possibilities. The same St. Paul who admonishes us to grow into the stature of Christ insists again and again that we are "saved by faith" and not "by works"; which is to say that our final peace is not the moral peace of having become what Christ defines as our true nature but is the religious peace of knowing that a divine mercy accepts our loyalty to Christ despite our continued betrayal of him.

It cannot be denied that these emphases are full of pitfalls for the faithful. On the one side there is always the possibility that we will not take Christ as our norm seriously enough, and that we will rest prematurely in the divine mercy. On the other hand an abstract perfectionism is tempted to obscure the most obvious facts about human nature and to fall into the fury of self-righteousness. The Protestant Reformation was in part a protest against what seemed to the Reformers an overly optimistic Catholic doctrine of human perfection through the infusion of divine grace. Yet modern Protestant interpretations of the same issue make the Catholic doctrine wise and prudent by comparison.

Once it is recognized that the stubbornness of human selfishness makes the achievement of justice in human society no easy matter, it ought to be possible to see that war is but a vivid revelation of certain perennial aspects of human history. Life is never related to life in terms of a perfect and loving conformity of will with will. Where there is sin and selfishness there must also be a struggle for justice; and this justice is always partially an achievement of our love for the other and partially a result of our yielding to his demands and pressures. The intermediate norm of justice is particularly important in the institutional and collective relationships of mankind. But even in individual and personal relations the ultimate level of sacrificial self-giving is not reached without an intermediate level of justice. On this level the first consideration is not that life should be related to life through the disinterested concern of each for the other, but that life should be prevented from exploiting, enslaving or taking advantage of other life. Sometimes this struggle takes very tragic forms.

It is important for Christians to remember that every structure of justice, as embodied in political and economic institutions, (a) contains elements of injustice that stand in contradiction to the law of love; (b) contains higher possibilities of justice that must be realized in terms of institutions and structures; and (c) that it must be supplemented by the graces of individual and personal generosity and mercy. Yet when the mind is not confused by utopian illusions it is not difficult to recognize genuine achievements of justice and to feel under obligation to defend them against the threats of tyranny and the negation of justice.

Love must be regarded as the final flower and fruit of justice. When it is substituted for justice it degenerates into sentimentality and may become the accomplice of tyranny.

Looking at the tragic contemporary scene within this frame of reference, we feel that American Christianity is all too prone to disavow its responsibilities for the preservation of our civilization against the perils of totalitarian aggression. We are well aware of the sins of all the nations, including our own, which have contributed to the chaos of our era. We know to what degree totalitarianism represents false answers to our own unsolved problems—political, economic, spiritual.

Yet we believe the task of defending the rich inheritance of our civilization to be an imperative one, however much we might desire that our social system were more worthy of defense. We believe that the possibility of correcting its faults and extending its gains may be annulled for centuries if this external peril is not resolutely faced. We do not find it particularly impressive to celebrate one's sensitive conscience by enlarging upon all the well-known evils of our western world and equating them with the evils of the totalitarian systems. It is just as important for Christians to be discriminating in their judgments, as for them to recognize the element of sin in all human endeavors. We think it dangerous to allow religious sensitivity to obscure the fact that Nazi tyranny intends to annihilate the Jewish race, to subject the nations of Europe to the dominion of a "master" race, to extirpate the Christian religion, to annul the liberties and legal standards that are the priceless heritage of ages of Christian and humanistic culture, to make truth the prostitute of political power, to seek world dominion through its satraps and allies, and generally to destroy the very fabric of our western civilization.

Our own national tardiness in becoming fully alive to this peril has been compounded of national selfishness and religious confusion. In recent months American opinion has begun to respond to the actualities of the situation and to sense the fateful destiny that unites us with all free peoples, whether momentarily overrun by the aggressor or still offering heroic resistance. How far our assistance is to be carried is a matter of policy and strategy. It could be a matter of principle only if it were conceded that an absolute line could be drawn in terms of Christian principle between "measures short of war" and war itself. But those who think such a line can be drawn have nevertheless opposed measures short of war. They rightly have pointed out that such measures cannot be guaranteed against the risk of total involvement.

The measures now being taken for the support of the democracies are a logical expression of the unique conditions of America's relation to the world. They do justice on the one hand to our responsibilities for a common civilization that transcends the hemispheres, and on the other hand to the fact that we are not as immediately imperiled as other nations. Whether our freedom from immediate peril will enable us to persevere in the reservations that we still maintain cannot be decided in the abstract. The exigencies of the future must determine the issue.

We cannot, of course, be certain that defeat of the Nazis will usher in a new order of international justice in Europe and the world. We do know what a Nazi victory would mean, and our first task must therefore be to prevent it. Yet it cannot be our only task, for the problem of organizing the technical civilization of the western world upon a new basis of economic and international justice, so that the anarchy and decay that have characterized our life in the past three decades will be arrested and our technical capacities will be made fruitful rather than suicidal, is one which must engage our best resources. We must give some thought and attention to this great issue even while we are forced to ward off a horrible alternative.

We believe that the Christian faith can and must make its own contribution to this issue. The task of building a new world, as well as the tragic duty of saving the present world from tyranny, will require resources of understanding and resolution which are inherent in the Christian faith. The profoundest insights of the Christian faith cannot be expressed by the simple counsel that men ought to be more loving, and that if they became so the problems of war and of international organization would solve themselves.

Yet there are times when hopes for the future, as well as contrition over past misdeeds, must be subordinated to the urgent, immediate task. In this instance, the immediate task is the defeat of Nazi tyranny. If this task does not engage us, both our repentance and our hope become luxuries in which we indulge while other men save us from an intolerable fate, or while our inaction betrays into disaster a cause to which we owe allegiance.

NOTES

1. "What I Believe," in *The Nation*, March 3, 1940.
2. Meno Simons (1496–1561) was the leader of the pacifist branch of the Dutch Anabaptists whose followers became Mennonites.
3. Luke xxii, 36.
4. Joseph Goebbels was the master propagandist of the Nazi regime and dictator of its cultural life for twelve years.

9

✝

Karl Barth

German Confessing Church
The University at Basel, Switzerland

O n September 30, 1938, just days after the Munich Agreement that surrendered Czechoslovakia into Nazi hands, Swiss theologian Karl Barth wrote in his diary: "Catastrophe of European liberty in Munich." He then sent a letter to Czech soldiers, explaining why resistance to Hitler was a service to Christ. Barth was out of step with the vast majority of religious thinkers on both sides of the Atlantic, who saw salvation at Munich: Patient diplomacy, they said, had averted another European war.

Barth claimed no prophetic gift, but he knew Hitlerism. He had studied and taught theology in Germany in the 1920s and 1930s and watched the emergence of the National Socialist Party—and fought it at every turn. He joined with Dietrich Bonhoeffer to play a leading role in the *Kirchenkampf*, the struggle to prevent the Nazi takeover of the German Evangelical Church. He refused to take the oath of loyalty to Hitler. And he wrote the 1934 Barmen Declaration, a defiant statement of Christian orthodoxy and one of the few corporate challenges to Nazi paganism. By 1935 Barth was dismissed from his teaching post in Bonn and settled in Basle, Switzerland.

Barth was also well aware of the church's entanglement with war and careless identification with nationalism. When World War I broke out in August 1914, he watched with disgust as ninety-three German intellectuals—some of them his former theology professors—issued a declaration supporting the kaiser's war aims as essential to defending Christian civilization. That "black day," as he called it, sent him on a spiritual journey. Along the way, he wrote *The Epistle to the Romans* and *The Word of God and the Word of Man*, towering works that reaffirmed the Bible's emphasis on God's transcendence and human weakness and finitude.

Liberal churchmen, Barth concluded, had reduced God to little more than an exaggerated projection of mankind. The result was an impoverished theology and a politics of moral ambivalence. Looking back years later on the events of 1938–41, he lamented the failure of will that liberal theology had produced. "The foe of Czech and European freedom proved in those days again and again that his force would have to be met by force," he said. "The peace at any price which the world, and also the churches, sought at that time was neither human nor Christian."

When Barth wrote the following letters to churches in Europe, he was the best known and most influential Christian thinker of his day. No one did more to revive Protestant theology in the twentieth century. Indeed, by the 1930s, Barth's "neo-orthodoxy" was having a profound influence on young American theologians, especially those arguing for American intervention. Some of the major themes of Barth's theology resonate throughout the letters: the lordship of Jesus Christ over the whole of life and the role of the state in expressing Jesus' sovereign rule on earth.

In his "First Letter to the French Protestants," written shortly after Britain and France had declared war on Germany, Barth argues that securing a just peace will be impossible without fighting and suffering for it. Opposition to war, based on the assertion that none of the countries involved are wholly innocent, is called a cynical evasion. "The apprehension of the truth that God alone is holy," he writes, "will not excuse us from the duty of putting up resistance today."

By the time Barth drafted his "Second Letter to the French Protestants," France had fallen into German hands. There was much talk about the necessity of "preaching Christ crucified," meaning a refusal to resist Nazi rule. Barth warns that the same spirit influenced German Christians in 1933, when the Nazis came to power. "Be perfectly clear that the demonic power of National Socialism . . . is connected with the fact that Christianity in Germany did thus retreat."

In the final letter, Barth assures his readers that the cause of Christians in England is the cause of the universal church. Though denying that the fight against Nazism is a war of religion, he nevertheless insists that it must be waged—"and waged ardently"—as an act of Christian obedience. "The obedience of the Christian to the clear will of God compels him to support this war," he writes. "The Kingly rule of Christ extends not merely over the Church . . . it also confronts and overrules with sovereign dignity the principalities and powers and evil spirits of this world."

First Letter to the French Protestants
December 1939

As you say in your letter, three-quarters of the French theologians whom I had the privilege of meeting and with whom I had the privilege of working in Biévres in January this year are to-day serving your country in a military capacity at the front or elsewhere. You invite me to send to them and to my other friends in France a message through *Foi et Vie*. I do so with great pleasure, since it gives me the opportunity of telling you what moves me at this present time as I think of you all.

Our situation here in Basle is such that we cannot possibly shut our eyes to the war. Only a few kilometres from here the fortifications begin. On the right are the German fortifications and on the left the French. The pilots of both sides are, I am afraid, in the habit of forgetting that they have no business in the air above our heads. It has even happened that certain undesirable objects have fallen from above upon our territory. In the midst of our streets the barricades and barbed wire of our defences bristle ready to meet an even worse menace. Such are the circumstances in which I have to expound the peaceful mysteries of Christian Dogmatics, just now the Doctrine of Predestination.

But what is that compared with the problems and cares which are your concerns to-day—you yourselves, your families, your congregations and the whole Reformed Church of your land? You may rest assured that I myself and many others in our still "neutral" part of the world realize what turmoils and hardships, what sacrifices and temptations events have brought and continue to bring to you. We know, too, that we are bound as Christians to share with you and with everyone in the belligerent countries in your anxiety and affliction: and we do this from the bottom of our hearts. You will not, dear friends, misinterpret the fact that we Swiss form at present an island of "neutrality" from a military point of view. At the moment there is no other possibility. The causes of the present war lie in the international decisions of 1919 in which our country did not take part. And since that date (as before) high politics in Europe have developed without our co-operation. Switzerland would become guilty of the same arbitrary methods in politics, the curbing of which is the task of to-day, if she voluntarily disregarded her repeatedly declared policy and entered the war as a belligerent without the compulsion of external pressure. For the moment we have a duty towards the whole of Europe—the duty of preserving the integrity of that piece of European order which has been entrusted precisely to us in the form of military neutrality. You will agree with me when I say that it is necessary and salutary for all nations, and not least for the Church of Jesus Christ in all nations, that there should be, as long as possible, such places through which it is possible to maintain contact between men and Christians in some sort of tranquility. Such a place is Switzerland for the time being. "Neutrality," interpreted in this sense, is laid upon us as an obligation for the time being. This neutrality signifies, not that we dissociate ourselves from The Event of our time, but that we associate ourselves with it in our own *particular* way. It signifies the special form of *our* responsibility in Europe. There are probably few Swiss who understand our "neutrality" in any other sense. At any rate I should like it to be known that I personally understand it in this sense and in this sense alone.

There can be no doubt that this war is for all of us, for belligerents and neutrals alike, a very special war, that it bears a totally different character from the war of 1914 and from nearly all the wars of previous centuries. France and England hesitated long (perhaps too long, but when one considers the grim character of this *ultima ratio*, this hesitation was certainly justified) before they took up arms to put an end to the arbitrary use of the law of might (*Faustrecht*) which the present German Government has openly proclaimed and put into practice with ever-increasing unscrupulousness. After having made Germany from end to end a land of fear and terror, Hitler's National Socialism has become to an increasing extent a menace to the whole of Europe. This menace has led to an awakening. In the midst of the sin and shame of all nations there still remains, through the goodness of God, something of law and order, of free humanity, and above all, and as that which gives meaning to all else, of freedom to proclaim the Gospel. Where Hitler reigns, even this remnant is destroyed. But Hitler is not satisfied to reign in Germany alone. When this last fact became sufficiently clear for even the blind to see, the war came. "Il faut en finir!" said your Prime Minister in the hour of decision, and his English colleague repeated this declaration. The question as to how deep this resolve and this determination go may safely be left to the sense of responsibility of these statesmen. It is certain that every Christian too, who has followed the last year with his eyes and ears opened, must, just because he is a Christian, give his own Yes and Amen to this "Il faut en finir!"

Undoubtedly, France and England have had in the past, and still have, their own imperialistic motives for waging this war. That, however, does not make any difference. Our generation would be answerable before God and before men if the attempt were *not* made to put an end to the menace of Hitler. In the end war remained the only means of achieving this purpose. France and England had to undertake the task, because they are chiefly responsible for the state of affairs which arose in Europe after 1919—because they are responsible, too, for making Hitler possible. But, now that they have undertaken the war, it cannot well be denied that in this war not only the interests of France and England are at stake, but also those of *all other* nations—in the end even the interests of the German nation itself. Herein lies the peculiarity of this war. It has arisen from the mortal jeopardy of all, and it must be waged in the defence of all. We "neutrals," too, are not neutral in so far as we know full well that the efforts and the sacrifices of this war are necessary to preserve for *us* too what is more indispensable for life than life itself. Our French and English friends, and our German friends as well, should know that we are grateful to those who, in accordance with their historical position and responsibility, have taken upon themselves the waging of this war against Hitler.

The Church of Jesus Christ cannot and will not wage war. She can and will simply pray, believe, hope, love, and proclaim and hearken to the Gospel. She knows that The Event by which we poor men are succoured in an effectual, eternal and godly way has come, comes, and will come to pass, not, according to Zechariah 4:6, by force of arms or by power or by any kind of human effort and achievement, but only by the Spirit of God. The Church therefore will not see in the cause of England and France the *causa Dei*, and she will not preach a crusade against Hitler. He who died upon the Cross died for Hitler too, and, even more, for all those bewildered men who voluntarily or involuntarily serve under his banner. But precisely because the Church knows about justification which we men cannot attain by any means for ourselves, she cannot remain indifferent. She cannot remain "neutral" in things great or small where justice is at stake, where the attempt is being made to establish a poor feeble human justice against overwhelming, flagrant injustice. Where this is at stake, there the Church cannot withhold her witness. It is the command of God that justice be done on earth; it is precisely for this purpose that God has instituted the State and given to it the sword; and, despite all the shortcomings of which it may otherwise be guilty, the State which endeavours to defend the right proves itself precisely by these endeavours to be a Just State, and may claim the obedience of everyone. It would be regrettable if the Christian Churches, which in previous wars have so often and so thoughtlessly spoken the language of nationalism and militarism, should just in this war equally thoughtlessly decide to adopt the silence of neutrality and pacifism. The Churches ought to-day to pray in all penitence and sobriety for a *just* peace, and in the same penitence and sobriety to bear witness to all the world that it is necessary and worth while to fight and to suffer for this *just* peace. They certainly ought not to persuade the democratic States that they are, so to say, the Lord's own warriors. But they ought to say to them that we are privileged to be *human* and that we must *defend* ourselves with the power of desperation against the inbreaking of open inhumanity.

The Churches owe the duty of witnessing to the Christians in Germany as well as to the whole German nation: Your cause is not just! You are mistaken! Have no more to do with this Hitler! Hands off this war! It is his war alone! Change your course while there is yet time! Why have the representatives and organs of the ecumenical movement preserved so diplomatic a silence in all these years, and even during the fatal developments of this summer and autumn, as if there were no prophetic ministry of Jesus Christ, and as if the Church had no duty of watchfulness? Why have we heard and why do we continue to hear, and that not infrequently, voices of an eschatological defeatism, a defeatism which, appealing to the truth that "the whole world lieth in the evil one," busies itself almost cynically with asserting that Hitler's present adversaries for their part are no saints either? The apprehension of the truth that God alone is holy will not excuse us from the duty of putting up a resistance to-day. On the contrary, the Church in every land will have to give much comfort in the dark times upon which, according to all appearances, we are entering. The Church, however, will only be able to give real *comfort* if she can also, without hatred or pharisaism or without any illusions concerning the goodness of any human beings, give *admonishment*, if she will earnestly and frankly say that to-day resistance is necessary.

And it will be particularly the Church of Jesus Christ that will at the same time no less clearly recognize and proclaim that other truth, that the ultimate in war—and in this war especially—cannot be war. War is like a painful yet purposeful surgical operation; it can only be waged in order to help, to heal and to secure life. The time may very soon come when there will arise in every country the urgent necessity of bringing this aspect of the matter into the foreground.

My dear French friends, you know how closely I am associated with Germany, with her Church and with her people. You will, I know, not take it amiss, if I ask you both individually and collectively, to concern yourselves even now with the question of what ought to happen if the disaster which Germany has brought upon herself is manifested in her defeat, a defeat which according to all human calculation is inevitable. At the beginning of the war the slogan was announced that the war was not directed against the German people but only against its present rulers. This was a noble formula, but it was an oversimplification of the problem. The new slogans, however, that every people gets the government it deserves, and that the whole German people must be held responsible for the actions of its government, is again too simple. The truth lies somewhere between these two poles. The German people are not wicked as a people, are not at any rate more wicked than any other people. The idea that to-day they must be punished as a whole is an idea which is impossible both from a Christian and from a human point of view. But Hitler's National

Socialism is most certainly the wicked expression of the extraordinary political stupidity, confusion and helplessness of the German people.

Let me just sketch the causes and the real significance of this fact as I understand them. The French people and the English people are no more "Christian" as a people than are the Germans. But the German people suffer from the heritage of a paganism that is mystical and that is in consequence unrestrained, unwise and illusory. And it suffers, too, from the heritage of the greatest Christian of Germany, from Martin Luther's error on the relation between Law and Gospel, between the temporal and the spiritual order and power. This error has established, confirmed and idealized the natural paganism of the German people, instead of limiting and restraining it. Every people has just such an heritage from paganism and from certain Christian errors which have strengthened this paganism. Consequently every people has its evil dreams. Hitlerism is the present evil dream of the German pagan who first became christianized in a Lutheran form. It is a particularly evil kind of dream, a dream which endangers the life both of the Germans themselves and of the rest of us as well. Apart from the torment which it has caused the dreamer himself, this dream has made the dreamer a menace for Europe. He must in the first place be rendered harmless.

It is essential that those who now face the German as an adversary in a war and all who may later find themselves face to face with him (if they will themselves think as Christians and not as heathen) should not lose sight of the fact that in this adversary they have to deal with *a sick man*. Particularly when the war is over—and even now we cannot devote too much thought to what must be done when the war is over—it will be necessary to treat him as a sick man is treated. Very firm yet very compassionate hands will then be necessary. Of course, it will be imperative to render physically impossible any further developments on the fatal course which leads from Frederick the Great through Bismarck to Hitler. It will be even more imperative to make manifest to the German people an illustration of that political wisdom which as yet is so foreign to them. By this I mean that there must be created for them *conditions of life* of such a kind that they will be prevented from going on dreaming that evil dream in some new form or other. The illusion that they can only stand their ground against other nations by terrorism must be eradicated from them by an unconditional resolve on the part of these other nations to *do justice* to Germany's real needs as they are conditioned by her geographical situation. That does not mean that Germany should be granted the freedom to become what Bismarck and Hitler wanted to make her. But it does mean that Germany should be granted the freedom to live by her own labour. It cannot be said that this freedom was granted to her in 1919, or in the period from 1919 to 1933. It is for this reason that every nation has its share in the responsibility for the rise of Hitlerism. I myself lived in Germany at the time of the occupation of the Ruhr, and, after that experience, I know what I am saying. It may be that the coming peace will have to be sterner than the peace of Versailles, sterner both politically and militarily. But it will have to be a wiser and a juster peace if all that we have gone through is not to be in vain once more. If this peace is to be wiser and more just it will have above all to show *more care and consideration*. We shall have to allow the population which occupies the wide area of Central Europe and which is set at such a disadvantage through the limitations of the natural resources in this area, to share in the means of life which other more fortunately situated nations enjoy. This must be done in such a way as will allow Germany to renounce that fatal course and to bring out her peculiar gifts—there can be no doubt of their wealth and significance—so that she may become to herself and to the other nations a blessing, and not ever and again a curse.

The long entertained desire to give Hitler "a chance" proved dangerous. But it would prove still more dangerous if, after the war, no readiness were shown to give the German nation an honest chance. The mistake of 1919–1933 must not be repeated. The present resistance to the German menace would otherwise be from the very outset without meaning. Otherwise it would be even physically impossible to destroy the German menace by political and military resistance. This is what people in France, too, should clearly realize.

But, my dear friends, I think it would be very unchristian, and therefore very imprudent, if we pondered all these considerations without at the end making the frank confession that man proposes—and it is man's duty to propose—but God alone disposes. We can and we should shoulder our responsibilities, our political responsibilities and, if need be, our military responsibilities. But it does not lie with us to determine what will be the eventual issue. And in no circumstances should we have the right to marvel or to complain if the issue were wholly different from the hope and intention, the plan and resolve which we envisage at the present. The outcome of this war is not to be predicted with absolute certainty by any calculation of man. I have no need to remind you that Germany is a doughty adversary. You must not think merely of her *capacity for military achievement*, but perhaps still more of the almost unaccountable *capacity for suffering* which the German people possess. This last is one of the best features of their natural and Lutheran heritages. And somewhere behind Germany stand the great enigmas of Russia, and of Italy too, enigmas which may find their solution in this way or that. Even if human calculation gave a hundred per cent. certainty, we as Christians have to remind ourselves that there are such things as "miracles of the antichrist," absolutely unexpected and astounding achievements of the "beast from the abyss," which

God has His own grounds for permitting, the occurrence of which could for the time being bring to nought all the calculations, not only of the "rational" portion of mankind but also of the Church and of Christians, be these calculations never so well grounded. We do not know whether Hitlerism is not capable of such a miracle—there is much in its development hitherto which tends in this direction. Perhaps a question mark is yet being set over against that admirable resolve, "Il faut en finir." Perhaps the nations of Europe may be destined to resist this enemy in vain and finally to have to live a life of dishonour under the rule of undisguised Lie, a life comparable to that of men and Christians in Germany to-day.

We are defending ourselves against this menace. We ought not to grumble if this threat were to become an accomplished fact despite all our wishes. We must realize that we shall then receive the due reward of our deeds. The use we all have made of that heavenly gift, that remnant of a free humanity, of democratic justice, and above all of the freedom of the Gospel, has not been such as to oblige God to preserve us from destruction. If we are preserved, it will be only by His grace. Are we prepared to be forced to recognize His grace even perhaps in His *not* preserving us? Are we prepared for a situation in which the defenceless confession of Jesus Christ is the only course left open to us? Are we prepared even then and under such conditions to remain loyal to our God and to rejoice in Him and to find our dignity in this and in this alone? On our answer to this question depends our title to defend ourselves now, depends our right to have a clear conscience in so doing, and our right wholeheartedly to ask God for His assistance. We must be prepared for God, just when we are acting in obedience to His command, to confront us with *His own* "Il faut en finir," and again by His command to lead us to something *wholly other*. We must be prepared to adhere *to Him* then and especially then, resolved upon a new obedience. Done in this spirit of preparedness, our work of resistance will then be a good work. Then and only then can it be offered with joy and confidence. We are both allowed and obliged to know that God will reign in any case and that He makes no mistakes.

When this letter reaches you, my friends, it will soon be Christmas. Then we, together, with the whole of Christendom, which is poor and yet so rich, and with all the angels in heaven, shall be privileged to rejoice in the presence and Kingly Rule of Him who is our salvation and blessedness wholly and in every situation. As the people that walk in darkness, we see a great light. That our duty and privilege is—each in his own place—to watch, to stand fast in the faith, to quit us like men and to be strong—let that be our message to you this Christmas.

KARL BARTH.
December, 1939.

Second Letter to
the French Protestants
October 1940

Dear Friends and Brethren,

On this occasion it was one of the youngest of the ministers of the Gospel in your country who took upon himself to urge me, as Pastor Westphal did last year, to address you in an open letter. In view of the developments which have taken place in the interval I have for long felt an obligation to follow up in some way what I wrote a year ago.

My last letter had in the main a friendly and understanding reception. I may therefore hope that what I now wish to write to you will not be regarded as the unwarranted interference of an outsider and non-participant.

In the need and task of our time there are no outsiders and non-participants. There may be many who think themselves such, but none are so in reality. This is much plainer to-day than it was a year ago. The war between the nations, which had then begun as a smouldering fire and has since become an all-devouring flame, is the necessary form of a conflict which is not confined by national boundaries, but cuts right across the nations (including the neutrals and not least the Germans themselves), and which everywhere in one way or another compels men to a clear and binding decision—to a Yes or a No, in full view of all conceivable consequences. We all find ourselves immersed in this conflict. We are all involved in its origin and continuance, and we are all, on one side or other of the gulf, involved in its solution, whatever this may be, as sharers in common action, common responsibility, common guilt and common suffering.

These being the grounds on which I take the liberty to address you again, dear fellow-believers in France, I can without further preface explain to you at once what are the question and the request I wish to put to you.

First, the question. It is true, is it not, my French friends, that we are agreed with regard to what has just been said? We were so a year ago. And surely we are so to-day—that is, after, as well as before, all that has happened? It is true, is it not, that the armistice concluded between France and Germany has not altered in any respect the fact that you too are still, and even more now, involved in the conflict which is the root cause of the war, and in the responsibility for the existence of the conflict and for its solution.

And now to add to this question my request. We know how much you are necessarily preoccupied at present with your particular national need and task. But you will not withdraw into it, as though it were your own private concern? You will not seek after solutions which would lead you to a neutral attitude in face of the great decision which now, as before, confronts you, as it does all of us, and on which in the last resort—for you in particular—nothing less than all depends? We count on you that, as Christians and as Frenchmen, you will not leave us in the lurch, but will stand with us on the same side of the abyss—stand with us both inwardly, with your faith and prayers, and—as a result of this—according to your insight and your ability, also outwardly, with your words and deeds, just as definitely as a year ago—nay, more definitely and convincedly, because of the added experience and knowledge of the past year. Just because we love and respect France now as much as before, we cannot and will not, for the sake of any specifically French concern, let you go. We need you. Do not separate your cause from ours, since ours, as truly now as formerly, is also yours.

I have been told that many of you after the events of last summer have remembered and pondered over the last part of my earlier Christmas letter, where I said that it was unchristian and unwise not to reckon with the possibility of the war taking a turn quite contrary to our wishes and expectations, with "signs and wonders of the Antichrist," with a coming judgment of God on ourselves, and that we must be ready to submit ourselves to the will and commandment of God even in such unwished-for circumstances. Then and only then, if we were prepared even for that, I wrote at that time, could the necessary work of resistance against Hitler's National Socialism be joyfully and confidently accomplished. That was in no sense an attempt to assume the role of a prophet. I wrote as I felt I must write in the circumstances of that time in the discharge of my responsibility to the Holy Scriptures. What actually took place in May and June I, just as little as others, did not at all foresee. It was certainly not a good omen that the French censor then thought it necessary to suppress the last part of my letter as "defeatist." It may be that the reason why the French resistance could not be so joyful and confident as to become effective was that men were too little ready to take into account that man proposes but God disposes.

However, be that as it may, the very thing that happened which we had all least desired and expected, worse than the worst we had imagined. I may tell you that my brother Peter Barth, who died on the evening of June 20th, in the extreme weakness of the last hour of his life exclaimed, "But we will not withdraw beyond the Loire!"[1] "We"—do understand, dear French friends, that many of us during those weeks were living in immediate union with you. Yet you (and we with you) had to withdraw far, far beyond the Loire. I need not here enter into details, which are better known to you than to me, and I for my part have no wish to use any of the harsh words which have been spoken and heard often enough in France itself to describe and explain that whole happening. Whatever the thing may be called, and whatever accusations or self-accusations may be made in regard to it, it was a simple fact that the military capacity of Hitler's Germany was able on this occasion to gain the upper hand, and that after Poland, Norway, Denmark, Holland and Belgium, France too is prevented for the time being from further co-operation in the necessary war against that Germany. It has come to pass that just in these circumstances you have now to submit yourselves to God's will and commandment.

But if, as is probably the case, you are more inclined to-day to remember especially that last part of my Christmas letter, I must also ask you to lay to heart that in the rest of what I then wrote to you there is nothing that needs to be taken back to-day. What change has there been, so far as you are concerned? This, certainly, that to-day for the time being (for the duration of the armistice) you have reasons—I refrain from enquiring whether they are good or bad reasons—for not wanting any longer, or at least not at present, to carry on the war. But there is one thing, surely, that has not changed even for you, but has rather been strengthened; the reason that is to say, which led you a year ago—led you as Christians—to endorse this very same war and to prosecute it with all earnestness. Need I remind you that a whole ocean of actual events, of enemy success and of our own failure, does not necessarily contain for us as Christians a single drop of truth? The recognition that we under-estimated others and over-estimated ourselves is a good and necessary thing. This recognition, however, has nothing to teach us about what is right or wrong or about the responsibility and decision which follow on our knowledge of right or wrong. I cannot think that your judgment of today about the fundamental situation between Hitler and the rest of us is different from a year ago just because in the meantime Hitler has had so many good days (vividly reminding us of Job xxi and Psalms x and lxxiii) and France, together with all those other countries, so many bad days. If that were your attitude, you would have surrendered, not merely to the German arms, but to that German philosophy which in 1933 broke out like a plague among the German people themselves. In that case, Hitler would have conquered not only your country but your souls.

I not only hope, but I know, that this is not so—in any case not so far as you, the sons and heirs of the French Reformation, are concerned. I know you are still able and willing to see through the terrible fog of a confusion between the Word of God and the language of brutal facts, just as in Germany itself I know people who have shown to this day the capacity and will to see through this confusion. I take it for granted that among your Roman Catholic brethren too, and also among the true heirs of the Revolution of 1789, there are not lacking those who have refused to be seduced by the false lure of the German realism of 1933. But to you, at least, the sharers of my own faith, I can press home the proposition that in regard to the grounds, the necessity and the right of the war against Hitler—even though it is at the moment not your war, but is being waged by others in the Channel, over London, in Egypt (and who knows where to-morrow?)—for you too nothing has changed, nothing at all. National Socialism itself, with its lies and cruelties, its arbitrary justice, its persecution of the Jews and con-centration camps, its attacks upon, and poisoning of, the Christian Church, its fundamental denial of freedom and consequently of responsi-bility for thought and speech, its conscious and wicked repudiation of spiritual values—National Socialism as "the Revolution of Nihilism," has not changed, even in the smallest particular. It has only proved itself to be more efficient in war than we thought and become more powerful than we wished. It has only conquered a certain number of nations, including your own, just as it first conquered the German nation, the most unfortu-nate as all. It has merely won a further opportunity of applying its meth-ods in Poland, Norway and Holland, and it seems probable that France too will quickly have the chance, if it has not had it already, of learning what they are.

Do you know what it is that at the present time exercises the minds of Christians in Germany belonging to the Confessional Church more than the whole war? It is the putting to death on medical grounds, of certain "incurably" sick persons, carried out as a system on a large scale and made immune from criticism by the power of the police. Rumour has it that up to the present there have been 80,000 victims of this system. This is Hitler. To withstand this Hitler, when after mastering his own people he began to hurl himself against other nations and countries, was the clear purpose with which England and France in the autumn of 1939, after long hesitation, entered into the war. The fact that since then things have gone so extraordinarily well for Hitler and so badly for his opponents, that he has found in Europe and Asia allies among those who by their own na-ture were bound sooner or later to become such, that to-day he exalts him-self like a god to force a new order of his own making upon the whole world, all this is no reason whatever for abandoning that purpose. For you also, even though you are at present no longer actually at war, all this is no reason for being untrue to that purpose. You must at least in your in-most heart be with those Frenchmen who have decided, and who have the opportunity of giving effect to the decision, to continue to carry on the war of the France of 1939. National Socialism is the same terrible, but at the same time inwardly empty and in the last resort utterly unreal, prod-uct of the underworld that it always has been. "One word shall quickly slay it," is as true to-day as yesterday. You, dear friends, can in fact remain neutral in this conflict no more to-day than yesterday.

If I have been well informed and understand the matter rightly, there is much talk in Christian circles in the France of to-day about the humility with which one ought to acknowledge and accept the "total defeat" as a divine judgment. And further, about the penitence which is now necessary.

And again, about a sorrowful silence in which one must address oneself to
the modest tasks which still remain, or are beginning to emerge, under the
provisional arrangements of the armistice. Much talk also about prayer,
about preaching Christ crucified, about creating, preserving and encouraging a new public spirit, as the only possible way for you to co-operate
to-day in matters which are the common concern of the Christian Church
and the legal State.

I understand all this, and I am doing my best to understand it with sympathy and trust. For I am a little disturbed by the fact that I seem to have
heard all this before; that is to say, in the Germany after 1933, when she was
overrun by National Socialism. At that time and in Germany it implied a retreat of Christianity from responsibility in ecclesiastical and political
spheres to the inner sphere of a religious attitude which, in order to maintain itself, no longer concerned itself with, or at least was not willing to fight
and suffer for, the right form of the Church, let alone that of the State. At
that time and in Germany, all this meant the sanctioning of National Socialism by a rightly or, it may be, wrongly interpreted Lutheranism. Be perfectly clear that the demonic power of National Socialism of which you
have now had experience yourselves, at any rate passively, is connected
with the fact that Christianity in Germany did thus retreat. By recalling
what took place in the Church struggle in Germany I certainly do not mean
to say that those who to-day in France use the language of which I have
spoken are already involved in this retreat. I only want to say that the
promulgation of these sentiments, however well intentioned and relatively
justified in the beginning, might be the first step in such a retreat, in which
the Church would play directly into the hands of the arch-enemy and, in
any case, of National Socialism. You will see to it that this does not happen.

Humility is an excellent thing. There is certainly no occasion for pride
and, if we have been proud in the past, we have during the last half-year
suffered a rude blow in the face. I am, however, troubled about the relation of this sudden emphasis on penitence both to the policy of the Vichy
Government and to the apathy into which, if I am rightly informed, the
great mass of your people has now sunk in the face of these fateful events.
Is it not almost too much of an accommodation to the spirit of the times
to fasten on humility as the preacher's theme to-day? But let that be as it
may. Let us only be sure that, if we preach about humility, it is a humility
before God of which we are speaking, and not a humility before facts and
circumstances, before Powers and Dominions, before men and human au-
thorities. Humility before God can have nothing to do with resignation,
nor with a stunned petrifaction before a destiny which we must recognize, at any rate for the time being, to be in a certain sense unalterable. If
we were to give way to this, we should have surrendered our faith and
the enemy would already have triumphed over us. The secret of Hitler's

being is that he knows how to produce this petrifaction all around him. Any true Christian preaching of humility in France to-day must keep far away from this kind of stupefaction.

It follows, if we are thinking of humility before God, that there can be no talk of *"total defeat."* Has not the idea too many painful associations with the "total" purposes and claims of our adversary? How have we Christians come to apply the word "total" to anything but God's omnipotent grace? When and how can a human defeat become "total," unless Christians involved in it were to lose their faith in the omnipotent grace of God, and with it their inward joy and the courage to bear their Christian witness? It is this that must never be allowed to happen.

It follows, if we are thinking of humility before God, that the acknowledgement and acceptance of *God's judgment* will certainly not mean that we shall grow weary and allow ourselves to become confused about what we previously recognized to be God's commandment and will, and tried to carry out in obedience to Him. God's judgment is directed not against our obedience, but against the endless disobedience with which we have again and again overlaid our little bit of obedience. If God has judged us, He has been gracious to us; He has not in judging us cast us out into a self-chosen neutrality, but given us a new beginning and encouraged us to a purer obedience.

It follows that the *repentance* which is needed will not be limited to an unfruitful, merely general, submissiveness or a passive regret for faults committed in the past; still less will it find expression in forms of renewal and innovation which will in fact help the old Adam to even greater triumphs. But true repentance (in regard, for example, to liberty, equality and fraternity) will make us wholly in earnest where formerly we were light-minded, joyful where we were sceptical, strong where we were weak and slack. Repentance will lead us to watch and not to sleep; it will guide our steps to life and not to death.

It follows that *silence*, which has certainly much to commend it, will not be a mournful silence, but the natural and fruitful self-restraint of those who have privately too much to do to indulge freely in talk.

It follows that *prayer* will not lead us away from political thought and action of a modest but definite kind, but will rather lead us directly into purposeful conflict.

It follows that the new *public spirit* will be not only a goal, not only the subject of all kinds of teaching, pastoral work and discussion, but, above all and at once, a beginning—the spirit of a Christian repudiation of defeat, the spirit of a Christian approach to a new and better resistance, the spirit of Christian hope which is not disposed to leave the field to the demons. How in the world can this spirit be created, maintained and encouraged except by practising it?

More than ever, and perhaps nowhere so much as in the France of to-
day will the *crucified Christ*, if we are thinking of humility before God, be
preached as the *risen Christ*—as the King, whose Kingdom has no boundaries, and whose servants can have no fear because He has overcome the
world.

If I could understand them in this way, and could correct them a little,
I should agree with these emphases. They would *not* mean that the *Church*
of France has concluded an armistice. It is just this that the Church cannot
and must not do, neither in the terms we have been considering nor in
any others. In the Church in France the spiritual war must still go on. She
cannot on any terms conclude a peace, or even an armistice, with Hitler.
And in the Church in France, it must be, and remain, perfectly clear that
even the military armistice which the Vichy Government made with
Hitler, can have only a provisional character.

Here I want to break off, though I know that it is just here that the practical questions begin. I lack the competence to take part in the discussion
of these questions. Above all, the question of "Vichy"! You may imagine
that I have my own opinion about it, and also an idea what my attitude
would be were I a Frenchman. But I am not a Frenchman, and I consider
it better in this matter, which is your special concern, to say only what I
must say explicitly—that precisely in this matter your attitude is of decisive importance in the answering of my question and the fulfilment of my
request.

I commend you, dear friends and brethren, to our God in all the difficult, temptation-strewn, dangerous ways which lie before you. May His
peace, which passes all understanding, keep your hearts and minds, and
the hearts and minds of us all, in Christ Jesus.

With brotherly greetings!
KARL BARTH.

Basel, October 1940.

A Letter to Great Britain
April 1941

I have been kindly invited by the Rev. A. R. Vidler and Dr J. H. Oldham to write you a letter in which I may tell you what is in my mind about those things which at the present time stir all of us. They both think that in this way I may be able to do something towards maintaining the link between the Christians of the Anglo-Saxon World and those on the Continent.

I accepted this invitation immediately, but I have been hesitating for a long time to comply with it. Now that I am about to do so, at the outset I want you to believe me when I say that without such an invitation I should hardly have dared thus to address you. I am by no means an Apostle; and, even if I were, after all I have heard and read about you in these last few years, I should feel inclined to say to you with the Apostle Paul: "I myself also am persuaded of you, my brethren, that ye yourselves are full of goodness, filled with all knowledge, able also to admonish one another" (Rom. xv. 14). My main reason for accepting the invitation to write you is that I want to express what I have been felling as I have shared with you the anxieties, hardships, tasks and hopes with which you are occupied, and to assure you that I shall continue to share with you in all that lies ahead.

But more than that: I want to make it clear that I consider the great cause which to-day lays hold of you to be in a special sense my own cause and the cause of the whole Church and of Christendom. For this reason I do not think that it is the interference of a stranger with your affairs if I tell you briefly my own personal thoughts on this subject. Kindly forbearance on your part will obviously be necessary. I am very eager to find the right door and to discover the right bell on that door: but that is anything but easy. For many years it has been my deep desire to gain a fuller understanding of the general life of your people and country, and especially of your Christian life. I have also studied with interest a good many specimens of your war-time political and theological literature. But I still do not find it easy to see exactly where you stand and to find the right message to send. And this is all the more difficult because the situation is now changing from month to month; and it may easily happen that to-morrow you will no longer be in the situation in which I had, perhaps rightly, thought you to be to-day. May I ask you very kindly to take all this into account, and to forgive me if I should show some misunderstanding of you in the course of what I write; and will you also forgive me if I should not succeed in making myself altogether clear? Should this happen, remember the sincere brotherliness of my intentions!

I have been invited as a Christian and by Christians to write this letter, and it is Eastertide as I put my hand to the task. Together, therefore, we hear the word of Jesus Christ: "All power is given unto Me in heaven and in earth." The fact that this word is true, and that in our own times it will remain and will prove itself true, brings us all and binds us all together. This it is which stirs you over there and stirs me here more deeply than anything else; this it is which lays hold of us more strongly than anything else; this it is which controls us more definitely than anything else. Taking our stand on the truth of this word, you and I look at the events and personalities of our time, and desire, in the face of these events and personalities, to take due account of our responsibilities. Because this word is true, you desire, in the midst of the storm and tumult of this war, to be and to remain good Britons, and you will do so; likewise, I desire to be and to remain a good Swiss, and with God's help I will do so. Everything which to-day we are together seeking to defend, though it may be in different places and in different ways, stands or falls with the truth of this word. I believe that, just because of the truth of this word and in spite of all human limitations, it will not be in vain if I speak my mind to you quite frankly, and if you of your charity will hear with an open mind what I have to say.

Let me begin with an assertion in which I think most of you will find yourselves substantially in agreement with me: we Christians in all lands find ourselves, as far as this war is concerned, in a situation strikingly different from anything that we experienced twenty-five years ago: that is to say, different in so far as we do not just accept this war as a necessary evil, but that we approve it as a righteous war, which God does not simply allow, but which He commands us to wage. And we hold this to be so in spite of the fact that it is not less terrible, and indeed may be much more terrible, than the last war!—in spite of the fact that we believe we have studied the Holy Scriptures since the last war not more superficially but thoroughly!—in spite of the fact that we think that since the last war we have given deeper consideration to the Christian obligations to the world!—in spite of the fact that since the last war our expectation of the coming of the Kingdom of God and its peace has grown not more feeble but more fervent! In spite of all this, we cannot resist the necessity of giving a different answer to what is to-day a different question.

We do not exclude the possibility that the well-known arguments of Christian pacifism, which twenty-five years ago we either made our own or which at any rate deeply disturbed us, may later, in a different situation and in a different form, once again bring us under their power. But on the other hand we cannot deny that at present those arguments, in the form in which we know them, have not this power. We long from the bottom of our hearts for conditions which will allow us men to exist and to live *for* one another, without being forced to exist and to live *in conflict with* one another, as we must when engaged in a dreadful war. Therefore we deeply deplore that war must be waged to-day. But we have no reason to say that it ought not to be waged; no reason to hinder those who are responsible for its conduct; no reason to avoid co-operating in its conduct. Rather we have every reason to acknowledge that this war must be waged, and indeed waged with determination and vigour; we have every reason to devote ourselves wholly to it. We hope that this war will end soon; but it must end in such a way that we shall achieve its object—its limited but essential object. We do not want a compromise, but a decision of the question about which this war is being waged.

We must not overlook the fact that this war is being fought for a cause which is worthy to be defended by all the means in our power—even by war; and, further, that this cause could no longer be defended by any other means than by war. Theoretically both governments and peoples could always settle their national, territorial, economic and strategic aspirations and claims by other than military action; and probably most of the wars which in the past have been waged for such reasons were not necessary—the war of 1914–18 included. But the war which was declared in September, 1939, is not being waged about such things, and it could not therefore be avoided. It is this that renders the pacifist argument unrealistic. People have made much of the various mistakes which after the last war—in the peace treaties, and in the following decade—were committed by the then victors, mistakes which have made this new war possible. But we can maintain no more than that these mistakes made this war *possible*. They did not make it *necessary*. They did not bring it about automatically. They were not of the kind that could be corrected only by the sword. Admittedly the victors of 1918 were astonishingly slow to correct them. But we must not overlook the fact that during those years they were equally slow in consolidating the predominant position which they had won in 1918.

Was not the fundamental mistake of those years this—that after the labours and sacrifices which the war had demanded of them, the victorious peoples and their governments tended to indulge their desire for as peaceful a slumber as possible, and consequently did not seriously fulfil their international obligations in any direction? But there are no grounds whatsoever for accusing them of striving to bring about another war in order to maintain and perpetuate the results of the mistakes which had been made. On the contrary, this new war was finally declared only after many years of continued hesitation and evasion, in order to check a movement which was alleged to be an attempt to put right the mistakes which had been made in previous years, but which was actually—and still is—a threat ten times worse than all those mistakes put together. This threat (I need not mention Mussolini, who has proved himself to be a mere lackey) was the attempt of Adolf Hitler to force his "New Order" on Central Europe to-day, on the whole of Europe to-morrow. The essence of this "New Order" is the assertion of the sovereignty of the German race and State, which in practice is that of the German "Fuhrer." Its establishment is to be achieved by the whole might of Germany's military power, which is impelled by the force of a heathenish religion of blood, despotism (*Autoritat*) and war.

This enterprise was met by toleration and yet more toleration, in a desire to atone (actually in a very unchristian way!) for past mistakes. It was perhaps through blindness to the true nature and power of this enterprise, perhaps in the weakness which came from a bad conscience about the past, perhaps because they realized they had neglected their duty to arm themselves for war in order to save peace, that the victors of 1918 negotiated with Adolf Hitler, as if those negotiations were concerned with questions which one can and ought to discuss for the sake of peace! They let Hitler and his serf in the South grow stronger and unhindered. They sacrificed Abyssinia and free Spain; and more especially they sacrificed Austria and Czechoslovakia, even though in 1919 they had made themselves responsible for their existence. And at long last, in order to put a stop to this enterprise, when Poland was also overrun in the autumn of 1939 they declared and started the war. It is not true that in this war the West wants to subjugate the East, or the "senile" nations the "youthful" nations, or the "haves" the "have-nots," or the Capitalists the Socialists. The imperialistic-militaristic demon would have acted somewhat differently from the men who were so slow to make up their minds to enter on this war, and only at long last took their decision! No! the question in this war was and is the very simple and practical one:

Is it right or wrong to exalt, or even to admit, "the Revolution of Nihilism"[2] as the ruling principle of conduct—that is, to adopt the mentality, the language, the standards and the methods of a den of thieves or, worse still, of the jungle—in order to remove some imperfection in the life of Europe, or to make it more perfect? As soon as some people in responsible positions began to realize that, as far as Adolf Hitler was concerned, what we have to do is simply and solely to defend the Right as such against the Wrong—a matter which did not admit of discussion but demanded the taking up of arms—as soon as they realized this, war broke out.

Since this is so, we Christians cannot say "No" nor "Yes *and* No" to this war; we can only say "Yes." We must postpone our objection to war as such to some future date, when it may once again have some reality. We must not evade our responsibility for seeing that this war is waged, and waged ardently. I say "we Christians" advisedly; meaning all those of us who seek to know God's Word and will in all things great and small, and desire to rule our lives accordingly. We should not, indeed, be Christians if we did not take into account the possibility that it may be God's will to punish us and the whole world, for having done so little to defend the Right, by a Nazi victory and the success of Hitler's evil enterprise. But neither should we be Christians if we were not convinced, just because we admit this possibility, that we must not on any account become Hitler's accomplices by assisting, either actively or passively, in the achievement of what he desires and purposes. Whoever to-day is for Hitler, or is not against him, or is even not wholeheartedly against him, deserves to receive by the will of God through "the Revolution of Nihilism" his due reward. That is the very reason why France—and, first of all, unhappy Germany herself—have by God's will fallen a prey to Hitler's movement. But it is not God's will that we should be likewise guilty and worthy of punishment. On the other hand, it is the clear will of God that we should recognize the true nature and power of the movement, in order to combat it with all our strength. The obedience of the Christian to the clear will of God compels him to support this war . . .

That an enterprise such as this ought to be resisted by political power using military methods is no new theory, devised merely to suit the present situation. It is precisely Christian thought which insists that resistance should be offered, and it is the Christians themselves who must not withhold their support. This implies, again according to the New Testament, that God has instituted for us Christians not only *the Church*, to build us up in Faith, Love and Hope, but also *the political hierarchy, the State* (for us, and also for the rest of the world), to testify to the Kingly Rule of Christ. Paul called the State in the most solemn way a "Minister of God" (Rom. xiii. 4, 6). He exhorted the Christians most emphatically to fit themselves into its framework and to pray for its good estate "that we may lead a quiet and peaceable life in all godliness and honesty" (I Tim. ii. I). The State which thus counterbalances the Church, and to which Christians are thus bound, is obviously a purely earthly institution. It cannot and must not be regarded as a second Church, much less as a beginning of the Kingdom of God (to which the Church itself can only look forward). When the State speaks we must not expect to hear a confession of Christian Faith, nor when the State acts must we expect to see a demonstration or an example of brotherly love. If we expect too much of the State, we shall fail to appreciate the little that there is to be found. The State embraces the life of all men in as much the life of all is actually and objectively under the sway of Jesus Christ, even in its unredeemed, and therefore dangerous, natural condition, even apart from the Faith, Love and Hope of the Christian. The State is therefore the sign of that consecration which the world has received through the resurrection of Jesus Christ: it is the sign of the patience with which God bears with, protects and upholds the world until the day when He shall make all things new.

Therefore the State is a constant reminder that the self-will of men, the imaginations and confusions arising from their self-conceit, the lusts which they may satisfy as they desire, are not without limits, and that these demons have indeed a master. For, according to Romans xiii. 1–7 and I Peter ii. 13–17, the task of the State is this: to discriminate between Right and Wrong in the lives of all men and to set certain bounds for their conduct. The State must keep constant watch on these bounds, and constantly defend them, first of all *on behalf of* everybody, since the life of all requires such bounds, and then, if necessary, *against* anybody who may be so arrogant as to seek to go round or to break through them. The State was instituted by God to do this, and, as it does this, it is the "Minister of God" in its own sphere and in its own way, just as much as the Church itself. The State bears the sword in order to fulfil this very function.

This fact is a solemn judgment on us, but it is God's changeless decree. Where the life of men will *not* be governed by the preaching of the Gospel *nor* by prayer, *nor* by Baptism or the Lord's Supper—in other words, where the bounds of the Church stop—there begins the realm within whose bounds God's fatherly care, which does not fail even there, must be maintained and imposed, if necessary, by the threat of the sword, and, in the last resort, by its use. We have no right to revolt against or to ignore this ordering of human affairs. And indeed, is there any order conceivable other than this so long as human life is not controlled by Faith, Love and Hope? We must be grateful to God that He has not simply given us up to disorder, but that He has given us this order, which is certainly stern but which has proved itself to be effective. Whatever we may say about it, it is an order which sets up a barrier not indeed against sin, but against the chaos into which sin would inevitably plunge us if God had not instituted the State, and if He had not entrusted it with the sword. The State would lose all meaning and would be failing in its duty as an appointed minister of God, and it would be depriving men of the benefits which God, by its function, had intended for them, if it failed to defend the bounds between Right and Wrong by the threat, and by the actual use, of the sword. We Christians cannot desire that the State should be guilty of failing in this duty. We Christians can only pray that it may be a righteous State, in the Biblical sense, whatever the circumstances and whatever the consequences, and we must wholeheartedly work to this end.

When the British government declared war on Adolf Hitler's Germany in the autumn of 1939, it acted as the Government of a righteous State according to Christian standards. And I believe this was true also of Switzerland when she resolved, at the same time, on the armed defence of her neutrality, the maintenance of which is her historic mission. Since this is so, there is but one decision left to the Christians of your country and of mine, and our Christian obedience compels us to make this decision. The cause which is at stake in this war is our own cause, and we Christians first and foremost must make our own the anxieties, the hardships and the hopes which this war demands of all men. The Christians who do not realize that they must take part unreservedly in this war must have slept over their Bibles as well as over their newspapers.

NOTES

1. A region in France and the scene of several important military battles in European history.

2. EDITOR'S NOTE: For the significance of this, readers may be referred to H. Rauschning's books: *Germany's Revolution of Destruction* and *The Beast from the Abyss*; also to the *Christian News-Letter*, Supplement No. 80.

10

✛

Stephen S. Wise

World Jewish Congress
Editor, Opinion

E ven before Adolf Hitler launched his economic pogroms against the
Jews, American Jewish leader Stephen S. Wise was warning the nation
and the world about Nazism. Wise had been watching closely the anti-Semitic rumblings in Germany since the 1920s. Others insisted that the
country be left alone to resolve its "local German question." But Wise argued in 1933—the year Hitler came to power—that "the conscience of humanity has made a world problem of the present situation" of the Jews.

Rabbi Wise already had built a career challenging the conscience of
America and the world on a range of social and political questions. He
took up his lifelong role as a Zionist in the 1890s, working closely with
Theodor Herzl and serving as American secretary of the world Zionist
movement. He helped draft the text of the 1917 Balfour Declaration,
which promised a political homeland for the Jews in Palestine. He
pleaded for the cause of the Armenians at the Versailles Peace Conference
of 1918. He was co-founder of the National Association for the Advancement of Colored People (in 1909) and the American Civil Liberties Union
(in 1920). He was active in groups such as the Child Labor Committee and
the Old Age Pension League.

By the mid-1930s, however, Wise was aiming his civic activism at the
anti-Jewish campaigns in Germany. In 1936 he organized the World Jewish
Congress to focus international attention on the problem. It proved to be an
uphill struggle: Anti-Semitism in America had reached a peak in the early
decades of the twentieth century. Within months of Franklin Roosevelt taking office in March of 1933, rumors abounded that Jews were running the
government. The Klu Klux Klan, the Black Legion, the Christian Frontists,

the Knights of the White Camelia, the National Union for Social Justice—these were just a handful of the groups determined to rescue the United States from the "atheistic-communistic-Jewish" conspirators. It's true that the religious press had begun to report on the persecution of Jews in the 1930s. Christian leaders and entire denominations issued statements condemning anti-Jewish bigotry. In 1941, a group of 170 Protestant ministers from New York City even signed a manifesto calling on all Americans to recognize anti-Semitism as "a threat to democracy and a denial of the fundamental principles upon which this nation is founded."

None of it, however, convinced the nation's political or religious leadership to take strong measures to rescue European Jews. Wise eventually appealed to President Roosevelt and the U.S. State Department to help stop the executions and support Britain's effort in the war. Yet he couldn't even persuade the government to loosen its immigration laws: Immigration policies actually tightened after America entered the conflict. As late as 1943—when the existence of the death camps was indisputable—most Americans opposed increasing immigration quotas for political refugees from countries under Nazi occupation. No Jewish leader in America did more to expose the viciousness of German Fascism and its wider threat to the norms of all civilized states. Nevertheless, the plight of the Jews barely figured into America's deliberations about World War II.

The following essays all first appeared in the journal *Opinion,* which Wise edited from 1936 to 1949. In "Five Mournful Years for Jewry," Wise reflects on the anti-Semitic campaigns under Hitler's chancellorship. He chides both Jews and Christians for failing to boycott German products—goods produced by the "foes of the human race." He picks up this theme again in "Enemy of Human Freedom," and calls it "the most sacred obligation" for free people to give moral, political and material assistance to Britain and France in order to defeat Germany. In "The Crime of Crimes," written after the fall of France, Wise laments that America failed to heed the warnings of Winston Churchill—the "one unappeasing leader" of the Western democracies willing to face the truth about Hitler. "With singular unintelligence, the world for the most part refused to heed the warning of his theories and his conduct alike, until he embarked upon a career of incredibly brutal conquest," Wise writes. "No day has seemed darker, no portent blacker than that of this hour."

Five Mournful Years for Jewry
Opinion, 1938

Five years have passed since that mournful 5th of March, which witnessed the so-called election of Hitler as Chancellor of the German Reich. It might long have been foreseen and perhaps even averted, had they been prepared, whose minds were under the moral obligation, to be ready. Save for Labor, and a handful of radicals who paid a terrible price, few resisted or even challenged the advent of the deadliest regime in a millenium. Least prepared were the Jews of Germany, about half a million, who had with most explicit insults been warned. At first some of the older and better circumstanced Jewish groups assented with incredible baseness to the diverting of anti-Jewish Nazi wrath to the newer East European emigrants who since war days had made their home in Germany. This was exactly as the Jews of Southern France more than a century earlier had attempted to burden their hapless Alsatian brother-Jews with the weight of putative Jewish iniquity.

Despite every escape mechanism, including cabled supplication to the leaders of the American Jewish Congress in our country, to desist from attack upon the new Nazi regime, what was threatened in pre-Nazi years has come to pass and German Jewry, which may no longer so style itself, lies prostrate and helpless beneath the iron heel of Nazi law and practice. In a review of five years of Nazism from the Jewish point of view, certain things stand out that justify special consideration. For years before Hitler's accession and for a time thereafter and in some part persisting to this day, certain groups of Jews have underestimated the gravity of the Hitler threat.

Again, it should be recalled that the German Jews took it for granted almost with unanimity that Hitlerism or Nazism was a passing phenomenon. After declaring that his access to power was incredible, they crowned their blunder by assuming that he would speedily vanish. German Jewry made no preparations as against the advent of Nazism and indeed up to the recent mournful utterances of Dr. Stahl before the Jewish Community of Berlin,[1] there had been no genuine and unafraid facing of ultimate and tragic facts by German Jewry. Such facing as came to light when the sagest of American Jews on March 13, 1933 a week and a day after the Hitler "election," declared "Jews must leave Germany." People scoffed at the impracticableness of this prediction rather than counsel. It is, alas, coming to pass. Had there, for example, been any concerted, wise facing of the facts by Jews in Germany, there never would have been one penny of foreign funds expended in Germany for relief to Jews. Morover, every well-to-do family that migrated to Palestine should have been invited or even compelled to take a poorer Jewish family with it, so that instead of leaving funds in Germany or transmitting them elsewhere, instead of 50,000 German Jews going to Palestine, the number might have reached 100,000.

I do not hold that the German Jews should have been expected to foresee all the more tragic and the remoter consequences of the Hitler regime. Still a word must be said about those who, prior to March, 1933, maintained that the fulfillment would not be as evil as the promise. "The threat is grave but it cannot be carried out." The truth is that the fulfillment is a thousand times graver than any threat of the pre-Hitler days. I am reminded of that German official who, in 1918, was asked by an English diplomat, "And if you had conquered France, how would you have treated the inhabitants after exchanging a million of the French population with as many of the German?" His reply was "*dann haetten wir die Liebenswuerdigkeit tuechtig und gruendlich organiziert.*" Verily the Nazis have in supremely thorough and competent fashion translated a campaign of hatred and vilification into the law and statute of their country. The Nuremberg Code stands as the incarnation of a nation's descent to the deeps of racial injustice and oppression of a minority.

What, of course, could not have been foreseen was that Germany would be permitted to disregard and to violate the Versailles Peace Treaty at every point, the most conspicuous example of such unchallenged violation being the surrender of Danzig to Nazism at its worst. Something more has happened within five years that is of moment not only to Jews in Germany but to Jews everywhere and that is the spread through the devilish instrumentality of the Ministry of Propaganda and Enlightenment of Nazi propaganda in all the lands of Europe and indeed in Asia, Africa, North, Central and South America. Tragic as has been the cold "Anschluss," virtually unrebuked by the democratic powers which long stood as Austria's guardians, there has been something worse than the annexation of Austria over a period of five empoisoning years, namely, the permeation of Eastern and Central Europe by Nazi propaganda. The device of the "Ghetto Benches" would never have been urged had it not been for bribery by Nazi funds and empoisonment by Nazi propaganda. Even the temporary accession of a pair of desperate and dissolute creatures such as Goga and Cuza to power in Rumania could not have been had not Rumania been a prey of Nazism for some years.[2]

One thing more requires mention. From the beginning, as that valiant anti-Nazi battler, Dr. Henry Leiper, has pointed out, the Christian communions of Germany imagined themselves to be secure and that Nazism was nothing more than yet another symptom of raging anti-Semitism.

The writer of these lines predicted in the home of Harry Emerson Fosdick in October, 1933, that, even though anti-Jewish Nazism screened itself behind the mask of racialism, in time the Protestant and Catholic churches would become the victims of the Nazi scourge. For the most part there was unbelief on the part of those who took it for granted that Nazism could not, would not dare to touch either of the mighty Christian bodies of Germany. Needless to say, my prediction has come true. The Catholic and the Protestant churches alike of Germany are in danger of having their influence minimized by the new paganism which has the sanction not only of Alfred Rosenberg but of most of the leaders of Nazi Germany.[3] In a word, Nazism is Aryan-racialism against Semitic Jews. With its protean capacity for hatred and injustice, it takes the form of a paganish revival against the great Christian church and communities of Europe.

Against the ever-growing might of Nazism in Germany, which unhappily has come into alliance with Rome and Tokyo, there has been no mighty uprising, whether political or religious or moral. Socialists and Communists and the free Labor Front of other countries such as England, France and America have uttered their impressions, but there has been no union of the church bodies of the Western world against Nazi paganism. Individual Christian leaders have spoken with power and inspiration under the early leadership of the golden-tongued Parkes Cadman, but there has to this hour been no voluntary union of the religious forces of mankind against Nazi paganism—it may be because Jews were its first victims.

Even more disappointing has been the constant yielding of the democratic powers to Nazi Germany's demands. The last two days in the House of Commons witnessed the almost unchecked triumph of the Nazi-Fascist axis. A handful of us, who have not wholly lost faith in the triumph of decency in the world, have felt it our duty to unite in a boycott against Nazi goods and services, a boycott being a moral revolt against wrong, making use of economic instruments. Timorous Jews and queerish Christians seem to feel that we are not justified in boycotting the foes of the human race.

Out of it all emerges the truth that we Jews have been taught that, unless we choose to go down to dishonor and even death, we will have to rethink our problem through. We will have to face what Nazism means to ourselves. The world will not think or act for the Jewish people unless the Jewish people think and act for themselves. We are not minors who require non-Jewish guardianship and even if we required it, we would not have an effective, dependable saving guardianship outside of ourselves. It may yet be that good will come out of the Nazi plague, the good of a democratic awakening, the good of a Jewish renaissance. The democracies may yet conclude that they will either stay the power of Nazism and

Fascism or be destroyed. Jews may yet come to understand that their position in the world is imperiled as never before in history. The alliance that alone might save them must be an alliance of the democratic forces challenging and battling against Nazism and Fascism, whether in Berlin, in Rome or in Tokyo, and Jews everywhere coming to understand that political tyranny anywhere means death, that political freedom and international justice alone can save them and make life worth saving for Jews and all peoples.

Enemy of Human Freedom
Opinion, 1940

For seven years *Opinion* has annually sought to convey a picture of the accumulating evil done by the Nazi regime. It may claim to have been among the first journals of the land to have discerned that the least grave, though in many senses the most foul, aspect of Hitlerism lay in its treatment of the German Jew. And still such treatment, far from being the objective of the Nazi regime, was little more than a bait held out to those susceptible to anti-Semitic passion to wreak themselves against the most defenseless group within the Reich.

Opinion so deeply felt at an early stage of the Nazi revolt against civilization that within some years Hitlerism would pit itself against all non-German races and against the whole of the Judeo-Hebreo-Christian world fellowship, that for five years it has followed the practice of arranging an annual symposium in which Christian and Jew should have part in setting forth the moral quality and the social status of the phenomenon commonly described as Hitlerism.

We never stood alone as victims of the Hitler odium. We were in the fullest and proudest company from the beginning. For such company included all women who chose to be free; the self-liberating trade union and workers' movement of Germany; every German idealist who had spoken and acted in the terms and on behalf of the movement of international peace and international integrity; the entire socialist movement long dominant in German politics; and every group that embodied the forward-looking and forward-moving hope of the German people that was.

And yet it was not long before the Catholics of Germany had the honor of winning the enmity of the Nazi regime. Rosenbergism, then ever more dominant than it is today, battled against the Catholic church and the youth within the Catholic Action movement with much of the ardor with which the unspeakable and forever speaking Goebbels enlisted all that was worst and foulest in German life against the security and the honor of German Jews. The name of Niemoeller is symptomatic of the wrath of Hitlerism against the Protestant churches because one indeflectibly loyal Christian group, under the spiritual leadership of Niemoeller, refused to do obeisance to a State which sought to exact such worship as followers of Christianity felt they would yield only to Divine Rule.[4]

In recent years Hitlerism has chosen to surround itself with a world of foes beginning with Austria, Czechoslovakia, and Poland. And it may, without exaggeration, be said that today the German Reich stands on the one side, and earth's civilized peoples on the other, save for Stalin's Russia, which has been beguiled into the unholiest of alliances, and Italy, which grows more deeply neutral in protest against the Hitler-Stalin alliance. At last the world has come to recognize what Nazism means. For years certain circles in France, dazzled by the hope of gain, were half tolerant thereof. England for five years and more could not be brought to understand the movement, and the imminence of the peril which it was unbelievably bent upon courting. But England and France are not alone in stating that Hitler and civilization cannot co-exist, that civilization must free itself of the Hitler menace, or else go down to cureless catastrophe.

There will be no more Munichs. The Munich of September, 1938, marked the last effort of the then unaware democracies of the West to traffic, at heaviest sacrifice of the national interests of others, with an unbelievable enemy of all civilization. In the meantime Poland has gone down to defeat, and the greatest sufferers within the old Poland are the Jews. Nearly a century ago General Grant returned his sword to General Lee. Hitlerism has undertaken to show the world that military defeat must be followed by the most awful visitations of fire and sword and plague. Inhumanity is written upon every item of every page of the German story of dispossession of Poland. Democracies that would be prepared to leave those monstrous evils uncorrected were little better than the regime they are bent upon challenging.

The question has ceased to be one of war versus peace, but is rather become a question whether unbridled might and unmoral power shall again rule over the destinies of men and nation. Insofar as England and France have taken up the gage, insofar as the two great democracies of Western Europe dared to say to Hitler after his threat to Poland, "Thus far shalt thou go and no further," it is for peoples who are, and for men who would remain free, their most sacred obligation to give moral, political, and material aid and furtherance to Britain and France. The wrongs of a world in which democracy will triumph may be corrected and cured, but the wrongs of a Nazi world would be cureless.

We Jews have no special stake in this war. Save possibly for the handful of Jews in the lands ruled and conquered by Germany, Jews are at one in their understanding of the truth. But Hitlerism is the enemy of human freedom, of human justice, of all those imponderable values and ideals which together constitute civilization. It is for that reason that every Jew on earth must take his place by the side of them that are resolved that Hitlerism and all that it is and means and portends shall perish from the earth, and that all those moral and social and spiritual ideals which it would destroy shall remain, as in truth they are, imperishable.

The Crime of Crimes
Opinion, 1941

Eight years since Hitler's so-called "election" as chancellor of Germany. It is not true to say that nearly eight years have "passed." Truer to say that eight years of fire and sword have seared the hearts of mankind, that these eight years have brought more hurt and grief to humanity than any similar period of time within a thousand years.

Recall to mind the state of the world before Hitler and contrast it with the state of the world that is today. In 1932, the world was ready to act on the Disarmament plan. It was the one proposal for world Disarmament in our lifetime which received serious attention throughout many nations and around which a conference in Geneva was built up, that gave high promise of the fulfillment of the long-time dream of Disarmament. In behalf of that program of Disarmament, the then President Hoover labored long and earnestly.

Hitler came and not only was the Disarmament dream shattered, but the world, its simple folk, at once and instinctively felt that the end of peace had come and that evil days lay before it.

The Nazi program sounded simple. But it was belied by every word he had written in Europe's best seller, "Mein Kampf." In that volume, he had laid down the theory of the master-race and the slave-race, speaking as contemptuously of the Latin race, including the Italians, his new Axis partner, as about the Slavic race, including Russians and Poles, as feeble, effete, and fit only to be ruled. Two immediate aims he named—the obliteration of Jews as of the inferior Semitic race, and the destruction of Marxian-Socialism. At once he robbed and crushed every Labor organization, which was an unmistakable sign of his deadly hatred of the normal and accepted instruments of democracy. As for Jews, he robbed them; he struck them down in their citizenship; he inflicted upon them every conceivable, and, up to that time, inconceivable humiliation, indignity and hurt, though Jews had lived and served Germany for a thousand years, including, in our own day, the names of Albert Ballin and Walter Rathenau and Albert Einstein.

There are men of ignorant unconcern with regard to the illimitable evil wrought by Hitler or who, in silent sympathy, almost welcome Hitlerism. These demand a Bill of Particulars concerning the Western world's indictment of Hitler and Hitlerism. Alas, nothing is easier than to single out a few of the more grievous blows which he has struck at the political and spiritual life of mankind. At one fell stroke, he smashed, as I have already said, the entire labor movement, stole its very considerable funds, including its insurance treasury. He compelled women to give up their high economic and political status and whipped them back into the kitchen and the nursery to feed his soldiers and to breed new recruits for his relentless armies. He not only ended the peace movement but exiled and doomed its leadership including such men as Gerlach and Bernstorff, whose crime had lain in seeking world peace through the League of Nations.

But over and beyond his destruction of these policies and programs which had made Germany one of the socially advanced countries of the last century, he sowed anew terrible policies which the world is harvesting today on blood-drenched battlefields. The world will not soon forget, though it will be eager to bury them in a sea of oblivion, the major and in a sense original items of the Nazi program.

He introduced what might be called intramural war, a war of a large element of the population against the smallest of its population groups—the war of a majority of the people against a minority, with the result that 99% of the Nazi population were incited to brutality, theft and murder against less than 1% of the population, its Jewish minority. But as if that crime of crimes were not enough, in "Mein Kampf" he proclaimed and after 1933 he proceeded to put into effect the doctrine of racialism. This meant that only one race on earth was fit to rule and to exercise mastery, and all other races, whether Semitic or Slavic or Latin, must accept the status of inferior and ultimately enslaved races.

Today, eight years after Hitler came, Europe presents the picture of an armed camp in which great and historic peoples such as the Czechs and Poles, Scandinavians and Rumanians, Belgians, French and Dutch, are nothing more than enslaved victims of the "master race." And the third plank of the Hitler program was summarized in the term *Gleichschaltung*, which means regimentation, placing the minds and moods and ideas and hopes of a people on the basis of unexceptionable uniformity. Regimentation meant the abrogation of every freedom of the individual, the mocking cancelation of all the great spiritual and political gains of the nineteenth century, the transformation of a great, reasoning and free people into a mighty and militarily usable army of machines.

But all this was preliminary to the great offensive now under way against democracy, which did not choose to war upon him but upon which he is resolved to war to the death. In his mad passion to rule a regimented world, he feels oppressed and hampered by the challenge of free and democratic peoples and seems resolved that the world shall not remain half Fascist and half democratic. Nothing in Hitlerism is more truly and completely psychopathic than the intensity of his passion against what he and his confederate Mussolini regard as the accursed challenge of democracy.

Five years and more, the world has watchfully waited. It did not even, for the most part, arm itself in a defense against him, who almost frankly announced his program of world conquest through the destruction of the greater Western democracies of which the English and our own alone survive today. With singular unintelligence, the world for the most part refused to heed the warning of his theories and his conduct alike, until he embarked upon a career of incredibly brutal conquest.

Austria was annexed in violation of written and spoken covenants. Czechoslovakia was overwhelmed in the Fall of 1938 and finally crushed and annexed in the spring of 1939, after all the pitiful drama of appeasement and conciliation had been played upon the Nazi boards by Englishmen almost ready to yield up even the self-revering honor of a mighty Commonwealth for the sake of peace. Nothing availed to stay the hand of him or them to whom neutrality was nothing more than child's play, sneered at and crushed like a house of cards. Armed as a nation never was in history, they violated treaties, they broke neutral nations, they imprisoned their peoples, they starved their populations and the Axis became, together with Japan and, alas, the Soviet Union in the dim shadow—a world alliance of bane and blight.

One unappeasing leader there was who almost from the beginning, as history will yet chronicle, understood and in an early day proclaimed the menace of the aggressor nations, of those dictatorships against which he felt civilized people, democracies of free men, should institute a moral quarantine. Had America heeded and followed his leadership, it might never have become necessary even to consider all-out aid to England, which is nothing more, perhaps, than an imperfect and inadequate substitute for such moral and political cooperation with all the democracies of Europe as would have stayed the march of the aggressors before it was too late.

England stands almost alone today, if a people can be considered alone which stands in the panoply of its majestic and unconquerable strength. *Not alone*, for there is little doubt that somehow and in a very real measure, if only it be not too late, our country will recognize the truth that the unthinkable invasion and downfall of England would mean menace and imperilment to our own American democracy. No day has seemed darker, no portent blacker than that of this hour.

And still on this tragic anniversary, I venture to prophecy that England will not fall, that democracy will not perish, that the immortal truth of Lincoln, "government of the people, by the people and for the people shall not perish from the earth" remains as true and valid today as it was when first spoken. Nay, more—after eight blood-filled, shame-laden, crime-accursed years of Hitlerism, Nazism and Fascism, we know as never before that it is for us to cherish, to safeguard the altar of democracy at which we Americans live and move and have our being.

NOTES

1. Dr. Stahl was the leader of a synagogue in Berlin.

2. As early as 1937, under the pro-German Goga-Cuza regime, Romania had enacted anti-Semitic legislation, only the second country in Europe (after Germany) to do so.

3. Alfred Rosenberg was the principal author of key Nazi ideological tenets, including the theory of racism and the persecution of the Jews and Christian churches. He was responsible for the spiritual and philosophical education of the Nazi Party and its related organizations.

4. Martin Niemoeller, as a pastor at Berlin-Dahlem, preached courageously against the Hitler regime after it came to power in 1933. He attacked Hitler's creation of the German Evangelical Church and became the leader of the German Pastors' Emergency League and of the Confessing Church, which publicly condemned Nazism. Briefly arrested in 1937, Niemoller was imprisoned again from 1938 until his liberation by the Allies in 1945.

11

John C. Bennett

Pacific School of Religion at Berkeley Union Theological Seminary

A twenty-eight-year-old John C. Bennett, fresh from theological studies at Oxford and New York's Union Theological Seminary, joined the newly organized Fellowship of Socialist Christians in 1930. Its purpose was nothing less than to implement "a socialist translation of Christian principles" throughout American society. A Congregationalist, Bennett represented a generation of "neo-liberal" theologians searching for an alternative to the modernizing forms of Christianity then in vogue.

In the early 1930s, Bennett's generation had one eye on Europe. By then Adolf Hitler had initiated the Nazification of the German churches. A nationwide conference of German Christians, attended by Nazi leader Herman Göring, set in motion plans for a "Reich" Church, a mix of neopagan tribalism and Christian symbolism. When leading theologians sided with the National Socialists as a way to restore national prestige, Bennett's break with liberalism was complete. In November of 1933, he wrote an article for *The Christian Century* about the intellectual and spiritual failure of mainstream Protestantism. Called "After Liberalism—What?" the piece powerfully captured the dissenting mood of a growing number of younger theologians and was widely discussed.

Through most of the war years, Bennett was a professor of theology at the Pacific School of Religion in Berkeley, California (later joining Reinhold Niebuhr at Union Theological Seminary). He had entered the decade of the 1930s as a pacifist and held out hope, even as Germany began its assault on Europe, that all-out war could be avoided. The fall of France, however, changed everything for him: The nature of German Fascism, he now believed, made diplomatic or political solutions impossible. It was time to reckon with the reality of human evil on the world stage. "The problem of man is not primarily an economic or social problem," he wrote in *Christian Realism* (1941). "It is finally the problem of finding meaning for his life in the face of sin and suffering and death."

During the Christmas season of 1940, editors at *The Christian Century* invited the nation's leading religious thinkers to explore the question of American involvement in the European conflict: "If America is drawn into the war, can you, as a Christian, participate in it or support it?" It was not an abstract question. Germany already had overrun Czechoslovakia, Poland, Denmark, Norway, and France. It had launched the Battle of Britain, assaulting London with more than two months of continuous bombing raids that left thousands dead. Political pressures were mounting for America to reverse its policy of neutrality and throw its moral and military might behind Great Britain. In September of the same year, President Roosevelt announced that the United States would exchange fifty destroyers for ninety-nine-year leases on British air and sea bases, marking the functional death of U.S. neutrality. The same month, Congress approved the first peacetime draft in American history.

The Christian Century asked John Bennett to write the opening salvo in the debate. Bennett disputes those who reason that any assistance to the Allies must mean a U.S. declaration of war, still a deeply unpopular position. Yet he insists that American neutrality is no longer possible because of the consequences of a Nazi victory—the extension of a totalitarian nightmare throughout Europe. The best policy, he says, is to gear up the national economy to give material aid to the Allies as quickly as possible. "Those who argue that we should do either nothing or everything to help Britain or China in order to persuade us to do nothing are willing to sacrifice the people of Britain or China on the altar of their own consistency." Bennett's compromise position probably represented the majority view among the interventionists until America's entry into the war.

The Darkest Political Tyranny
The Christian Century, December 4, 1940

The Editor asks, "If America is drawn into war, can you, as a Christian, participate in it or support it?" I assume that the question refers only to a war against one or more of the Axis powers in the present world situation, and so, my answer is "Yes." My affirmative answer does not mean that I am advocating full participation in the war by this country (at a later point I shall explain my reasons for not advocating it). I do approve our present policy of intervention. In doing that I must face now the possibility that such a policy may lead to our involvement in the war in the future. One cannot support intervention now and refuse to support the American government in war in case war should come as a result of that intervention. Therefore, the most important question of principle is now settled in my mind. Moreover, those of us who honor the Chinese and the British for their resistance can hardly withhold support from our own government in case this country becomes involved in the same struggle. The fact that Christians in America do not now face the issue in the same form in which it confronts Christians in China and in the British Commonwealth is an accident of geography.

CONSEQUENCES OF A NAZI VICTORY

I confess that if the editor had sent the same question to me a year ago I should have given a different answer. It would have been a "no" based, not upon absolute pacifism, but upon the judgment that modern war is so destructive and so futile that whatever the issues may appear to be, to limit its area is more important than to insure the victory or defeat of either side. In an article in *The Christian Century* in November 1939 I gave expression to that point of view in relation to the present European war. Since that time I have been forced against my will and contrary to my habits of thought and feeling to change my mind. I have publicly expressed this change of mind with great regret. I find myself in a minority among those groups of Christians with whom I have usually felt most kinship but with the majority in the nation. No one can be in that position without great danger to his soul!

I can put the essential reason for this change in mind in a sentence. *The fall of France and the immediate threat of a German victory opened my eyes to the fact that the alternative to successful resistance to Germany is the extension of the darkest political tyranny imaginable over the whole of Europe with the prospect that if Europe can be organized by Germany the whole world will be threatened by the*

Axis powers. Before the events that followed the invasion of Belgium and Holland I was living in a world of illusion. It was a world in which the only pattern that I could take seriously was the pattern of the last war and its consequences. It was not a lonely world in which to dwell and it is still thickly populated by those who allowed their attitude toward war to become crystallized at the close of the last war and who refuse to see that the world today is threatened by something far more dangerous than a German victory might have been in that war and far more disastrous than the peace of Versailles. Those who still live in that world of illusion concentrate their attention upon the causes of Hitlerism and they refuse to act on the realization that Hitlerism is now a force that has great momentum of its own, that its consequences cannot be overcome by repentance concerning its causes.

A final German victory would mean the exposure of all the peoples of Europe to the German secret police. It would mean the systematic destruction or at least the silencing of the leadership in all conquered countries. It would mean a fate beyond description for the anti-fascist exiles who have found refuge in those few oases that remain. It would mean the loss of cultural and religious freedom. (The Treaty of Versailles did not subject central Europe to this kind of foreign control and it did apparently leave room for national recuperation.) The press and the universities in conquered countries would share to a great degree the fate of the press and the universities in Germany. Even the churches would lose their freedom to speak about this world. The defeat of Britain would enable the nazis to organize Europe to support their attempts to extend their power over Africa and South America and such a victory for Germany would enable Japan to consolidate her power in Asia. We in North America might be able to ride out the storm but we could do so only by turning this continent into a fortress. But whether we can do that or not, Christians who seek to be responsive to the demands of love must recognize their responsibility for saving others from tyranny, for the restraining of violence which is already let loose upon the world.

If this is a fair picture of the probable consequences of a final German victory, the assumption that seemed natural in the nineteen twenties, that it makes little difference who wins a war because all lose, hardly fits our situation. If the threat of such a series of consequences is less vivid than it was a few months ago the reason is the success of British resistance.

FLAWED ASSUMPTIONS

In order to make this position clearer I shall now consider three assumptions which are common among us and which, for many Christians, disguise the real situation.

1. It is often said that what is taking place is a revolution or "the wave of the future" and that we must learn to like it. It would be more accurate to say that in nazism we have tendencies which represent a remote past rather than the future. The success of nazism means the undoing of the results of the previous revolutions. There is ample worth in the idea that the success already attained by the nazis is a judgment upon the democratic nations, upon their policies following the last war, upon their imperialisms, upon the capitalistic mind that has so largely controlled them. But let us remember that British imperialism is in the process of decentralization, that it contains many means of self-correction, that it permits criticism of itself from those nations under its rule and that it encourages criticism of itself at home. It is imperialism with a troubled conscience. To substitute for that imperialism this new totalitarian rule that stifles all criticism, that acknowledges no standards, that deliberately seeks to make non-German peoples politically, culturally and economically subject to the "superior" race, is a revolution, but to use that magic word does not make the actual thing less hateful.

   This development may be a revolution against capitalism. It does involve the organization of economic life for the sake of a collective purpose. But to say that any form of collectivism is good is as stupid as the blind resistance to all collectivism that is so common in this country. Collectivism so concentrates power that it enhances the possibility of "demonic" developments in society. It is good for men to cooperate for a common purpose but if the purpose be evil, the very goodness in the process of cooperation multiplies the evil results of the purpose. National Socialism does not represent "the wave of the future." It is supremely reactionary because, as I have said, it discards the gains of past revolutions. Collectivism that becomes total tyranny is worse than the inefficiency and the injustice of capitalism. Collectivism which is the organization of economic life to maintain the power of an elite or to provide false glory for a nation is a betrayal of the masses to whose interest in security it first appeals.

2. It is often said that if Germany wins one can expect that her rule will become more moderate as she becomes more secure. Such a speculation points to the truth that there are limits to tyranny. In the long run God will not be defeated in history. I do not believe for a moment that Germany can build a permanent structure on the present basis. Sooner or later there will be division at the top or revolt from the bottom. But it would be a disastrous error to form our policy on the basis of a hope that moderation will render German rule less hard to bear. We must remember that modern forms of power enable a small minority to rule for a long time by sheer coercion. As a last resort

those who are willing to act with complete ruthlessness can use air power to keep a defenseless population in subjection. The fate of Rotterdam suggests that such complete ruthlessness is never far away.[1]

If Germany consolidates her power in Europe for a decade she can break the continuity of institutions, she can demoralize the population, she can destroy the leadership around which opposition might rally, she can begin to pervert the minds of the rising generation. There will be an end to it but that end will probably take the form of civil war made possible by a split among those who control the military power. There would be a new revolution against the results of this revolution. The question that now engages us concerning the use of force by Christians to prevent the consolidating of nazi tyranny will then become the question concerning the Christian's support of revolution against that tyranny. The principle would be the same in both cases.

3. There are some American Christians who now take at their face value the statements of European Christians who are under nazi rule or who live in neutral countries that are within the orbit of nazi rule. Some of those European Christians are saying that their own fate is a judgment upon the sins of their churches and upon the sins of secularist democracy. They hope that the present catastrophe may lead to a cleansing of Europe and the development of a more Christian culture. Marshall Petain is credited with that hope.[2] But this judgment which Christians must make concerning the religious meaning of their own fate should not be turned into a political judgment by observers, enabling them to look more complacently on that fate.

The outside observer can see clearly that the alternative to secularist democracy now available is not some kind of Christian authoritarian society but a blatantly secularist tyranny. He may also recognize that while those who are suffering persecution may have a right to take satisfaction in the purging effect of persecution, the other side of the picture is that a church driven underground loses touch with the rising generation where the state controls education. The church in the catacombs has an obligation to come out of the catacombs at the first opportunity to mold the mind of the community. The church that is made silent by oppression has the responsibility to seek for the development of a social structure in which it can break that silence.

NEGOTIATION EQUALS SURRENDER

In the face of the real alternatives that are available to us, the Christian is caught in a tragic dilemma. The American Christian can in some measure evade the dilemma but that evasion is more apparent than real. Those

Christians who favor aid to Britain and China are morally committed to the use of military force. Those Christians who oppose such aid to Britain and China are in part responsible for the extension of tyranny. The latter may cover up that fact to their own satisfaction by their belief that if only we or the British were sufficiently moral it would still be possible to have a peace now by negotiation that would prevent the full tragedy of a German victory as well as the tragedy of continued war. When you are dealing with the Axis powers negotiation is but a euphemism for surrender and for the abandonment of Germany's present victims to their fate. Conceivably the time may come when negotiations would be better than fighting to a bitter end but that would depend upon a balance of power in the world that could insure the keeping of agreements, especially the agreement to evacuate conquered territory and restore full independence. That balance of power would depend upon the success of the British in demonstrating that Hitler cannot win.

Pacifism as a political policy for this nation would encourage a German victory, would probably make impossible that balance of power on which negotiations in the future would depend. Pacifism as non-violent resistance can be effective only when victims and oppressors occupy to some extent the same spiritual world, when there is enough freedom of expression so that victims and oppressors can face the same facts. But pacifism as non-violent resistance cannot penetrate the walls built by censorship behind which whole populations are blinded by propaganda. The pacifist says that in the last resort those who adopt a policy of non-violence can themselves bear the suffering that results from their policy. But even that is not possible. When American pacifists agitate against aid to Britain, the suffering that would result from that policy would be borne not by them but by people in London.

For the Christian to support violence even if he believes that submission to tyranny may in some cases be worse than violence is for him to become party to intolerable evil. His is a tragic decision. If the only alternative to absolute pacifism were the uncritical support of war, with hatred and without repentance, it would be better for a Christian to be a pacifist regardless of the consequences. But there is another alternative. It has already been tested in experience by many Christians in China and England. It was once embodied in Abraham Lincoln. The marks of it can be briefly summarized as follows:

Those who represent this form of non-pacifist Christianity have no illusions about war while they support it. They know that military force may prevent something from happening but that it cannot make anything constructive happen. They know that their own nation shares the guilt for the war and so they do not locate all evil in the enemy nation. They know that it is never right to indict a whole nation, that though a whole nation may seem to suffer from a collective neurosis, the people of that nation must be healed and force cannot do the healing. They do not allow themselves to forget that the last war was a failure and that everything depends upon the peace which follows a war. They realize that this war is an explosion resulting from unsolved problems and that the new order that follows this war must overcome international anarchy as well as the insecurity caused by the failure of capitalism to turn productive power into distributed abundance. They are determined to preserve the bonds which unite Christians of all nations in the world church and they desire to begin now to build the bridges that can be completed after the war's end.

Those who represent this outlook welcome the fact that there are pacifists in the church and the nation who concentrate on the redemptive tasks of the Christian, leaving to others the political problem of restraining aggression and tyranny. They know that the urgency of this political problem and the pressures of public opinion are only too likely to cause them to forget important aspects of the Christian perspective. They will be reminded of those aspects more surely by pacifists who themselves admit that their own decision to leave to others the political problem is also a tragic decision and that they have no strategy available to the nation for coping with the threat of Axis domination.

SELECTIVE INTERVENTION

At the beginning of this article I said that my affirmative answer to the editor's question does not mean that I advocate full participation by America in this war. I do not believe that the most important issue is the legal status of neutrality or belligerency but rather the degree of responsibility that America should now assume for the defeat of Germany on the continent of Europe and for the defeat of Japan in Asia. Those who argue that if we do anything important to help Britain now we are obliged to enter the war do not distinguish between the responsibilities of an individual and those of a nation. Individuals can throw themselves into crusades with abandon. Governments which are trustees for the welfare of whole nations must move more cautiously because of the complexity of their responsibilities. Those who argue that we should do either nothing or everything to help Britain or China in order to persuade us to do nothing are willing to sacrifice the People of Britain and China on the altar of our own consistency. I believe that the American government is right at this time in seeking to give what help it can to the centers of health in other continents without assuming unlimited liability for the policing of those continents.

It seems to be a fact that we can give the most important aid to Britain and China now without declaring war and without assuming the unlimited liability of which I have spoken. This aid should be increased in volume. It should be given and not sold. Our country should organize its life so that the aid can be given with all the efficiency possible. If we were in the geographical position of Sweden or Yugoslavia such a policy would mean war for us. But in our position it means only the risk of a further degree of participation with still a chance to choose the extent of our liability in the war. Not to take this risk of war now is to run a greater risk of war later if Germany and Japan succeed in consolidating their power. America has an important stake in what happens in Europe and Asia but America does have a destiny that is not to be identified completely with what happens on either of those continents. An American government will be most true to all of its responsibilities if it adheres to its present course of selection intervention and attempts to keep this country from being bogged down for a generation in the struggles of Europe or Asia.

One thing is clear: the American people are determined to avoid full participation in this war. In this they are morally no better or worse than other peoples because no democratic nation goes to war until it is convinced that its own security can be safeguarded in no other way. In the long run we may welcome this strong inhibition against foreign military adventures as a safeguard against a new American imperialism in the broken world that this war will leave. Those who feel as I do that America should have a troubled conscience about being a beneficiary of the struggles of others should not seek to trick or over-persuade the nation into full participation in the war. On the other hand, American Christians who reject all war on grounds of Christian pacifism would do well to keep themselves under criticism when in order to buttress their pacifism they are tempted to be unfair to those people who are bearing the brunt of the struggle to prevent the Axis powers from organizing the world.

NOTES

1. Rotterdam, a major port city in southwest Holland, endured terrible bombing raids by German forces in 1940. Germany invaded Holland in May 1940 and conquored the small nation in five days.

2. Marshall Petain was a French military leader who headed the Nazi-collaborationist regime of Vichy during World War II. He handed over most of northern France to the Germans and moved the capital to the city of Vichy in southern France. He instituted numerous Nazi practices, such as arbitrary arrests and political censorship. When France was liberated in 1944, Petain fled to Germany but was forced to return in 1945 to stand trial for treason. He was found guilty and imprisoned for life.

12

Henry Pitney Van Dusen

Union Theological Seminary
Christianity and Crisis

H enry Pitney Van Dusen had planned to follow his father's footsteps into law, but an experience of "personal religion" as a member of the Princeton YMCA caused him to change course. He pursued theology, became an ordained Presbyterian minister, and eventually made his mark on world Christianity as a leader of the ecumenical movement. Toward that end, he traveled extensively—touching down in sixty countries across six continents—and played a key role in the founding of the World Council of Churches. Van Dusen also enjoyed a thirty-seven-year career at New York's Union Theological Seminary: as dean of students, professor of systematic theology, and finally president. Under his leadership, the school became a major center for theological study and one of the most influential seminaries in the world.

Van Dusen had gotten off to a rocky start. When he stood for his ordination in 1924, he tangled with conservative Presbyterians who opposed him because he refused to affirm a literal understanding of the Virgin Birth. Eventually, however, it was liberal Christianity that drew his strongest criticism: The latest fads in theology and science, by idolizing human understanding, revealed "the most consummate and childish egotism." Van Dusen sought a new approach, and in 1933 organized a Theological Discussion Group, attracting about thirty leading religious thinkers and educators, including German exile Paul Tillich. Meeting twice a year throughout the decade, they brought a Christian perspective to social and political problems based on a deeper understanding of the ambiguities of human nature. Most subscribed to some aspect of the "Christian realism" being advocated most powerfully by Reinhold Niebuhr.

Perhaps most important, Van Dusen and his colleagues regarded themselves as internationalists: America, they agreed, must accept the moral obligations of its world power status—and the Christian church would help define those obligations. When war broke out in Europe, Van Dusen joined with John Foster Dulles to form the Commission on a Just and Durable Peace, an effort to engage the churches in helping to prepare for the postwar world. The goal was not to achieve an utter transformation in global relations but to lessen the risk of another international conflict. In the meantime, however, Hitler's war machine was devouring European democracies with no end in sight, and Van Dusen found himself increasingly at odds with the pacifism of his peers. He became so disgusted with the neutrality arguments of *The Christian Century*, for example, that he helped found *Christianity and Crisis* with Reinhold Niebuhr and served on its editorial board. In 1941, he joined the Fight for Freedom Committee, a group of clergymen and prominent Americans agitating for direct U.S. intervention in the war—a deeply unpopular stand in a nation enamored with isolationism.

In the first essay included here, "Irresponsible Idealism," Van Dusen laments American inaction in 1938 and 1939, when Hitler seized Czechoslovakia and began his occupation of Western Europe. He scornfully dismisses the peace proposals then being made by liberal clerics, even after the fall of France. "During nine of the most tragic months in human history, large numbers of American Christians have been waiting from day to day for the summoning of the proposed peace conference," he writes. "There is not the slightest scintilla of possibility that such a move . . . could now end this war or bring enduring peace." In the second essay, "The Christian as Pilgrim and Citizen," Van Dusen explains the dual responsibilities of the believer: She is a member of the universal church, concerned about the spiritual freedom of fellow believers, but also a citizen of a democracy, concerned for the liberty and welfare of all people. Both sets of obligations are seen in light of the global consequences of a Nazi triumph over Great Britain. "No one who has observed at first hand the meaning . . . of Axis domination in Europe and Africa can question that immeasurable human values hang in the balance."

Irresponsible Idealism
The Christian Century, July 24, 1940

A year and a half ago, through the columns of *The Christian Century*, Dr. Albert W. Palmer initiated a campaign for the summoning of a world economic conference to forestall the threatening European conflict. *The Christian Century* supported Dr. Palmer, made his proposal its own, and ardently pressed for such a conference as the one promising preventive of war. During six and more of the most critical months in human history, large numbers of American Christians lodged their hopes for averting world conflict in the projected world economic conference.

Yet there was never the most minute iota of possibility that such a conference could have been held or that, if it had assembled, it could have turned back the inexorable march of events. Every intelligent student of world affairs knew that. This was true even within the church. I can recall vividly the expressions of incredulity on the faces of foremost Christian leaders from every corner of the world when the proposal first came to them at Madras. And again in Paris a month later when the plan, now transformed into a *Christian* world economic conference, was urged upon the provisional committee of the World Council. Was it possible that reasonable and responsible men could seriously sponsor such a suggestion in the face of what all knew to be the true actualities of the world's crisis? One of the senior leaders of the world church, a man of uncommon grace and charity of spirit, voiced the view of nearly all when he referred, with unintended alliteration, to "Palmer's preposterous proposal."

ONLY ONE THING POSSIBLE

The proposal sprang in the first instance from a sincere and noble concern—a sense that the nations were heading toward holocaust, and that something ought to be done about it. As one of the advocates of the plan cried passionately, "The world is about to burst into flames. Surely there is something we can do!" Yes, there was one thing, and *only* one thing, which the American people could have done through the winter of 1938–39 which might possibly have averted the European conflict. If the United States had then promised to the democratic powers the unlimited material and moral aid which is actually being given today, war might have been averted. If the people of the United States had then been willing to indicate that they could not witness unconcerned the repeated and ruthless despoilment of weak and unoffending peoples and that, if such aggression continued, this nation would feel compelled to enlist its full strength in defense of the victims, war would almost certainly have been averted. This should, of course, have been combined with proposals for world economic readjustments. That was the only line of action which could possibly have affected in any significant degree the development toward the present tragedy. Every intelligent student of world affairs knew that.

It is not for one moment suggested that the American churches should have advocated such a national policy. It *is* contended that, if the churches or their leaders essayed to advise the American public as to moves they might yet make to avert war, they should have told them this. For this was the truth, and churches and their leaders are under obligation to truth. To advance any other measure as an effective preventive of conflict was to fire people's hopes by expectations without the slightest foundation, and so to prevent them from facing the real facts. The proposal for a world economic conference, whether at the call of President Roosevelt or the World Council or the Federal Council, was escapism. Escapism the psychologists define as the creation of a world of illusion to evade confronting reality.

ESCAPIST JOURNALISM

Since the outbreak of hostilities in September, *The Christian Century* has been urging, almost weekly, that the United States bring the conflict to a speedy end by sponsoring a peace conference. With persistent and unwearying reiteration, it has been suggesting to its public that the realization of this high end waits only upon the initiative of President Roosevelt supported by other neutrals. As late as May 15, its leading editorial entitled "What Can America Do For Peace?" proposed that the President should send deputations to eighteen "neutral" European capitals inviting their governments to join a standing peace conference to remain in session at Rome or Madrid for the duration of the war. When the editorial was written, fourteen of the eighteen nations were so bound to one or another of the belligerents as to forbid independent diplomatic action; every intelligent student of world affairs knew that too. Before the editorial could reach its readers, two of the remaining had been overwhelmed and reduced to servitude. Within another fortnight, the proposed seat of this continuing peace conference had become the latest center of unprincipled aggression.

Now Dr. Palmer returns to support the proposed strategy. "Why wait any longer to make definite proposals to stop the war?" he inquires. "Let the United States call the remaining neutrals together at once and outline the main points of a decent post-war order."[1] I have been studying a world map to discover the composition of the projected world peace conference. Apparently the participants, in addition to nations of the Western hemisphere, are to be Switzerland, Portugal, Iran, Iraq, Siam, Afghanistan and possibly one or two others which have eluded attention. "Would Hitler consider such a proposal?" he goes on to ask. "Does anyone know until it is put up to him?" Or, "Will Hitler now abdicate in favor of Bruning and a restoration of constitutional democracy in Germany? Does anyone know until it is put up to him?"[2]

Presumably during nine of the most tragic months in human history, large numbers of American Christians have been waiting from day to day for the summoning of the proposed peace conference. There is not the slightest scintilla of possibility that such a move would have ended or could now end this war or bring enduring peace. The proposal has less meaning than Alice's Wonderland, for the latter had at least symbolic reference to reality; this has none. It is an appeal to the church's favorite instruments—protestations, pronouncements, the calling of conferences, talk—in a world in which those instruments have ceased to wield significant influence. If it is possible to subtract from nothing, the present suggestion has less relation to the world of today than the projected world economic conference a year and a half ago. Now, as then, if the American people are determined to take effective action toward the reestablishment of peace, one and only one course opens to them—the enlistment of their full national resources in assistance to Great Britain.

THE TASK OF THE CHURCH

Again, it cannot be too strongly stressed that the advocacy of such a course is no task of the churches. There is a place—I should hold, an honored and indispensable place—for Christians who in service of conscience declare that they can have no part in this or any war. There is a place for wide difference of view among Christians as to the course which the United States should pursue in the present crisis. There is, I submit, no place within the church and its leadership for persistent misleading of Christians as to what the truths of that crisis are or for the encouraging of expectations which have no discoverable relation to the facts. That is escapism—the creation of a world of illusion to evade confronting reality. More serious, it is a betrayal of truth. And the world can be saved only by truth.

These are harsh words. It is not easy to say them. Especially when they appear to bear heavily upon men for whose sincerity one holds deep respect and for some of whom one feels warm affection.

UNFORGIVABLE BLUNDERS

I believe they must be said. This is a day when sincerity, e.g., good intentions, is not enough. There is demanded of responsible Christian leadership a more difficult virtue—disciplined and rigorous fidelity to reality, however disagreeable. We are not permitted the delightful dream-worlds, the irresponsible fancies, the recourse to resolutions and conferences which are the stock-in-trade of the pulpit and which are allowed to pass as harmless in ordinary times.

What is at stake here is not simply a deficiency of information or difference in judgment or latitude for free expression of personal whim. It is resolute unwillingness to face known and indisputable facts. And that unwillingness leads on to radical falsification of issues and the gross misleading of those who do not have access to the facts. In any Christian, escapism is always pitiable. In one charged with influence over the views and decisions of others in days like these, it is unforgivable.

Those who wield public leadership at this hour are not merely toying with ideas. They are handling issues and decisions which will control the fate of multitudes. What may be at stake is the lives of tens of thousands of people, the deepest existence of millions—now and for countless years to come.

The Christian as Citizen
The Christian Century, December 4, 1940

I know no better summary of the Christian's dilemma in the present situation than the statement recently issued by five Christian pacifists and five nonpacifists:

> There are two judgments which all Christians are called to make concerning a given war. One is the judgment upon the relative right and wrong as between the parties at war. The other is the judgment upon war per se. In both judgments concerning this war, virtually all thoughtful Christians are in accord.
>
> In any particular war the Christian will define his attitude and act according to his view of the comparative weight and urgency of these judgments. One Christian may feel constrained to take up arms; his friend may find himself compelled to take the contrary course. The one may believe that the immediate issues for his fellow men are so great that he cannot refrain from going to their succor, even though he may have to recognize that he may be a party to all the evils of war. The other may believe that he cannot take part in any war, even though he may have to recognize that his abstention may prolong great sufferings.

"There are two judgments which all Christians are called to make concerning a given war. In both judgments concerning this war, virtually all thoughtful Christians are in accord." If this is true, and I believe it is, it is a striking and significant fact. The divisions among Christians occur mainly at the point where they must decide which of two judgments on *both* of which all are agreed is to determine action.

"One is the judgment upon war per se." That judgment has been given with inescapable clarity and authority by the Oxford conference: "War is a particular demonstration of the power of sin in this world, and a defiance of the righteousness of God as revealed in Jesus Christ and him crucified. No justification of war must be allowed to conceal or minimize this fact."[3]

"One is the judgment upon the relative right and wrong as between the parties at war." If the fundamental thesis is correct, it ought to be possible for Christians to achieve almost as full agreement in this judgment as in their common judgment concerning war per se.

AN ISLAND OF DEMOCRACY

Each of us approaches the question of America's relation to the present conflicts in three perspectives. First as an American citizen, knowing full well that the policy of his government in so vital a matter as war and peace will be finally determined by considerations of national self-interest. Second, as a citizen of the world, believing in a moral order, concerned for the liberty and welfare of all peoples, and committed to the realization of world community grounded in justice. Third, as a churchman, viewing all men as brothers, strongly persuaded of the unique importance of the Christian world movement and bringing to the issues of the conflict the Christian ideal of peace and the Christian judgment upon war.

The Christian must view the conflicts as an American citizen knowing well that, whatever his desires, his nation's policy will be determined by national self-interest. In the past six months, slowly but inexorably, there has *begun* to filter into the consciousness of the American people a realization of what is at stake for their national existence in the outcome of the conflicts. I say "begun." Even today we have hardly made a beginning at confronting the full implications. The following is an attempt to summarize the more important of them.

On the day on which Great Britain falls, the United States will be confronted by naval power in the hands of nations which have formed an alliance specifically directed against her with two to three times her naval strength. These nations will possess shipbuilding facilities five to seven times those of the United States. They will command access to unlimited supplies of all necessary raw materials. Current talk of a "two-ocean navy" has in view a fleet in both the Atlantic and the Pacific superior to any hostile fleet in either ocean. If the British fleet is captured or immobilized (it could be saved *only* by basing it in American harbors—a direct act of war), the United States will never have such a "two-ocean navy." All but the minimum fleet necessary to hold Japan off the west coast and possibly Hawaii will be withdrawn from the Pacific. Our main naval strength will be concentrated in Atlantic and Caribbean harbors in the hope of establishing a protective chain of steel a few hundred miles from the eastern seaboard. Meanwhile every national resource will be commandeered for our shipyards in a frantic effort to overtake a hostile naval superiority which will steadily increase.

Within six to nine months after the day of British capitulation the United States will be confronted by more than two-thirds of the geographical surface of the earth, inhabited by over three-fourths of its population, containing measureless resources of every important raw material including virtual monopolies of two vital products (rubber and tin), serviced by four-fifths of the merchant shipping of the world, and protected by vastly superior naval power—all knit into a single totalitarian economy. Within that economy will be the sources of 50.3 per cent of the United States' normal import trade and the recipients of 61.4 per cent of her normal export trade. That economy will have as its principal purpose the ousting of its only remaining competitor from world markets. It will have at its disposal the leverage of overwhelming economic superiority. It will have at its governing controls the principles set forth in *Mein Kampf* and authoritative nazi economic literature, and given effective demonstration in the economic subjugation and unification of Europe.

All of the above is premised on the continued independence and friendship of the British dominions, China, the Philippines and all the Latin American republics. But that is a very dubious supposition. South Africa, Australia and New Zealand with no protection save their own strength can hardly withstand united Japanese and German pressure. How long can China hold out against an enemy with the resources of such an economy at her command? The Philippines will be left to their own defense—with what outcome few students of the Far East have serious question.

What of Latin America? Its cultural and historical affinities are with the continent of Europe. The commercial interests of its southern states are intimately enmeshed in the European economy. (Eighty-one per cent of their exports go to Europe, 11 per cent to the United States; 57 per cent of their imports come from Europe, 20 per cent from the United States.) They desire to remain outside the Axis orbit and to look to the United States for friendship and cooperation. But they know that preferences cannot stand up against the pressure of inexorable economic and political considerations. Within six months of British capitulation, there will be fascist coups in three or four of the strongest Latin American states. The United States will confront totalitarianism, not across the comfortable expanse of oceans, but as an immediate neighbor hard up against our most vulnerable frontier. Talk of "hemisphere solidarity" and "hemisphere defense" is premised upon continuance of the status quo in Europe. With Great Britain's defeat, "hemisphere defense" will shrivel almost overnight into a lonely and precarious "continental defense."

In summary: Within six months to a year of Great Britain's fall, the United States will find herself an island of democratic ideals and institutions in a world united into a single economic structure and political alliance dominated by antithetic principles—outnumbered in military strength, outclassed in possession of and access to raw materials, outdistanced in world trade, severed from effective cooperation with all but her immediate neighbors—in a position of extreme economic and military precariousness and of well-nigh intolerable intellectual and spiritual isolation—every citizen and every national resource and facility under command of government and directed in frenzied struggle to keep the domestic economy functioning and to maintain military establishments adequate for minimum protection of the national borders.

Those who have not troubled to apprize themselves of the facts may dismiss this picture as the exaggeration of a hysterical imagination. There are many imponderables no one can measure, many eventualities no one can foresee. Nevertheless it is, I believe, the most accurate possible forecast of the probably development of events should Britain fall before the nazi assault.

We hear much of the danger of concentration of power, of tethering of civil liberties, of totalitarianism in the event of American involvement in the conflicts. In the world which will succeed British defeat, I do not believe there is a fighting chance to avoid American totalitarianism in which every liberty and person will be conscripted to a single national purpose. There will be a *fighting* chance of American survival, and America will desperately take that chance, but the final outcome will be highly problematical.

THE FATE OF MANY NATIONS

The Christian must also view the present conflicts as a citizen of the world, believing in a moral order, concerned for the liberty and welfare of all peoples and committed to the realization of world community grounded in justice.

Let us be quite clear. Great Britain and her allies in Europe, China in the Far East, are not fighting primarily for any other peoples. They are fighting for their own existence, for their right to live freely. It is a fact, however, that the future of peoples for whom they are not deliberately fighting will be determined by the success of their struggle—the peoples of Norway and Denmark and Poland and Belgium and Holland and Czechoslovakia and France, of Korea and Malaya and Indo-China and the Netherlands Indies and the Philippines, of Greece and Rumania and Bulgaria and Yugoslavia and Turkey and Egypt, of north Africa and west Africa and south Africa and east Africa and central Africa, of the Near East and the middle East and India. On the outcome of the conflicts in Asia and Europe hang the basic conditions of existence—of the possibility of even a modicum of liberty, of justice, of self-determination, of self-government, of self-directed advance, and of free and constructive relations with other nations—for not less than 1,000,000,000 human beings.

Victory for China and the Allies will not assure Utopia for these peoples. It will not even guarantee freedom, democracy, advance for all of them. It *will* assure their possibility. Defeat for China and the Allies will destroy that possibility. No one who has observed at first hand the meaning of Japanese overlordship in the Far East or of Axis domination in Europe and Africa can question that immeasurable human values hang in the balance.

For example, Singapore is often described as a citadel of empire. The description is true. Rather, it is a half-truth sometimes more dangerous than outright falsehood. Few passionate nationalist leaders of India, of Malaya, of the Philippines, of Indo-China, of the Dutch Indies think of it so today. To them, Singapore is primarily a symbol, and a considerable part of the reality, of all that stands between them and the fate which has already overtaken Korea, Manchuria, north China, Ethiopia, Finland, Czechoslovakia, and Poland. The most important fact about the promised "New Order in Asia" is this: however much the peoples of the Orient may chafe under Western political rule or resent white economic exploitation, there is not a single one of them from Siberia to New Guinea to Suez which would not infinitely prefer its present status to the only live alternative—Japanese or Russian or German domination.

THE END OF RELIGIOUS LIBERTY

The Christian will consider the present conflicts finally as a member of the Christian church, viewing all men as his brothers, persuaded of the importance of the Christian world movement, but bringing to the issues of the conflict the Christian ideal of peace and the Christian judgment upon war.

I wish to state with all possible insistence my conviction that the implications of the conflicts for Christianity, great as they are, should not be permitted to influence by one iota the Christian's advocacy of national policy. The Christian movement must accept the exigencies of political change without dependence upon political or military support. Nevertheless, the Christian cannot blind his mind to facts which concern so vitally the movement in which his hope for mankind's future largely centers.

The meaning of the conflicts for Christianity may be summarized in this sentence: Within a short time after Britain's capitulation, the Western hemisphere, possibly the North American continent, will be the last considerable area on the earth's surface where men and women will be permitted to gather for worship without police surveillance; where the elemental truths of Christian faith can be preached without imminent threat of concentration camp; where it will be permissible to pray for all nations and peoples, especially the needy and oppressed; where it will be legal to declare one's belief in all mankind as of one blood under the fatherhood of one God.

During these latter years many have discovered the significance of the Christian world movement, now spread to every continent and almost every land through the influence of Christian missions. No one can forecast the precise effect of an Axis victory upon that vast world-circling and world-uniting movement. The more or less official publication of the nazi party, *Grosse Volkerkunde*, puts it quite bluntly, "We will forbid all religious missions." The *Schwarze Korps*, official organ of the S.S., contains an article with these proposals:

> The Negro must remain what he is and not be spoiled by European missions. As he is, he is in his own way perfect, as perfect as every natural creation with which men have not interfered. Christian missions mean a survival of the inferior and the degenerate. We will re-create that situation which was the presupposition of natural selection before the white slave traders and missionaries interfered with God's handiwork. The most complex doctrine of spiritualized Christianity is a teaching with which the children of the virgin forest do not know what to do. Moreover, Christianity with its theory of equality and redemption is a hindrance for the sovereignty of white men. The greatest danger of the dethroning of white men and their political power comes from the teaching of missions. Every doctrine of equality and redemption, every teaching that one can become perfect by industrious praying, every propagation of the idea that by prayer one can become white, must destroy the prestige of white men. There is, therefore, no further place for missionary societies in the German colonial empire. Missions are institutions which have outlived themselves and must be replaced by something else.

Christianity will not perish from the earth. No earlier tyranny or persecution has succeeded in extirpating it. Nor will this one, despite its more powerful weapons and more ruthless ingenuity. But we must face the fact that, should the Axis designs prevail, the type of Christian faith and life which the overwhelming majority of American Christians regard as authentic will cease to function as a living factor in the public life of three-fourths of what we call "the Christian world."

Am I suggesting, then, that this is a "holy war"? Nothing of the kind. Moreover, the national policy must *not* be influenced by the interests of the church. But it is simple fact that, in the outcome of these conflicts, issues of quite incalculable magnitude for the freedom of Christian peoples and the opportunity of their movement to make its contributions to a better world are involved.

NO ALTERNATIVE TO WAR

Face to face with this dilemma—the Christian judgment upon war *and* the Christian's appraisal of the issues for humanity at stake in the outcome of this war—each of us must make his decision. Two alternatives lie open.

"He may believe that he cannot take part in any war, even though he may have to recognize that his abstention may prolong great suffering."

That decision I profoundly respect. It is a position which must always stand as a challenge to those who do not take it. Were there not many holding this absolutist ideal before us, some who now follow another course might feel constrained to take it lest the world be without the "perfectionist" Christian witness.

If one take this decision, he may do so with an attitude toward the issues of the conflict in no essential respect different from that of his Christian brother who is willing, if need be, to fight. He recognizes that those who attack peaceable populations today will not be restrained by Christian ideals of justice and peace, that the whole existence of tens of millions of innocent peoples will be determined by the outcome, and that governments charged with the welfare of these millions have no alternative but to resist by force. Some Christians must take responsible action within those governments and their armed forces. Other Christians must hold rigorously to the ultimate ideal of non-violence.

"The other may believe that the immediate issues for his fellow men are so great that he cannot refrain from going to their succor, even though he may have to recognize that he may be a party to all the evils of war." In the event that the United States does become involved against the Axis alliance, that is the course I shall follow.

I should do so with profound respect for fellow Christians who, recognizing the realities of our common dilemma, decide otherwise. I should wish the final word to fall upon our unity. In the words of the declaration with which this paper began: "They should honor each other's decision and be careful under all circumstances to maintain their community in Christ. And both alike should regard their perplexity as a symptom of the sin in which with all men they are involved."

NOTES

1. *The Christian Century*, June 19, 1940.

2. Heinrich Bruning was a major political force in Weimar Germany and a strong advocate of constitutional democracy. He was appointed chancellor in 1930, but was dismissed in 1932 as the nation's economic crisis deepened. He fled to Holland in 1934 and remained an outspoken critic of Hitler and Nazism.

3. The Oxford Conference of 1937, held in Oxford, England, was a major ecumenical gathering of Protestant and Orthodox Christians to discuss the theme of church, community, and state. Many of the delegates belonged to churches supportive of the emerging totalitarian regimes in Europe, and were unprepared to confront the implications of Communism and Fascism either for the church or for society.

13

Lynn Harold Hough

Drew Theological Seminary
Methodist Clergyman

A fter the carnage of World War I, an entire generation of ministers and religious leaders became utterly disillusioned with war. Thousands signed pledges never to endorse another armed conflict. Not Lynn Harold Hough. The Methodist minister and historical theologian emerged from those years with his theory of a "just war" very much intact. In 1918 he published *The Clean Sword*, a principled rebuke to pacifism and a moral defense of the use of force by civilized nations to check tyranny. "The international sword is not a substitute for conscience," he wrote. "It is an expression and vindication of conscience upon the most significant arena of the world's life."

Hough served a stint as president of Northwestern University, but his love of preaching sent him back into church pulpits and then to Drew University, where he was dean of the Theological School from 1934 to 1947. A theologian, philosopher, and gifted preacher, Hough exerted influence in America, England, and Australia. Early pastorates in New York and Baltimore helped shape his "evangelical humanism," a blend of the historic doctrines of Christianity with the Western classical tradition. In one of his later works, *The Dignity of Man*, Hough acknowledges that much of the evil in the world is a result of ignorance or even heredity. But there is another kind of evil, located in the human heart, for which man must take responsibility. "From the very centre of his being he must repent because he has so misdirected his life," he writes. "Education can do nothing about this deeper and darker problem."

Active in the ecumenical movement, Hough reported on the 1925 World Missionary Conference in Stockholm as a contributing editor to *The*

Christian Century. He was one of 700 Christian delegates from around the world who met to discuss economic issues, social problems, education, and international relations. Hough noted a widespread hatred of war among the delegates, yet also resentment among the Germans and anxieties over national security among the French. "How can these suspicions be quieted?" he asked. "How can peace be brought to the minds and hearts of men?"

With the rise of National Socialism in Europe, such questions were becoming moot. Hough believed that the seriousness of the Fascist threat facing the West was being badly misdiagnosed. As a leader in the Methodist Church—the most pacifist denomination of the 1930s—he opposed colleagues who thought that every international crisis could be resolved by negotiation. Hough served on the executive committee of the Federal Council of Churches, the largest and most important association of Protestant church bodies in the country, and clashed with committee members over American involvement in the war. Outspoken pacifist Albert Edward Day, for example, took over as FCC vice president in 1941, and hoped to steer the organization on a course of unconditional nonintervention.

By the spring of 1941, however, absolute pacifism was on the defensive. An unbroken string of Nazi victories had begun to rattle American isolationism. Even Franklin Roosevelt, who pledged to keep the United States out of war, saw the conflict in almost apocalyptic terms. As he put it in a May radio address: "Today the whole world is divided between human slavery and human freedom—between pagan brutality and the Christian ideal." In the following article, written for *Christianity and Crisis* in April of 1941, Hough anticipates Roosevelt's admission. He insists that the crisis in Europe now demands two qualities of political and religious leaders: sober moral judgment and the courage to act on it. With energetic prose and steely logic, he assails those invoking the faults of Britain as a cover for inertia in the face of Nazi aggression. "The perpetual tendency of corpulent and intellectually dull men and nations is to treat wolves as if they were pleasant domestic animals," he writes. "There is no excuse for the mental bewilderment in the United States since the fall of France. The evil which has been set loose upon the world must be crushed. And we cannot wait for perfect men or perfect nations to crush it."

Defending Justice
Despite Our Own Injustice
Christianity and Crisis, April 21, 1941

Men have a way of becoming morally modest when this modesty de-
creases the pressure of responsibility. They have a way of becoming
morally arrogant when their privileges are at stake. They are ready to
shout all the watchwords about the rights of men when these rights may
be used to buttress their own claims. They are ready to talk vaguely about
the difficulty of applying moral principles, the complexity of society, and
the relativity of all human judgments, when the principles in question
might be used to buttress the rights of others. They are ready to call in
dreams of a perfect society for the dislocation of the relationships of an order where they have what they consider an inadequate share of the goods
of life. They suddenly remember the universal and inevitable distribution
of evil when they are asked to go forth in battle array for the sake of giving justice to others. They do not doubt their worthiness when they are
about to make demands for themselves. They have sudden compunctions
about their worthiness to do battle for the sake of giving justice to others.

For this reason it becomes necessary to inspect with complete candor
the motives which lie behind moral scruples of all kinds which emerge at
the moment when some sort of action is demanded. A survey of the whole
field where this variety of casuistry appears is a matter of real importance
when we live in the sort of world which conditions our present activities.

Admittedly perfect beings could apply perfect standards with complete
and immediate effectiveness in a world where no imperfect beings had
appeared. But we do not live in such a world. At some points every human being is soiled by the evil of life. At some points every human institution reflects evil qualities. In no end of ways society is corrupted by the
cumulative evils which have been flourishing through the centuries of
man's life on this planet. From unsuspected dark corners evil is always
arising to turn to frustration the purposes which are good. So deeply true
is this that the man who sets about standing for justice is always plagued
by injustices of his own. The institution which lifts the flag of righteousness is always shamed by unrighteousness inherent in its own life. The
nation which goes forth to fight in the name of some sort of moral order
is always plagued by some of the pages of its own history. If we have to
wait for completely immaculate men before we make any demand in the
name of justice, we will have to wait forever. If we have to wait for perfect institutions to be the instruments of moral values, all hope of moral

advance is completely lost. If we have to wait for nations with a perfect past before we make any attempt to secure civilized decency in the present, we might as well give up the whole endeavor once and for all.

But this very putting of the question makes clear the way we must take. Since we cannot wait for stainless men to fight the evil in the world, we must use such men as we have. Weather-beaten men upon whom many a storm of evil has blown, bearing the marks of much failure in the storms of life, must go forth in spite of their own imperfection to fight against the lies which destroy the soul and the actions which degrade and disintegrate the good life of man. Institutions which have made their own compromises with evil must yet come to the place where they say "Thus far, and no farther" to evils both within and without their own corporate life. Nations which look back upon many a sorry tale in their own past must come upon days of stern resolution to resist the evil which presses upon them from without even as they must resist the evil which presses onward from within. Only so is some sort of justice and decency achieved in the individual life. Only so is some sort of honor and nobility given a place in the structure of corporate life. And only so do nations set themselves to move from the jungle toward the goals of truly civilized life.

When once we persuade ourselves to think of the matter honestly we see that such soundness and such justice as have become a part of human life have been achieved in just this fashion. The apostle Paul was very proud of his Roman citizenship. He understood perfectly the relative good—and a very high and commanding good it was—which the Pax Romana had given to the world. But he was able to write with stinging satire of the dark evils which belonged to that same structure of life. He was ready to perceive and appropriate and cooperate with the good of the structure. He was also ready to draw the sharp arrows in his great bow for the piercing of the evils in that very structure. And both in his hearty appreciation and in his deadly criticism he was ready to recognize that he himself was a man with evil fibers in the very structure of his own life, safe to think and safe to act only through the great grace of God.

Feudalism achieved very great things, not only in the region of justice, but in respect of the graces which appear only when golden thoughts command the minds of men. But the feudal societies had their own evils, their own dark disloyalties to the very standards by which they lived. When the tale of chivalry was put into lovely poetry we find that imperfect men with a shining dream made up the knighthood of King Arthur's Round Table. Here was the glory and the tragedy of chivalry both as history and as poetry. But if imperfect men had not dreamed the dream, there would have been no beginnings of more gracious life. All would have been the black plight of ugly brutality.

From this standpoint we can understand the grim and hostile criticism and the glowing and tender appreciation of the same institutions by different students. One student sees the idea of justice and fine living which fires the best spirits. So he writes in glowing appreciation. Another student sees the betrayal of this ideal and watches the decaying processes which rot the ripening fruit. He writes with something like irritated scorn. Our own period has produced a vast quantity of fierce young scholars so occupied with the fashion in which human evil has betrayed man's passion for justice that they have become completely unable to see how genuine good is ever attained in a society in which dark evils flourish.

If we accept the leadership of these men whose eyes are simply eyes of gloom, we travel straight toward complete paralysis and final frustration. Unable to see the gallant fight of justice in evil hearts and in evil societies hope dies out of their eyes and finally perishes in their hearts. It is a curious situation when a man's passion for perfection produces the complete breakdown of his will in the presence of the evils which characterize the world in which he lives. He has become so color-blind that he cannot see the good which exists because of his preoccupation with the evils which betray that good. A man determines wrathfully that he will not tell himself lies in order to make himself comfortable in an evil world. And straightway he begins to tell himself lies by misreading the good in front of his own eyes. If it is both stupid and evil to call wrong or right black or white, what shall we say of the man whose passion for a destructive interpretation of all existing human life and all historic human orders leads him to use every ingenuity to find evil motives for good deeds and dark purposes back of fair action?

The truth is that only the man who sees the good in the midst of evil and the evil coiling its dark way toward the heart of good is a safe guide. He knows how precarious is our fight for goodness in an evil world. He also knows how glorious are the achievements of good in spite of all the insistent and pervasive evil.

The peril of psychopathic judgments is one of the most sinister of the dangers confronted by men of our time. In the period between the conclusion of the first World War and the outbreak of the present cataclysm, untold millions of young people were brought up to look for a worm in every apple in the tree of life, and to go shouting with strange glee at the discovery of each new worm. The leaders and teachers of youth were so much engrossed by their own psychopathic glooms that it did not occur to them that man cannot live by the discovery of worms alone. And so a generation was produced which ceased to believe in any sort of goodness in the fruit hanging on the tree of life. Even their poetry became a dark and slimy poetry of worms. They had become so passionately engrossed with the presence of evil in the world that they became unable to see the perpetual and dauntless battle of good with evil in every human heart and in every human institution. This power to see the actual good in a world where there is so much evil is a necessity if we are not all to come to a state of complete incapacity for action. The attack on the sources of belief in life is the most deadly of all attacks upon man's heritage. The one central insight a man must have if he is to be of any sort of worth in a world like ours is just the insight that, soiled though your life may be, you can yet give yourself to the fight against some intolerable evil and the battle for securing of some good necessary for a decent life for men. And this insight is secured as we insistently tell the truth about the good which has been actually achieved in an evil world by men whose lives were stained by the evil of this grim world and yet had capacity for deathless loyalty to some clearly seen good and deathless hostility to some clearly understood evil.

There is no more fascinating or sardonic sport than the indoor analysis of the failure of democracy. If it merely consists of an honest criticism of a form of life which must perpetually be held up to standards from which it is tempted to fall away, this is very good indeed. But all too easily it becomes a cynical delight in the failure of democracy and at last an unhesitating condemnation of democracy itself. The democrat, because he is a creature whose loyalty to good fights its way through compromises with evil, carries his treasure in an earthen vessel. But it is a treasure. And it represents something which once and again has become very glorious on the highways of mankind. We must be honest about its failures. But in God's name we must be honest about its successes. We must tell the truth about its evil alliances. But at the peril of the very integrity of our own minds we must tell the tale of its refusal to make compromises and its spurning of alliances which were evil. It is possible for imperfect creatures to achieve a certain standard of decency and freedom in the world. And it is so not as a matter of faith, but of any honest interpretation of history.

The preoccupation with man's tendency to injustice leads to the confusion of the understanding at every point where a decision must be made. When there is a great war in the world, it enables you to claim that both sides are equally evil and so you are saved from moral judgment and from moral responsibility. Sometimes in the process you are reduced to a state of intellectual dishonesty which is enough to make angels weep. It seems beyond belief that any sincere man could follow the tale of Hitler's activities in Poland, Denmark, Norway, Holland, Belgium, and France, every step a movement in treachery and faithlessness to the plighted world, every step accompanied by remorseless barbarity and cruelty, every step a new slaughter of freedom in the name of conscienceless power—it seems impossible that any sincere man could follow this tale of complete and unabashed evil and then turn to the British Empire, with its tale of democracy increasing century by century until it holds a supreme hope for the good life for men, without feeling a contrast so complete that the very facts themselves carry the necessity for the decision that in this war the cause of Britain is the very cause of mankind. To any one capable of straight thinking in the light of the facts, the situation is clear enough. Something utterly disintegrating and uncivilized has been let loose in the world. It has won dangerous victories. Britain stands between the rest of the world and incalculable tragedy.

But the thinker, with a passion for perfection, sometimes especially alive when that passion can be used to show a way to escape responsibility, now begins to speak. He reminds us of every evil thing he can find in the history of England since the Norman Conquest. He makes a very brave attempt to blacken England in order to be able to say that since both contestants are equally evil, we can just stand aside and watch. He uses every strategy for the misinterpretation of England. He overestimates the evil. He ignores the good. And even so, after his best efforts, Britain remains a dull grey against the bitter black of Hitler's Germany. The history of parliamentary democracy is ignored. The broadening liberties of the British Empire are forgotten. The word *imperial* is used in such a fashion as to black out intelligence and to set every fact in a false perspective.

Nobody—least of all the British—would deny the dark spots in British history. But they do not represent the defining matters in the British tradition. The British Navy has been the protector of the liberties of the world. It has not been a menace to the freedom of man. The three thousand miles of unfortified boundary between the United States and Canada is itself a symbol. The British Commonwealth of Nations has been made up of very human beings; sometimes evil leaders have lifted false flags, and sometimes popular demand has involved moral compromise. But on the whole, what a splendid achievement in freedom and law is represented by the British flag! Men with all their injustice can achieve extraordinary results in maintaining justice. The British Empire is proof of it.

But that is not the whole story. The dark evils will go to incredible lengths if they are not resisted by men who care for some sort of freedom and decency, imperfect though these men may be. The two outstanding characteristics necessary for the meeting of such a crisis as the one in which the world finds itself are, first, a sense of the significant facts, and second, unhesitating courage in dealing with the facts. Dr. Van Loon has used the phrase "fact blindness" to describe the quality which has led to the fall of many nations.[1] The perpetual tendency of corpulent and intellectually dull men and nations is to treat wolves as if they were pleasant domestic animals. And when it is too late, the dull men and the dull nations awake to the nature of what they have done. There is no excuse for mental bewilderment in the United States since the fall of France. The evil which has been set loose upon the world must be crushed. And we cannot wait for perfect men or perfect nations to crush it.

If intellectual acuteness is necessary, the courage to act is also necessary. And in every age many men have been ready to make themselves a human wall against a threat to any sort of just life for man, even though they knew that they were themselves men whose lives needed much moral surgery. Indeed, the moment when an imperfect man gives himself to a necessary fight for the maintaining of a decent life for the world, he takes another step toward the triumph of justice in his own life. And the nation which like Britain becomes the fortress of the human cause achieves in that hour a justice and a nobility greater than any it has known before.

The first step toward moral achievement for the individual and for the nation is the hour of commitment to something more perfect than the individual or the nation has yet achieved. Jesus put the heart of the matter into an immortal epigram when he spoke of those who were evil and yet could give and would give good gifts. We, though evil, may give the good gift of a great loyalty to the cause of man. We can achieve some sort of justice in spite of the injustice in our hearts and in our national life.

NOTE

1. Hendrik Willem van Loon was a popular historian whose 1922 work, *Story of Mankind*, became a best-seller.

14

Lewis Mumford

Writer and Philosopher

Time magazine featured author Lewis Mumford on its cover in April of 1938, following the publication of his latest book, *The Culture of Cities*. The article praised Mumford for "his specialist's conscience," his attention to the ways in which modern cities affected human values and relationships. At about the same time, however, *The New Republic* thrashed Mumford for his troubled conscience about events in Europe: Adolf Hitler had just taken over the German Army, established himself as total dictator, and annexed Austria. Mumford published an article calling for immediate national action to confront him, and the magazine's editors savaged him for it. "Strike first against fascism, and strike hard," he wrote, "but strike."

Mumford must have seemed an unlikely commentator—and hawk—on U.S. foreign policy. He had studied philosophy, biology, and literature without earning a degree. He was a student of New York City, systematically covering the city on foot to observe its architecture. He was a prolific and wide-ranging author, with significant contributions to literary criticism, architectural criticism, the history of cities, technology, American studies, and other areas. Historian, philosopher, writer, artist—Mumford would be called "the last of the great humanists."

It was his humanistic ideals, in fact, that caused Mumford to share the optimistic assumptions of his generation immediately after World War I. As he once described himself, he was among the many "yearning utopians" who looked to Woodrow Wilson as their Moses: They fully expected the Treaty of Versailles to pave the way to a new promised land of international peace and security. "The innocent world that existed before 1933 is gone," he wrote in the summer of 1940. "We had glibly assumed that barbarism was a condition that civilized man had left permanently behind him: that certain kinds of cruelty, certain kinds of bestiality and violence, could never occur on a large scale again."

All these assumptions, he added, had smashed on the rocks of totalitarian brutalities. Mumford had seen it coming: While in Germany in 1932 researching a book, he noticed copies of *Mein Kampf* in the bookstores in Munich; he saw how Nazi Brownshirts had taken over the streets in Lübeck; and he listened at dinner parties as upper-class Germans praised Hitler's program against the Jews. He soon believed that the democratic nations might have to go to war to stop the dictator. At a peace rally in the spring of 1935 at Dartmouth, Mumford stunned the young crowd into silence when he took the podium and said the day was coming when they would be required to put their lives on the line to defend freedom.

Mumford shocked and angered many of his colleagues as well. A man of letters, Mumford's closest friends—among them architect Frank Lloyd Wright and historian Charles Beard—were intellectuals and noninterventionists. He soon found himself in the company of Reinhold Niebuhr, and eventually joined Herbert Agar's hawkish Fight for Freedom Committee. He expanded his *New Republic* article into a book, *Men Must Act*, and followed it a year later with *Faith for Living*. In both works he criticized the failure of liberal thinkers to admit the existence of "radical evil"—a provocative position for a humanist. "We are not merely faced with evil conditions: we are faced with the doctrines and the works of evil men," he wrote. "One of the reasons that liberalism has been so incapable of working energetically for good ends is that it is incapable of resisting evil: in its priggish fear of committing an unfair moral judgment it habitually places itself on the side of . . . fascism's victories."

Similarly unsparing criticism appears in the selections included here. In a chapter from *Men Must Act*, Mumford explains the distinguishing marks of fascism: its glorification of war, contempt for the weak, contempt for science, hatred of democracy, hatred of civilization, and its delight in physical cruelty. It reads like a recruiting manual for the al-Qaeda terrorist network. In the second essay, written for *Christianity and Crisis* in March of 1941, Mumford argues that liberal thinkers in the West based their political and social beliefs on a grievously mistaken idea: the dogma of the natural goodness of man. It was this doctrine that allowed his contemporaries to watch—"without the faintest tremors of suspicion"—the savage despotisms growing in Soviet Russia and Nazi Germany. These regimes, it was thought, would respond to reason, diplomacy, and negotiation. The catch phrase of the hour was "world disarmament," a concept invoked even by President Roosevelt contemplating the postwar world. As an approach to foreign policy it struck Mumford as dangerously naive. "Disarmament can proceed as fast as the non-democratic states transform themselves into constituent republics, obedient to international law: no faster," he writes. "On any other terms, disarmament is an invitation to banditry and a pledge of insecurity."

In 1944, Mumford's son, Geddes, died fighting for the Allies.

The Barbarian Alternative
Men Must Act, 1939

Behind fascism's moldy resurrection of despotism is something far more sinister: its deliberate appeal to the raw primitive and its positive glorification of barbarism. As a political system, it might be regarded as an error of politically undeveloped countries, such as Italy and Germany historically were and are: now more than ever. But as a system of ideas its capacity for mischief is of a much wider order.

To understand the growing popularity of barbarism, one must indeed understand the weaknesses of our contemporary civilization. During the last two centuries Western Civilization, developing too quickly, too ruthlessly, under the tutelage of the inventor and the capitalist, has often demanded sacrifices out of all proportion to its visible benefits. In precisely those points where it has achieved a certain equilibrium, its results have proved unsatisfactory in many respects to the common man. Each day brings with it a burdensome routine: the anxious efforts at punctuality, the necessity for speed and machinelike efficiency in production, the need to suppress personal reactions in an impersonal process, the painful sense of universal insecurity and impotence that an ill-organized, socially irresponsible system of production has brought about—all these things have created a deep malaise. Automatism and compulsion become pervasive: the human personality becomes dwarfed. Totalitarian dictatorships, in one sense, only mobilize this sense of defeat and direct it to their own ends: an attack on civilization itself. . . .

Fascism distinguishes itself from earlier forms of despotism, which grew out of more primitive means of aggression, in that it proudly associates itself with this deliberate return to barbarism. Whatever coherence fascism has as a system of ideas derives from the cult of barbarism: that is the point where its brutal practices take on an "ideal" tinge. The marks of fascism, as a system of ideas, may be briefly summed up:

FIRST: *glorification of war*: war as the permanent state of mankind and as the perfect medium for fascist barbarism. The belief in war as an attribute of all virile nations is a primary mark of fascism: it is bellicose even when it is chicken-hearted. Any attempt to lessen the possibility of war is from this standpoint a confession of weakness and futility. In practice, war is conceived as a one-sided method of butchering the weak and looting the submissive: hence the display of arms and the belching of fascist eloquence sufficiently satisfies the fascist demand for martial glory, provided the victim is inclined to purchase "peace" by surrender. But war remains the basis of the state: the drilling of the soldier is a holy duty; for the aim is to make a whole population obedient to command, like an army. Life for the fascist reaches its highest point on the battlefield: or, failing that, on the parade ground.

SECOND: *contempt for the physically weak.* Whereas Christianity made the meek, the humble, and the weak the very basis of its system of love and charity, fascism does just the opposite: the weak are either to be exterminated or to be used as the objects of sadistic sport. While Christianity elevated to a high place the domestic virtues, fascism has mercy only for the strong and pity only for the more powerful: the fascist prides himself upon being a carnivore, as Spengler proclaimed, though in actual fact man is the chief of the domestic animals: his first achievement in domestication was himself. Politically speaking, all minorities are in the class of the physically weak: hence they are detestable to fascists except as objects of aggression.

THIRD: *contempt for science and objectivity.* Because fascism is based upon a series of shabby myths and pseudo-scientific pretensions which would disgrace the intelligence of a well-educated modern schoolboy, it must reject science. By what rational means could it possibly establish the existence of an Aryan race, the divinity of a Duce or a Fuehrer, the purity of national blood, and the universal degeneracy of Jews, Liberals, Socialists, Catholics, and all non-white races except those distinguished Aryans, the Japanese?

Objective science naturally reduces these imbecile claims to ashes: hence science must submit to official rape before it may be pursued in fascist countries. For science is a means of arriving at results by methods of measuring and testing that all other men in full possession of their senses may, with similar preparation and discipline, follow. It leads to action on the basis of proved knowledge, rather than action in the basis of mere dream-fantasy and irrational impulse. Fascism, on the other hand, rests upon an addled subjectivity: what the leader desires is real: what he believes is true: what he anathematizes is heresy. These fiat truths bring about a debasement of the entire intellectual currency.

Since science requires patient effort and keen discipline and long training, fascism provides a cheap vulgar substitute: with the sword of its obsessive dogmas it cuts the Gordian knot of knowledge, too. The operation is quite as successful here as in political life: that is, it extirpates real knowledge and leaves the minds of its docile pupils open to whatever propagandist concoctions the needs of the prevailing crisis may dictate. Italy's sudden discovery of its Aryanism was timed exquisitely to harmonize with the need for strengthening the Rome-Berlin axis. To see things as they really are—which is another phrase for objectivity—is the last thing that a dictator would have happen: for it is the danger of all dangers to the system of illusions upon which his power is established.

FOURTH: *hatred for democracy.* The chief source of this hate I will go into later: here it is enough to record that the hate is a double-faced one; for despotism is, as Aristotle knew, a bastard child of democracy. Even now, through its absurd plebiscites, fascism occasionally goes through the motions of casting a ballot, though the population has lost the right of election. By playing upon the more infantile illusions of the masses the fascists hope to stave off the development of popular groups that will challenge their power. But democracy, in the sense of responsible popular control and popular initiative, is the chief obstacle to smooth fascist leadership. Hence fascism uses democracy's own healthy skepticism as to its weaknesses and mistakes as a weapon for undermining its own self-confidence. The essential difference between democracy and fascism, as concerns mistakes, is that fascist governments have the privilege of covering them up. *By definition, the leader can make no mistakes.*

FIFTH: *hatred for civilization.* If fraud is better than honesty, if propagandist lies are better than objective truth, if arbitrary force is better than rational persuasion, if brutality is preferable to mercy, if aggressive assault is preferable to co-operative understanding, if illusions are better than scientific facts, if war and destruction are better than peace and culture—then barbarism is better than civilization, and fascism, as the systematic inculcation of barbarism, is a grand gift to humanity. Fascism, both by its proclamations and its actions, leaves no doubt as to its source or its preference. Though whatever energy fascism exhibits is due to the fact that it still can live parasitically upon the remains of civilization, its own specific contributions are barbaric ones.

Fascist civilization, in short, is a contradiction in terms. We have not yet witnessed a fascist civilization; and we are not likely to do so; for if civilization comes again in Germany and Italy, it will be as the result of overthrowing fascism. What the visitor is usually shown as fascist achievements are the results of the common culture that fascism has inherited and not yet completely despoiled. What will finally emerge, if fascism continues to prevail in Europe, will be a system of barbarism: its stunted, emasculated minds: its grandiose emptiness: its formalized savagery. Fifty thousand hoarse voices shouting *Sieg Heil*: that is fascist music. A parade ground for a hundred thousand goose-steppers, drilled into flat-footedness: that is Nazi civic art.

Hatred for civilization is a hatred for mind, sensibility, or feeling that shows any degree of complexity or exhibits any wider connections with the world outside the crude parochial ego. What the fascist calls order is the order of Procrustes: the systematic elimination of the differences and variations which give to a true culture its inexhaustible variety: the fascist prefers to cut off the leg that will not fit the fascist bed.

SIXTH—and finally: *fascism crowns its imbecilities, its superstitions, and its hatreds with one mastering obsession: delight in physical cruelty.* This is one of

the true stigmata of fascism. From the castor-oil treatment first adminis-
tered by the Italian fascists to the merciless beating and gougings and
maimings practiced in Nazi concentration camps and prisons, a strong
bent toward sadism is even more characteristic of fascism than sheer aggression: for aggression against an equal always carries with it the possibility of incurring suffering as well as inflicting it: fascists do not attack
equals. For nations to qualify as fascist victims they must be small enough
to be stamped on and smeared with blood without risk to the fascist aggressor (hero).

Make no doubt of it: barbarism is the easy way of life. One has only to
let go: to shout when one is angry, hate aggressively when one is frustrated, destroy when one is puzzled. In return for this letting go, one must
take orders: but this, in fact, is another kind of letting go—permitting the
leader to do one's thinking and to give the answer to questions that would
otherwise have involved thought, conflict, responsible decision. Fascism
therefore calls to those who have not yet emerged from infantilism and to
those who would like speedily to return to it: it is the way of regression.
It is a political system that appeals to rapacious industrialists, disappointed political arrivistes, and frustrated mediocrities. Civilization on
the other hand is the hard way: it is the way of disciplined growth: it involves efforts beside which the fascists' repetitious drills and routines,
however strenuous, are mere child's play. The relapse into barbarism is a
recurrent temptation. Only *men* can resist it.

The Aftermath of Utopianism
Christianity and Crisis, March 24, 1941

THE RETREAT FROM RESPONSIBILITY

One of the difficulties about the present war is this: people have never faced with candor the issues and results of the great World War. Our contemporaries read *Under Fire, All's Quiet on the Western Front, The Road to War*; they brooded over the horrors and tortures of fighting; they became acutely conscious of the ineptitudes and blunders committed by the victorious powers, and in particular, they recognized the implacable selfishness of the ruling classes. But they lost sight of what the war itself was about; what it actually *did* achieve, and what it eventually *could* achieve.

Even those who had entered eagerly into the World War did not as a rule survive the shock of the postwar deflation. They had hoped for a new heaven and earth to descend from the skies; and when they found that they had only cleared the ground for the City of Man, they were unprepared to survey the site or to set the cornerstone. The two decades that followed the first World War will be known to posterity as a period of ebbing energies and dwindling hopes. Its efforts for peace and cooperation were half-hearted: there was a general retreat from responsibility, symbolized at its worst by the passive non-committal observers the United States sent to the League of Nations.

The agreement to treat the World War as an altogether disastrous and meaningless episode in the life of mankind was a bad preparation both for facing the duties that rose out of the war, and for avoiding the present repetition—this time with the odds heavily weighted against freedom and democracy, by reason of the very cynicism which was encouraged by that agreement. But why did this mistaken judgment become popular? Why was this retreat from responsibility all but universal? Why did the war leave only an image of vindictive imbecility on the minds of most people; so that those who were on the victorious side were ashamed of their cause and looked back sheepishly to their participation, as to a dementia that had unaccountably seized them?

These questions are worth asking, for they cast a light on our present weaknesses. The answers will, I think, bring out a fatal naiveté in the social and ethical philosophies that still govern the behavior of most democratic peoples; and in particular, the more enlightened, the more humane, the more liberal groups.

For a dozen years after the war I shared many of the typical attitudes of my generation: our beliefs were symbolized by the polemics and the predictions of Randolph Bourne.[1] So I am entitled to speak with candor about the sins of the postwar generation: in part they were my own. Bourne had prophesied a permanent disaster from America's participation in the war; he thought, in contrast to Thorstein Veblen and John Dewey, that it would bring an end to all social progress here. His view proved false. Many evils indeed accompanied the war and persisted long after it had ended. But the worst disaster of all was not the direct result of fighting: it was the consequence of our withdrawal from social and political responsibility. America's participation in the military struggle had given us the right and the duty to take part in the establishment of a more just and stable world order. But we refused. Perhaps the greatest catastrophe of the war was that those who emerged from it accepted, consciously or unconsciously, the romantic defeatism that Bourne had preached in 1917.

My generation, old and young, smug and cynical, was wrong; it expected too high a reward for its virtue and sacrifice; and it was prepared to give too little. Above all, it failed to understand the task that history had given it; and it thus did not rise to the demands of peace as those who had been maimed or killed had risen to the demands of war. In an orgy of debunking, my generation defamed the acts and nullified the intentions of better people than themselves. If only to prevent a similar miscarriage of effort from happening today, it is important that we should understand the reasons for that earlier failure.

GREAT EXPECTATIONS

Those who attempt to account for the disillusion and cynicism that followed the World War usually think they have accounted for everything if they refer it to the Treaty of Versailles. They contrast the high hopes and the ideal expectations that had been enunciated by Woodrow Wilson with the terms of the treaty. And they find in that contrast an excuse for the bitterness, the apathy, the resentment, the indignant sense of betrayal that followed.

But this explanation is more in need of an explanation than the fact it supposedly explains. Did people reject the war itself because the Treaty of Versailles was not a perfect treaty? Or because they discovered, by May 1919 that the politicians who pieced the treaty together were not saints and philosophers? Or, again, was it because they suddenly discovered that the moral and humanitarian claims of the Allies were disfigured by the rankest sort of national egoism, and by undisguised lust for economic and financial power? When one examines the attitude that grew up among the democracies as to their own share in war and peace, one discovers that a great part of the disappointment arose out of the illusions they had nourished about human nature and society. The mistakes that were committed in the peace treaties were due to conflicting economic interests, to political ignorance, and to sheer stupidity and chicane. But the people who were appalled by these things did, apparently, hope for a peace treaty that would, after six months' conference, be perfect: they did indeed believe that capitalism, enormously over-stimulated by war production, would affably bow itself into oblivion and permit the Bolshevik revolution to spread; they did indeed hope that national egoisms, swollen to the bursting point by the very act of fighting, would suddenly dissolve, and permit a quick, worldwide cooperation.

These were singular hopes and expectations. They suggest that the liberal and progressive groups in the democratic countries had told themselves a fairy story. They indicate that people expected more to be achieved through the peace treaty with regard to international affairs, than had been heretofore achieved through peaceful education and cooperation with any one country. Unfortunately, in 1919, the world was full of pert young men who believed that in less than six months, immediately on top of a war of unparalleled brutality, rancor, and violence, a perfectly just and generous treaty could be composed. These indignant people did quite as much to sabotage the post-war political tasks as the most vindictive isolationists, like Senator Lodge.[2] They formed an unholy alliance with the forces of reaction, comparable to that formed in our own day between the groups of the extreme right and those of the extreme left.

In short, the war-weary countries were full of yearning utopians who looked upon Woodrow Wilson as a savior, capable of transforming the souls of his contemporaries. But Wilson's fellow-statesmen were limited men, who saw in the great leader only what he actually was—another limited man. The war generation was bitterly disappointed because their Moses did not lead them into the Promised Land; but that disappointment was highly premature. Moses's followers were forced to endure forty years of wandering in the wilderness: the utopians were not prepared to endure forty months.

THE DOGMA OF HUMAN PERFECTION

What was the source of this wishful utopianism? What brought on this long period of morbid disillusion? The answer lies a long way behind the first World War: it lies in the social and religious philosophy that became popular in democratic countries from the eighteenth century on. Though the war itself, with its ugliness and its heroism, temporarily displaced this utopianism, the latter attitude finally had its revenge.

For the last two centuries the liberal and humanitarian groups in the Western World have been governed by two leading ideas. One of them was the belief in mechanical progress, more or less openly accompanied by the conviction that there was a positive relation between material improvements and moral perfection. The other was the belief that, through the free use of human reason, the world was ripe for a sudden transformation that would establish peace and justice forever.

The first of these ideas buoyed up the capitalist classes and gave a sort of missionary fervor to their most routine activities. The second set of beliefs accompanied all the reformist and revolutionary movements of the nineteenth century; its promise of social salvation had a millennial undertone even in the prophecies of Marx, for whom the classless state was a final resting place which suspended all the dialectical movements and oppositions that preceded it. The first doctrine was gradualist; the second was apocalyptic. Both rested implicitly on a third doctrine, the dogma of the natural goodness of man. Theologically speaking, the last belief is, of course, the Pelagian heresy.

According to this belief in natural human goodness, the purpose of social reform is to shake off evil institutions and restore man to the primeval paradise in which he could once more "be himself." The self, as such, was above suspicion. Rational men, once they are in possession of the facts, will act in accordance with reason on behalf of the common good: given enough rational men, one might enact the millennium; or, if one needed force to effect the change, the need for it would disappear as soon as the last king was strangled by the entrails of the last priest.

This optimistic belief in the automatic reign of reason found steady reassurance, from the eighteen-fifties on, in the succession of improvements that took place in mechanical industry; the perfection of machines and the ennoblement of man seemed parts of a single process. Did not Mark Twain, a naive mouthpiece of the age, couple the birth of the "steam press, the steam ship, the steel ship, the railroad" with the emergency of "man at almost his full stature at last"? Though rational invention was not nearly as automatically beneficent in its general social applications as the utilitarian philosophers proclaimed it to be, the sense of power that was derived from conquering space and time and commanding great energies spread into every department of life. If machines could be improved so easily, why not men? In Bellamy's *Looking Backward*, that typical mixture of humanitarianism and mechanism, utopia is voted in at a Presidential election.

None of these hopes was altogether absurd if one accepted the basis premises. Before 1914, people watched the spread of socialism from country to country, without the faintest tremor of suspicion that socialist ends might become the excuse for the most savage despotism, as in Soviet Russia, or that socialist ends might become the agents of barbarous and archaic ends, as in Nazi Germany: in both cases, a hideous travesty of rational hopes. Only reactionary writers like Dostoyevsky were acute enough to predict that a humanitarian materialism might result in Shigalovism (*The Possessed*). That human nature might go wrong, that people might consciously cultivate barbarism and restore torture, was before 1914 unthinkable; indeed, so unthinkable that those who still cling to this older ideology in its original purity will not let themselves admit the existence of barbarism and torture today.

On the same humanitarian premises, again, it was equally difficult to accept the war itself. Into this world of mechanical progress and human amelioration, the World War came like a baleful meteor from outer space: a meteor that landed, not in a Siberian desert, but in the midst of a populous city. What was shocking about the war was not merely that it cut across the path of social improvement. What was even more dreadful, from the standpoint of rational utopianism, was that it brought into action emotional drives, animal loyalties, irrational surges, outrageous capacities for bloody exploit that had long been hidden from popular view: acts that were supposed to belong to the unenlightened past. Man's complete nature, not his rational side alone, now became visible. Plainly he was a creature with greater capacities for good and evil than the utopian had pictured. In war, he reached sublime heights of heroism and self-effacement; he also sank to depths of brutal egotism and animality that only the dregs and outcasts of society had explored.

The discovery of man's seamier nature was to many people a deep humiliation; what is more, it contradicted many of their most sacred beliefs and hopes. But instead of understanding themselves better, they made the war bear the burden of their frustrated idealism. If this barbarous ordeal was to justify itself to reason, it must become the repository of all men's idealisms. If the war were not to mock them forever, it must produce the rainbow; and the rainbow must also point to an authentic pot of gold. Unless all this was assured in millennial terms, the whole business was just a futile horror.

THE FALLACY OF ABSOLUTISM

In short, a good part of our contemporaries accepted the World War on condition that they should be given, for fighting through it, a free pass on an express train to the Promised Land. Their desires for the future were in proportion to their shock and outrage over the brutal present. For them, only an absolute good could justify such an absolute evil.

Need I point out the twofold misconception? First: the war itself was not in its outcome an absolute evil. Those who opposed Germany's tribal plans for conquest, though not guiltless themselves of exploiting economically a domestic no less than a colonial proletariat, nevertheless stood on their records as the exponents of far more humane and cooperative and democratic methods of government than Germany exemplified. Germany had not undergone the liberating processes of the English, the American, and the French revolutions: hence the German government, backed by a long line of German thinkers from Luther to Fichte and from Treitschke to Houston Chamberlain, stood for conquest as a mode of life, and the beast of prey as the pattern for a conquering ruling class.

Compared with Germany, the Allies stood for universal principles of justice: principles that would eventually liberate India, Africa, China, no less than the internal proletariat of their own countries. The immediate result of the Allies' victory was the restoration of dismembered Poland, the redemption of submerged Czechoslovakia, the liberation of the Baltic states from Germany's recent conquest, the lifting of the yoke of slavery from Belgium, and finally—not least—opportunity to throw off the incubus of Junker military rule from the new republic of Germany itself. All these were beneficent results; they prepared the way for a more cooperative international society.

The second misconception was the belief that the peace treaty, to justify the high aims that Wilson had uttered, must be absolutely good; that only a perfectly just peace, without stain, without blemish, without human error, could justify the four long years of slaughter. This belief in an absolute good is the fabrication of people who have no understanding of the human personality, of the processes of human society, of the inevitably relative and mutable quality of all human effort. For the kingdom of absolutes is not of this world; human life knows only partial or momentary fulfillments. The post-war settlement was full of specific evils and specific goods. On the whole, the goods greatly overbalanced the evils, because a method of cooperation and the beginnings of a system of effective public law between nations had been laid down. If the mechanism of the League of Nations was feeble and imperfect, it was no worse than the Articles of Confederation which came out of our own Revolutionary War.

The notion that the World War had been fought to no purpose by the Allies and in particular by the Americans—who might have stayed out of it—is false both in theory and fact. Life presents one with innumerable situations in which one's most strenuous acts and duties produce nothing good: at most by taking up one's burdens, one keeps something worse from happening. A surgical amputation is not in itself good; it is a frightful evil; but it is usually preferable to the complete loss of life. A flood is an evil that might often be prevented by human foresight; but once the flood breaks, salvage and rescue become one's duty; and one does not help matters by crying out loudly against the Legislature's failure to provide reservoirs and reforestation belts in time.

So with the World War. Its long list of negative results is no proof whatever of its unreason or its purposelessness. This was an irrational solution of unbearable military and political tensions that had been forming for fifty years. Had Germany accepted repeated British offers of cooperation, the war might have been averted: that choice lay in human hands. But once the war itself had broken out, the duty of decent, intelligent men was to keep this irrational event from being pushed by a German victory to an irrational conclusion: a conclusion in which power alone would triumph over reason and justice. The Treaty of Versailles did not fully succeed in this aim: but one has only to compare it to the German-dictated treaty of Brest-Litovsk to realize that both wisdom and justice were preponderantly on the Allied side.

To perform the duty of resisting collective aggression, it is not necessary to hold that the morally worse cause is altogether evil, or that the better cause is wholly pure. When one helps one's neighbor to resist the assault of the gangster, the assault itself is open evidence to the relative merits of the two parties; even when one is ignorant of the gangster's history: but one need not deceive oneself as to the moral beauty of one's neighbor's character. The fact that he needs succor does not prove he is a saint; and the fact that he is not a saint does not establish one's right to withhold succor. In helping one's neighbor one vindicates the dignity of the human soul, in its refusal to submit to unreason and injustice. No reward has been promised for such an action; no reward can be demanded. But a penalty is attached to a non-action in such a situation; for a human society in which men will not help their neighbors to resist evil and struggle for justice, will presently cease to exist as a society, since it will lack even the animal loyalties that are necessary for survival.

The second point against the argument that no good came out of the World War is that two tremendous results, both potentially beneficent, did indeed come out of it. One of them was the world-wide disgust and hatred for war, as an instrument of asserting and enforcing the will of nations. The hatred became so deep in the common people of the world that it has already had a fatal result: it has caused them to treat peace as an absolute good and to surrender to evil, rather than to resist it at the price of war. Thus this salutary reaction against war has lent itself to perverse manipulation by the totalitarian tyrants: Hitler has boldly exploited its capacity for demoralization.

The other great positive result of the war, achieved in the very act of fighting, was the world-wide cooperation against the Central Powers. This was a unique event in mankind's history. It made possible the League of Nations, and had the United States accepted its share of responsibility as a world power—even to the extent that it is now belatedly doing—it might have made possible a far more effective union of mankind than the League of Nations. This was no small triumph. It was the first recognition of the fact that mankind had, for practical no less than for religious purposes, become a working unity. Hence aggression and injustice in any part of the planet must eventually be a threat to law and order and peace in every other part of the planet. Through this worldwide cooperation, the Central Powers were defeated by a moral as well as a military coalition.

Here was an occasion for profound rejoicing. Its moral meaning and its further political uses should never have been lost sight of in the years that followed.

Apart from all the particular goods that did in fact come out of the war, these two larger results would, if carried through, have justified the tragic sacrifices that men had made. But because our more idealistic contemporaries hoped for an immediate, wholesale regeneration of mankind, they shirked the further duties and further renunciations that the situation demanded. What is worse, in order to justify to themselves their own irresolution and irresponsibility, they cast the blame wholly on the diplomats, the capitalists, the munitions manufacturers—as if the natural and inevitable conduct of these people did not precisely constitute the great challenge of the post-war situation. So the outraged utopians held that since perfection was not achieved, nothing whatever was achieved; and that since low aims as well as high ones had characterized the victorious powers, the high aims were non-existent, and the low ones alone had reality.

MORAL FOR THE PRESENT

The natural letdown that followed the World War was debilitating enough in itself. But such a letdown is almost the inevitable physiological result of the hypertension and superhuman effort such a great crisis demands. What made the letdown worse was the fact that the results of the war were measured, not against human probabilities, not against the dire results that would have followed a German victory, but against "ideal" results, born out of exorbitant hopes and expectations, founded on a juvenile conception of human nature. A good part of the liberal gullibility about the achievements of the Russian revolution, in the face of its patent tyranny and totalitarianism, was due to the fact that, having been cheated of an absolute at home, the utopians needed a surrogate heaven which they could worship at a safe distance.

Unfortunately, the spirit of utopianism has not yet been exorcized. It still continues to infect much of the thinking that has been done about the present war. And it is therefore necessary both to see its mischievous effects in the past and to anticipate them once more in the future. Unless we head off these false hopes, lazy wishful attitudes, and perfectionist illusions, we will continue to defeat all our legitimate expectations and deplete the moral energies we will badly need to achieve the relative goods that will be open to us.

We must remember, to begin with, that the immediate aftertaste of the present war will, without doubt, be repulsively bitter, even if the Axis powers should be decisively beaten, beyond any possibility of their plotting a second comeback. Consider the peoples of Europe; peoples who have been bullied and blackmailed, robbed and raped, bombed and tortured and enslaved, who have been flung here and there like so much rubbish, peoples who have been betrayed by their Quislings and Lavals, and who have been ruled by the cold sadists that Himmler has created for his universal inquisition.[3] The sense of intolerable wrong and outrage felt by the people who come under the totalitarian rule will not at once disappear. If their hearts are to be softened, the Germans must show a capacity for repentance commensurate with the wrongs they have inflicted: an attitude of humble contrition that they gave no sign of, as Friedrich Foerster reminds us, after the last war. Humility, contrition, repentance will probably not come quickly in a land where the human soul has been barbarized and defeated to the extent that has by now happened in Germany.

In the meanwhile, the democracies, if victorious, will be condemned to take over the ignominious duty of policeman and jailer, exercizing a strict vigilance, not only over millions of Nazi gangsters, well-hardened in crime, but over large tracts of the earth that have become barbarized and demoralized by the actions of these people. We must not expect the victims of Nazi rule to shake hands with those who have terrorized them: on the contrary, we must make allowances for the resentments the totalitarian governments have awakened, and we must not be unduly impatient when hot hatred or uncharitable impulses of revenge stand in the way of rational plans and reorganizations. We cannot expect more of the peoples of Europe than actually came from our brothers in the South after their country had been overrun by Grant and Sherman. And if it took fifteen years to get rid of the poisons generated politically in the first World War, it will probably take twice that time to recover from the present conflict. Only charlatans will promise a quicker recovery; only inveterate sentimentalists will let themselves even privately hope for it.

With similar realism we must face the demand for immediate world peace and disarmament. I mention this matter here because the failure to fulfill the original promise of disarmament is often taken as one of the most outrageous breaches of international promise that followed the Versailles Treaty, and as one of the great failures of the League of Nations. Even so astute a statesman as President Roosevelt has repeatedly publicized the view that world disarmament must take place after the present war. If "after" means during the next twenty years, the demand is based on a serious misconception. The fact is that security, under law, is bound up with the existence of force; as law becomes more universally observed, more habitual, the need for force is diminished, though never entirely removed. Disarmament is not a cause of security; quite the contrary, security is the condition of disarmament. Not merely must one disarm the gangsters and bandits before one can establish the reign of international law; one must be careful *not* to disarm those who will be responsible for keeping the gangsters from building up another racket.

Before universal disarmament can take place, the states of the world will have to submit to the reign of law. They must embody their desire for law and justice in an ordered international government, with an executive, a legislative, and a judicial authority; and this government must be capable of superseding the wills of individual groups and states. Disarmament cannot precede the establishment of a world authority; and since the working out of a planetary organization is an extremely complicated and difficult task, the maintenance of armaments by the democratic states who will serve as a nucleus for world order is vital to the success of a peaceful constitutional regime. Disarmament can proceed as fast as the non-democratic states transform themselves into constituent republics, obedient to international law: no faster. On any other terms, disarmament is an invitation to banditry and a pledge of insecurity. The moral of this should be plain. The end of the present war must not repeat the pattern of the World War; and to avoid that tragic error, we must banish the spirit of immature utopianism that proved so self-defeating when the first great catastrophe was ended. If the ideal goals we must work toward are to be achieved, we must be prepared for a century of resolute struggle. There will be delays, mistakes, mis-managements, weaknesses. Unless we take these things in our stride—along with the human partialities and prides that threaten all good efforts—we will be disheartened once more with the nature of the materials with which we have to deal and we will once more shrink from the burden of responsibility.

When the war is over we will not enter utopia; we will pass into the next phase of life. Such goods as we achieve will not be ultimate and absolute: they will always be relative; and we shall be in danger of losing them at the very moment they seem most secure. There are no final solutions to human problems: what seems a final solution is only the courage to take the next step.

NOTES

1. Randolph Bourne was a literary critic and an essayist who wrote for *The New Republic* and the radical magazine *Masses*. He returned from a trip to Europe just at the outbreak of the First World War, and became a committed pacifist.

2. As chairman of the Senate Foreign Relations Committee, Henry Cabot Lodge led the opposition to U.S. acceptance of the Treaty of Versailles and blocked the efforts of President Woodrow Wilson to link the treaty to American entry into the League of Nations.

3. Vidkun Quisling, a fascist leader in Norway, became a puppet prime minister during the Nazi occupation. His name has since been applied to anyone who aids an enemy. Pierre Laval was a French statesman and deputy to Marshall Petain, who openly collaborated with the Germans. After the war, he was tried for treason and executed in Paris.

III

THE GATHERING STORM
Awakening a Slumbering Democracy

15

A Summons to the Church and a Manifesto from the Faithful

INTRODUCTION

Disturbed by the ambivalence of American churchmen to the war in Europe, *Fortune* magazine published an editorial taking them to task for their flip-flopping: Religious leaders had enthusiastically supported the Allied cause in World War I, but not now. Why? The threat to civilization, the editors argued, was far greater. The magazine, an icon of free-market capitalism, went on to make a somewhat astonishing accusation—that the churches were abandoning their commitment to absolute spiritual values. The reflexive pacifism of Christian leaders, and the arguments being made to defend it, sounded no different to the editors of *Fortune* than the rationale of secular isolationists. "The voice of the Church today, we find is the echo of our own voices. And the result of this experience, already manifest, is disillusionment."

Not all of the nation's religious leaders, however, agreed with the pacifism that had become a new dogma of American Christianity. A group of prominent churchmen—including figures as religiously diverse as Henry Sloane Coffin, Lynn Harold Hough, John R. Mott, and Reinhold Niebuhr—drafted a national manifesto urging "quick and resolute action" to meet the Nazi menace. At a time when most Americans wanted no part of the European conflict, they called on the United States to provide all material help possible to assist the Allied forces. Their document delivered a grave warning about the consequences of a German victory for democracy on both sides of the Atlantic. "This is the hour when democracy must justify itself by capacity for effective decision, or risk destruction or disintegration," they wrote. "Europe is dotted with the ruins of right decisions taken too late."

War and Peace:
The Failure of the Church to Teach
Absolute Spiritual Values
Will Undermine Christian Civilization
Fortune, January 1940

DEMOCRACY is too easily assumed to be a pattern of government based upon certain special political bodies and offices. It is true that democracy has its parliaments and legislatures, its ministers, secretariats, and courts of law. Yet these elements, no matter how arranged, and no matter how controlled or balanced, cannot make a democracy. A monarchy, such as that of Britain, may be democratic: an elective system, such as that of the U.S.S.R., may not be. Democracy is a spirit, not a form of government. It is embedded in intangibles: it consists largely in assumptions, one man about another, one nation about another. And in our civilization these assumptions are Christian assumptions.

As the leading democracy of the world, therefore, the U.S. is perforce the leading practical exponent of Christianity. The U.S. is not Christian in any formal religious sense: its churches are not full on Sundays and its citizens transgress the precepts freely. But it is Christian in the sense of absorption. The basic teachings of Christianity are in its blood stream. The central doctrine of its political system—the inviolability of the individual—is a doctrine inherited from nineteen hundred years of Christian insistence upon the immortality of the soul. Christian idealism is manifest in the culture and habits of the people, in the arguments that orators and politicians use to gain their ends: in the popular ideas of good taste, which control advertising, movies, radio, and all forms of public opinion; in the laws, the manners, and the standards of our people. If these applications of Christianity are materialistic, they are nonetheless real; they are nonetheless removed from the barbaric, the pagan, the un-Christian: they are nonetheless humanitarian rather than terroristic, kind rather than cynical, generous rather than selfish. The American has always been, and still as, at home among ideals.

FAILURE OF THE CHURCH

NOW, manifestly, the American owes all this to the Church. He owes it to the fight that the Church put up during long, dark centuries in Europe; and he owes it to the leadership that the Church provided in the settlement, founding, and political integration of his incredibly bounteous land. But while his original debt to the Church is thus profound and utterly without price, it cannot be said that, for the past hundred years or so, it has been much increased. It cannot be said that this period, characterized by the greatest material progress that man has ever made, is characterized by an equivalent spiritual progress. It cannot be said that the Church has faced with any conspicuous success the new material conditions brought about by the industrial revolution. Indeed, just the opposite can be said. It can be said that the Church has been unable to interpret and teach its doctrine effectively under these conditions; and that as a result there has been a declining emphasis on spiritual values and a rising emphasis on materialism as a doctrine of life.

We have, therefore, the peculiar spectacle of a nation which, to some imperfect but nevertheless considerable extent, practices Christianity without actively believing in Christianity. It practices Christianity because the teachings of the Church have been absorbed into its culture or ethos: but it fails to believe because it is no longer being effectively taught. The Christian leadership has passed from the hands of the church to the hands of the active and practical laity—the statesmen and educators, the columnists and pundits, the scientists and great men of action. And this is another way of saying that there is no true Christian leadership at all. Hence the future of Christianity and of its derivative political and social doctrines has become imperiled.

SPEAKING AS LAYMEN

FORTUNE comes to this subject as a layman. W cannot presume to know what the Church's solution is. We cannot enter into the great underlying conflict between God and mammon, or suggest what reconciliation there may be between them, if there may be any. As laymen dedicated to the practice of Christianity we can merely record our certainty that in order for humanity to progress it must *believe*; it must have faith in certain absolute spiritual values, or at least have faith that absolute spiritual values exist. The Church, as teacher and interpreter of those values, is the guardian of our faith in them. And as laymen, we do not feel that that faith is being guarded.

RECORD OF INCONSISTENCY

IN SUPPORT of this criticism it would be possible to bring forward considerable historical evidence, such as, for example, the Church's stand toward slavery for decades prior to the Civil War. Neither in the North nor in the

South did the Church embrace the doctrine, inherited from its own teachings, that all men are free, whether black or white. Instead, it rationalized slavery during the entire period of the "irreconcilable conflict" and did not change its position *until the people forced it to.* It did not, that is to say, preach absolute values, but relative values. It failed to provide spiritual leadership.

But for examples of this failure to define and interpret absolutes it is not necessary to have recourse to history. The most trenchant example is to be found in our own time in the Church's attitude toward war. In 1914, the U.S. Church was solidly opposed to war, which it characterized as un-Christian. The U.S., it asserted, must on no account be drawn in. But in 1917, on the grounds that certain Christian values were at stake, the pastors mounted the pulpits to declaim against the Huns and bless the Allied cause. As Elijah commanded the fire to come down from heaven, so did they. It used to be said among the troops, with a kind of clairvoyant bitterness, that if the Y.M.C.A. didn't' win the war, then the preachers back home surely would. Such hatred for the enemy as there was in the front lines produced no oratory to compare with the invective hurled against Germany by the men of Christ. The spirit of Elijah stalked the land.

But the reaction from that war to end war was as extreme as the invectives that had urged it on. Nowhere could men see any good in the war; nowhere would men give any credit to the peace. The boys had died in vain. And as for the Church, it descended from its pulpits to meditate. Collectively or individually, publicly or privately, it retracted; it was ashamed of having called down the fire; a number of its members turned to extreme pacifism; and when the war of 1939 broke out it was *again* opposed to participation almost to a man.

THERE are two points to observe concerning this complete circle that the Church made in the brief span of twenty years.

FAILURE OF ABSOLUTES

FIRST, the values used by the Church in reaching its decisions could not have been absolute spiritual values because by no spiritual logic is it possible to get from one of these positions to the other. The threat to Christianity from the Kaiser in 1917 was far less than the threat from Hitler is today. The regime of the Kaiser was militaristic, ambitious, and bold; but it embodied also an old-world culture from which neither religion nor certain political rights were excluded. The regime of Hitler, on the other hand, is nihilistic, in that it derives its strength from the denial of all values except the self-evident value of personal power. It is godless. Yet the men who urged U.S. soldiers in 1917 to face death against an ordinary emperor, whose chief sin was worldly ambition, now conclude that it would be wrong to fight a virtual Antichrist whose doctrines strike at the base of the civilization which the Church has done so much to build.

In reply to this the pastors plead human fallibility. Indeed no one can expect them to be infallible, but an examination of their plea sheds light on their predicament. In an effort to clarify the situation last October, FORTUNE wrote to 139 pastors of the nine major denominations and asked them to elucidate their attitudes toward war. From this request we received an amazing 65 per cent reply, mostly in long, painstaking letters: there can be no question as to the Church's sincerity and earnestness. But the vast majority of these earnest respondents had a peculiar complaint, namely, *disillusionment* after the World War. This, they said, accounted largely for their change in attitude between 1917 and 1939.

But it is pertinent to ask: disillusionment in what? It was fair enough for the doughboy to be disillusioned because nothing turned out for him the way it was promised. It was fair enough for taxpayers and bondholders to be disillusioned because they lost their money. It was fair enough for statesmen, even, to be disillusioned, because they tried to set up an international system of peace—and failed. Disillusionment, indeed, might be expected of the laity, who had tangible hopes for a better world, which were not fulfilled. But is disillusionment a proper plea for the Church to make? If the pastors had had genuine spiritual grounds for urging our participation in the last war they would not now be disillusioned; for the spiritual fight is an endless fight, the kingdom of heaven is infinitely far, and the loss of one battle, no matter how costly, cannot be accepted as definitive. After nineteen hundred years of struggle we cannot surrender our spiritual values, and if we must be killed in order to preserve them— which is what the Church said—we must not be disillusioned by temporary failure. It is for the flesh to be disillusioned, not for the soul.

FAILURE OF LEADERSHIP

SECONDLY, if pastors were not reasoning from absolute spiritual grounds last time, how can we be sure that they are doing so this time? Their position today is almost exactly what it was in 1914; and their arguments are almost the same. How much will it take to get them over on the other side of the fence? The answer would seem to be clear: the pastors will go over to the other side when, as, and if the people go over to the other side.

Indeed, the pastors are not talking about the soul at all, they are talking about the flesh. They are talking about the same thing that the American industrialist talked about when he too urged us into the last war, and the same thing that he talks about now when he urges us to stay out of the present one. In both cases—but especially in the present one—industry has provided a leadership at least as effective, and based essentially upon the same arguments, as that of the Church. Industry wanted to save democracy in 1917 by fighting. If its point of view is more materialistic than that of the Church, its goal is identical. And so far as the record goes, the American people would do as well by their souls to follow the advice of the industrial leaders as to follow the advice of the spiritual leaders.

THUS the flock is leading the shepherd. And this circumstance in turn has two results, which, if they are not corrected, will carve themselves deeply into human history.

THE RISE OF MATERIALISM

THE first result is, as already indicated, a rise in materialism. No matter how well intentioned our lay leaders may be, this result can scarcely be avoided. By definition the layman is primarily concerned with material affairs. Industrialists are not, should not be, and certainly do not claim to be spiritual leaders. The best they can do is to adapt such spiritual truths as they have been taught, to the requirements of the arena of action. Their progress in this direction is inevitably slow. But it will vanish entirely unless the initial teaching is strong, convincing, related to the contemporary scene, and consequently effective. In this regard it is all-important to observe that the solutions to material problems are not to be found within materialism. This is just as true as the fact that democracy is not merely a collection of political bodies. By no conceivable set of circumstances could materialism have produced the great "solution" of the eighteenth century that we have come to know as the American system. The American system has its origin, on the one hand, in passionate religious sects who believed in the spiritual absolutes that today are lacking: and on the other hand in those rationalists of the Golden Age of the American colonies for whom Reason was not merely mechanistic but divine. Similarly, by no conceivable set of circumstances will it be possible to solve by materialism the titanic problems, domestic and international, with which humanity is faced today. The ultimate answers to the questions that humanity raises are not, and never have been, in the flesh.

Therefore it may be safely predicted that if these matters are left in the hands of the laity, to be solved on basically materialistic grounds, a gradual devolution will set in, and civilization, instead of going forward so breathlessly, will seem to recede. Without spiritual leadership the maladjustments of our politico-economic system must inevitably increase; unemployment, lack of opportunity, maldistribution of wealth, and lack of confidence will symptomize a long retreat; collectivism will grow; and what remains to us of the Golden Age, when we were able to *believe*, will be consumed in revolutions and wars. For the solutions to these things do not lie within these things.

THE SPIRAL OF DISILLUSIONMENT

SECOND, so long as the Church pretends or assumes to preach absolute values but actually preaches relative and secondary values, it will merely hasten this process of disintegration. We are asked to turn to the Church for our enlightenment, but when we do so we find that the voice of the Church is not inspired. The voice of the Church today, we find, is the echo of our own voices. And the result of this experience, already manifest, is disillusionment. But this is not the disillusionment that the pastors complained of in their letters to FORTUNE. This is not a disillusionment in the ability of men to win wars, or to make peace after wars. This is a profound and absolute spiritual disillusionment, arising from the fact that when we consult the Church we hear only what we ourselves have said. The effect of this experience upon the present generation has been profound. It is the effect of a vicious spiral, like the spiral that economists talk about that leads into depressions. But in this spiral there is at stake, not merely prosperity, but civilization.

THERE is only one way out of the spiral. The way out is the sound of a voice, not our own voice, but a voice coming from something not ourselves, in the existence of which we cannot disbelieve. It is the earthly task of the pastors to hear this voice, to cause us to hear it, and to tell us what it says. If they cannot hear it, or if they fail to tell us, we, as laymen, are utterly lost. Without it we are no more capable of saving the world than we were capable of creating it in the first place.

America's Responsibility in the Present Crisis
May 1940

The undersigned members of the Christian church in America previously affirmed their common conviction that in the European war ethical issues are involved which claim the sympathy and support of American Christians. Developments, then unforeseen by many, require the elaboration of that declaration.

Each day makes the deeper significance of the European conflict more inescapable.

1. A decisive German victory, now an ominous possibility, would menace not only democratic government but the most elemental securities and liberties for the peoples of the whole of Western Europe. This is true not merely for Great Britain and France but even more decisively for the peoples of the smaller nations. What has occurred in Finland, Denmark, Norway and Holland, as well as in Poland and Czechoslovakia, makes the issue transparent: It is the preservation of freedom for life, for worship, for thought and the basic essentials for humane living for tens of millions of citizens in progressive and peace-loving nations.

2. Both the interests and the ideals of the United States are imperiled. A decisive German victory would leave the Untied States the only powerful democratic nation in the world. This country would confront the continents of Europe and Asia under the domination of ruthless tyrannies. There is some evidence that Nazi ambitions do not stop short of Latin America. German victory would render obsolete our accustomed conceptions of America as a continent secure in geographic isolation. It would doom this nation for a generation to a stupendous program of national preparedness in which virtually all interests, individual and social, would be subordinated to the single purpose of rendering this hemisphere secure against attack.

3. The hour has come when the American people must decide whether they are prepared to face the future in a position of virtual isolation, surrounded by powerful victors made strong by practices destructive of American ideals or whether they will lend to the European nations struggling desperately against the German threat such support as may yet enable them to halt that aggression.

However, more is at stake than national self-interest. A German victory which would destroy the liberties of free peoples and subordinate all life under the rule of political totalitarianism would endanger every value embodied in western civilization by the Christian faith and by humanistic culture.

We reaffirm that all nations including our own share responsibility for the conflict and that Allied victory would not of itself assure the establishment of justice and peace. But we are committed to the realization of a community of nations founded in justice as the only firm hope for the peace of the world, and we hold that the halting of Nazi aggression is prerequisite to the possibility of world order.

When men or nations must choose between two evils, the choice of the lesser evil becomes a Christian duty. That is the alternative confronting the American people now.

In light of these facts, we urge that the United States immediately enlist its moral and material resources in support of the Allied nations. Such assistance, we believe, offers the best hope of avoiding either military involvement in this war or a later single-handed encounter with victorious totalitarian powers, east and west. Only by concentrating every effort upon preparing herself for defense and by proffering wealth and supplies to the nations now struggling desperately to stem the tide can America hope to keep war from the Western Hemisphere and safeguard liberty, justice and honor for all nations, including herself.

Lastly we would urge the necessity of quick and resolute action. This is the hour when democracy must justify itself by capacity for effective decision, or risk destruction or disintegration. Europe is dotted with the ruins of right decisions taken too late. Not a day can be spared."

The following signatures were attached to the pronouncement: John Coleman Bennett, William Adams Brown, Charles C. Burlingham, Henry Sloane Coffin, Sherwood Eddy, Henry W. Hobson, Ivan Lee Holt, Lynn Harold Hough, F. Ernest Johnson, W.P. Ladd, Mildred McAfee, John A. Mackay, Elizabeth C. Morrow, John R. Mott, William Allen Neilson, Reinhold Niebuhr, Justin Wroe Nixon, Edward L. Parsons, Howard Chandler Robbins, William Scarlett, Charles Seymour, Henry K. Sherrill, Robert E. Speer, Charles P. Taft, Henry St. George Tucker, Henry P. Van Dusen and Henry M. Wriston.

Bibliography

Abrams, Ray H. *Preachers Present Arms*. New York: Round Table Press, 1933.

Bainton, Roland H. *Christian Attitudes toward War & Peace*. Nashville, Tenn.: Abingdon Press, 1960.

Bennett, John C. *Christian Realism*. New York: Charles Scribner's Sons, 1941.

Berman, Paul. *Terror and Liberalism*. New York: W.W. Norton & Company, 2003.

Burleigh, Michael. *The Third Reich: A New History*. New York: Hill & Wang, 2000.

Butler, Jon, and Harry S. Stout, eds. *Religion in American History*. Oxford: Oxford University Press, 1998.

Carroll, Vincent, and David Shiflett. *Christianity on Trial*. San Francisco: Encounter Books, 2002.

Churchill, Winston. *Memoirs of the Second World War*. Boston: Houghton Mifflin Company, 1959.

Cole, Wayne S. *America First: The Battle against Intervention, 1940–1941*. Madison: University of Wisconsin Press, 1953.

Elshtain, Jean Bethke. *Just War against Terror: The Burden of American Power in a Violent World*. New York: Basic Books, 2003.

Fox, Richard Wightman. *Reinhold Niebuhr: A Biography*. Ithaca, N.Y.: Cornell University Press, 1985.

Holmes, John Haynes. *Out of Darkness*. Harper & Brothers, 1942.

Hough, Lynn Harold. *The Clean Sword*. New York: Abingdon Press, 1918.

———. *The Dignity of Man*. New York: Abingdon-Cokesbury Press, 1950.

Johnson, Paul. *Modern Times: The World from the Twenties to the Nineties*. New York: HarperCollins Publishers, 2001.

Keller, Rosemary Skinner. *Georgia Harkness: For Such a Time as This*. Nashville, Tenn.: Abingdon Press, 1992.

Langer, William L., and S. Everett Gleason. *The Challenge to Isolation, 1937–1940*. New York: Harper & Brothers Publishers, 1952.

Lewis, Bernard. *The Crisis of Islam: Holy War and Unholy Terror.* New York: The Modern Library, 2003.

Lippmann, Walter. *A Preface to Morals.* New York: Time Incorporated, 1929.

Manchester, William. *The Last Lion: Winston Spencer Churchill; Alone: 1932–1940.* New York: Dell Publishing, 1988.

Meyer, Donald. *The Protestant Search for Political Realism, 1919–1941.* Middletown, Conn.: Wesleyan University Press, 1960.

Miller, Donald L. *Lewis Mumford: A Life.* New York: Grove Press, 1989.

Miller, Robert Moats. *How Shall They Hear without a Preacher? The Life of Ernest Fremont Tittle.* Chapel Hill: University of North Carolina Press, 1971.

Mumford, Lewis. *Men Must Act.* New York: Harcourt, Brace & Company, 1939.

———. *Faith for Living.* New York: Harcourt, Brace & Company, 1940.

Muste, A. J. *War Is the Enemy.* New York: Pendle Hill Pamphlet Number Fifteen, 1944.

Niebuhr, Reinhold. *Christianity and Power Politics.* New York: Charles Scribner's Sons, 1940.

Page, Kirby. *Jesus or Christianity: A Study in Contrasts.* Garden City, N.Y.: Doubleday, Doran & Company, 1929

Pells, Richard H. *Radical Visions and American Dreams: Culture and Social Thought in the Depression Years.* New York: Harper Torchbooks, 1973.

Rasmussen, Larry. *Reinhold Niebuhr: Theologian of Public Life.* Minneapolis: Fortress Press, 1991.

Ross, Robert W. *So It Was True: The American Protestant Press and the Nazi Persecution of the Jews.* Minneapolis: University of Minnesota Press, 1980.

Sittser, Gerald L. *A Cautious Patriotism: The American Churches and the Second World War.* Chapel Hill: University of North Carolina Press, 1997.

Warren, Heather A. *Theologians of a New World Order: Reinhold Niebuhr and the Christian Realists, 1920–1948.* Oxford: Oxford University Press, 1997.

Index

About the Editor

Joseph Loconte is the William E. Simon Fellow in Religion and a Free Society at the Heritage Foundation. He previously served as deputy editor of *Policy Review* and is the author of *Seducing the Samaritan: How Government Contracts Are Reshaping Social Services*. Loconte is a regular commentator on religion for National Public Radio's *All Things Considered*. His articles have appeared in the *New York Times*, the *Wall Street Journal*, the *Los Angeles Times*, the *Weekly Standard*, *National Review*, and the *Public Interest*. He holds a B.A. in journalism from the University of Illinois, Urbana, and an M.A. in Christian history and theology from Wheaton College in Illinois. He lives in Washington, D.C.